Where in tl

Astro*Carto*Graphy
& Relocation

Erin Sullivan

The Wessex Astrologer

Published in English in 2020 by
The Wessex Astrologer Ltd
PO Box 9307
Swanage
BH19 9BF

For a full list of our titles go to www.wessexastrologer.com

Cover design by Jonathan Taylor

A catalogue record for this book is available at The British Library

ISBN 9781910531440

First published in 1999 by the CPA Press in England under
ISBN 9781900869119

Dedicated to Jim Lewis

Table of Contents

Part One:
Astro*Carto*Graphy

Part Two:
The Astrology and Psychology of Relocation – Finding Your Place In the World

Part One:

Astro*Carto*Graphy®

This seminar was given on 28 September, 1997 at Regents College, London, as part of the Autumn Term of the seminar programme of the Centre for Psychological Astrology.

Introduction

Good morning, everyone! Today, I won't be talking about relocation charts specifically, although the psychology and manifestation of relocation are contained within the bigger picture of Astro*Carto*Graphy®. It is in next week's seminar that we will talk about relocation – moving from one city to another. When we do actual relocation charts for specific places – and those of you who are coming next week should bring your Astro*Carto*Graphy maps as well as relocation charts – we will focus on the relocation of your natal horoscope to a place other than the birthplace.

However, this week I want to concetrate primarily on the global view so elegantly illustrated by A*C*G – the big picture. For the diploma students, please bring acetate horoscopes next week for any relocations that you have found remarkable, and want to share with the group. Literally, a move from London to Manchester would make a difference, albeit slight. Many of you have come to London from other cities, indeed, other countries, and have stories to tell, and that is all part of the work for next Sunday's session – for you to be actively involved in the workshop as the afternoon moves on. [1]

---

[1] Henceforth, "A*C*G" will be used periodically and interchangeably with "Astro*Carto*Graphy", and the registered trademark only observed in this first

In today's seminar on Astro*Carto*Graphy, I am not going to blind you with science, but hopefully show how a complex astrological technique is eloquently reflected in personal experience. There are some explanations of the technical side of Astro*Carto*Graphy in Jim Lewis' book, *The Psychology of Astro*Carto*Graphy*.[2] This book is a result of various notes of Jim Lewis', collated and organised by me from the extensive notes and tapes and various articles he had written in the course of his twenty years working on Astro*Carto*Graphy. The final book was written after Jim's death, when Ken Irving then took the bulk of Jim's work and created the book.

This book is an essential, as it offers not only a "cookbook" interpretation of lines and crossings, but also some of Jim's fascinating mundane, personal and political stories. Today I will offer some new ways of looking at maps, and later on we'll hear some unique and rather amazing experiences from those of you who have been kind enough to volunteer your own stories about various lines you have in your maps.

Now, I am not going to do a workshop on myself. However, because I have travelled extensively, lived in several countries, and had profoundly explicit experiences related to the lines upon which I have lived and travelled, I am going to use my own A*C*G map in some instances as an example. My most recent experience to date was last weekend in Berlin, where I went to do a workshop. I had to lecture for ten minutes or so, then be paraphrased in translation. Fortunately, the man who did it was not only an excellent astrologer, a highly intuitive person, and fluent in both English and German, but we also had the advantage of my Mercury and his Moon being conjoined, so there was a nice third house flow. A good translator is a Sun/Descendant experience, and Berlin on is my Sun/Descendant line.

Another odd aspect of this line manifested in tiredness; I thought to myself, "This is a new take on Sun/Descendant." It was rather like feeling as if the Sun was setting all the time – hence it must be time

reference. All rights to use the terms associated with Astro*Carto*Graphy have been granted by the Astro*Carto*Graphy Living Trust.
[2]*The Psychology of Astro*Carto*Graphy*, Jim Lewis with Kenneth Irving, Arkana, Contemporary Astrology Series, London/New York, 1997.

to go to sleep. I actually did spend quite a bit of time sleeping, in an hotel called "Mercur" – the psychopompos at work. It was rather nice. One way of perceiving your Sun/Descendant line is that it is Vespers, time to sleep, time to enjoy the evening side of your life.

On a more serious note, the Sun/Descendant line is where one is more responsive to the masculine side of one's own nature, in relationships and in the environment; more aware of the heroic, adventurous and exploratory aspect of one's own nature. I felt the undercurrent of the history of Berlin. For all the rote interpretations you might find about A*C*G lines, you must always incorporate the knowledge of the condition of the natal horoscope – that is, a Sun line is not "on its own", but implicitly carries the condition of the natal Sun in its manifestation.. Thus, if one has a Sun/Saturn square, then the Sun line is coloured with that information. Similarly, if it is a Sun/Jupiter opposition, then that too must be implicated into the interpretation of the Sun line on the map.

While in Berlin, I was taken to a dance production – one which is deeply meaningful to me. My host had no idea of my tastes in art, music, or entertainment, yet he had booked tickets to a performance by Ishmael Ivo, a Brazilian dancer portraying the paintings of Francis Bacon – a notoriously "dark" figure. My host did not know the work of Bacon, but I did, and very well. He was my hero when I was at the Vancouver School of Art in the mid-1960's. And many years later, upon moving to London, I became somewhat familiar with him because we frequented the same private club in Soho. The influence of Bacon on my work as a young girl occurred on my Sun/Ascendant line, my knowing him took place on the Moon/Neptune/Descendant line (in a private club bar), and then, upon my first trip to Berlin, I experienced the most stunning choreographed performance of Francis Bacon's work.

Clearly, there are many ways of looking at how we exist. That is partly what drew me into astrology, well over thirty years ago – the myriad ways in which individuals express their archetypal existence. Even as a small child, I was deeply curious about how the human mind worked and what motivated people. By the time I reached adolescence, I was particularly intrigued by psychopathology and the "invisible", that is, the metaphysical and the unconscious seed-self, as I now perceive it.

On the psychological level I was interested in multiple personality phenomena, schizophrenia, and altered states of perception. I enjoyed stories like *The Three Faces of Eve* – anything that illustrated multiple dimensions of awareness or apparently disassociated experiences. On the metaphysical, I found myself gravitating instinctively toward authors such as Jung, Freud, R. D. Laing, Richard Alpert (Ram Dass), Paul Reps, Aldous Huxley, Alan Watts, and other futuristic thinkers. From an early age, I was thoroughly convinced that the mind had the capacity to exist on more levels than the obvious.

I began reading Freud and Jung quite early on, as well, and thought Freud was especially interesting in relation to the subconscious. But I thought Jung was particularly adept because he opened the doors to a concept which, hitherto, had been unconsidered – that it was possible for the entire collective of humanity to be unified by an unconscious link, and that individuals were linked in their psyche to every individual who lives and has ever lived.

At the quantum level, where energy and mass are one, we are all of us connected, and astrology is unique in that it allows us to see aspects of our nature as they are arrayed in the heavens (collective, global) from a specific central viewpoint – a fixed locus – that being one's own self (individual, personal). When you look at someone's natal horoscope, you are looking at a global picture, as seen from a local frame of reference. Simply stated, the natal chart is local, whereas the A*C*G map is global.

Here and now: everywhere

Let's open the door to thinking in a global context. As I sit here right now, the Moon is in a particular place to the degree, minute and second. In fact, the Moon is at 29° 30′ Leo. But for my friend in Melbourne, Australia, nine hours east of us here in London, the Moon also is at 29° 30' Leo.

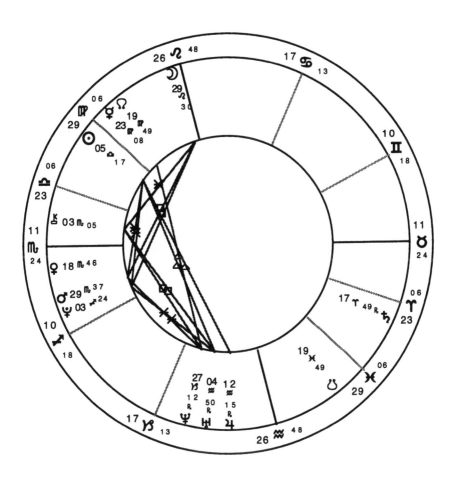

Figure 1
28 September, 1997
London (51N19, 0W10)
10.28 am BST (09.28.00 GMT)
Placidus cusps

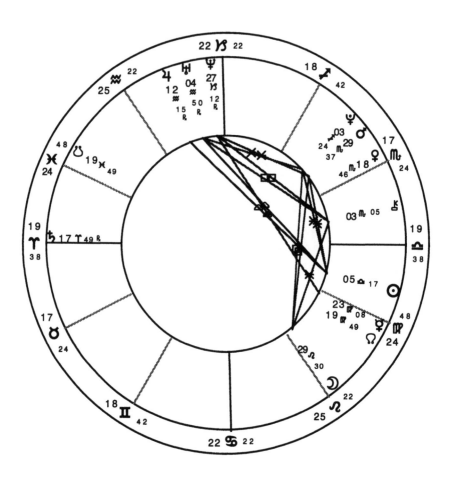

Figure 2
28 September 1997
Melbourne, Australia (37S58, 144E58)
7.28 pm AEST (09.28.00 GMT)
Placidus cusps

Right now the Moon is in that degree from every vantage point around the globe. The global planetary view incorporates the entire array of the planets at a single moment in time. However, when we set a horoscope, we then "fix" it to a location. Thus, if we set a chart right now for London at 10.28 am on the 28th of September, 1997, it then fixes our own personal and local viewpoint. And it also freeze-frames our consciousness, based upon how we are viewing the world from that local point.

As we sit here in London, 11° 30′ Scorpio is in the Ascendant and 26° 48′ Leo is at the MC, and the Moon is in the MC/10th house.

Setting the chart for right now in Melbourne, we have the same zodiacal longitude for the planetary positions exactly as they are here. However, those planets are being seen in different sectors of the sky. Thus, as we begin our day here in London, people in Melbourne are out in their back gardens just after sunset, playing with the dog and watering the bird-of-paradise and bougainvillaea. As I speak, 19° 41′ Aries is rising, and 22° 22′ Capricorn is at the MC. The Moon is in the 5th house, and as the Earth turns, the angles are "moving" the Moon toward the 4th house, and the Sun has just set and is seen in the 6th house. That is location.

Notice that, in London, the Moon is angular now – at the MC – while, in Melbourne now, Saturn is angular – at the Ascendant. We are feeling this concurrent time very differently in each place. Were these natal birth charts, they each would cast very different figures in the psyches of the individuals, resulting in very different subjective and objective experiences of life. Even with the identical zodiacal planetary degrees, those planets are found in places which charge the soul and ego with vastly different tasks.

With A*C*G, it is fundamentally the same thing, in that the A*C*G map is calculated based on the same data as a horoscope – date, time, and place of birth – but, as we shall see, A*C*G focuses *only* on angularity. A*C*G shows what is rising, setting, culminating and at the IC all over the world at the same moment in time. Philosophically, A*C*G is about being born in the world, not in London or in Vancouver, BC or Durban. When we look at an A*C*G map, we might be a bit daunted at this array of lines projected onto a map of the world, but in fact it is as simple as a horoscope. There is a minimum of forty lines. All eight planets and the luminaries are represented at the four angles – MC, IC, Ascendant and Descendant. If you include Chiron, there are then forty-four lines. Increasingly, Chiron is being included, and should be, in my estimation – and if the Moon's nodes are included, it adds even more.

At first glance, to the untrained eye, it might look a bit much. However, it is much simpler than a horoscope, because it doesn't involve houses. As I said, A*C*G depicts only the four angles – Ascendant, MC, Descendant, and IC. Those four places as we use them in natal astrology are our local frame of reference. Projected on the map of the world, they present a picture of what is rising, setting, culminating, and at the nadir all over the world simultaneously. When you are born, your horoscope is set in accord with the latitude and longitude of the location. Although we start our life on earth according to the time of the stars – sidereal time – we have to live it out on Earth – local time and local space. These areas – MC, IC, Ascendant, Descendant – are the only places in the house division of the horoscope that are "real" points – observable astronomical points of reference. The intermediate houses are mathematical calculations or visualisations dependent upon the mathematics that the various ancient astrologers derived.[3] I don't really mind what house system you use in calculating horoscopes.

Audience: What house system do you use?

Erin: Over the years, I have come to use Placidus exclusively for natal charts.

The creator of the Astro*Carto*Graphy maps which you have in your hands was Jim Lewis, although he was not the first to see this concept. Jim was strongly influenced by Cyril Fagin and Donald Bradley, both of whom were siderealist astrologers. In the 1950's, for mundane purposes only, Donald Bradley was already drawing maps showing where the planets were as they rose and culminated, and, based on these drawings, worked with various political and mundane

---

[3]For more understanding of houses and the house systems, see *Astronomy for Astrologers*, John Filbey and Peter Filbey, Aquarian Press, Thorsons, London, 1984. For interpretations, see *The Twelve Houses*, Howard Sasportas, Aquarian Press, Thorsons, London, 1989.

situations. Jim was impressed by this view of astrology, and though he was deeply influenced by these fellows, he remained a tropical astrologer. He was not a siderealist as were Fagan and Bradley. In 1957, in American Astrology magazine, Bradley published, for the first time, the first sort of astrocartographical maps and ideas. In the mid-1960's and early 1970's, Jim Lewis found himself in various parts of the country and started to think, "My God, something happens here in this part of the country that doesn't happen to me over there in that part of the country." And he began to develop his own responses and ideas.

For instance, he had a place in the US that he called his "flat tire zone" – Salt Lake City, his Mars/MC line, unbeknownst to him at the time. Whenever he went through this place, something ridiculous would happen regarding his car. In other places it would be a personal attack. He started to become aware, as any good Gemini can, that it is possible to exist not only within yourself, but also in other parts of the world at the same time, as if you are everywhere at once. As I alluded to earlier today, I too knew this to be a phenomenon, and often experienced myself in "different" places or dimensions at a very early age. When I met Jim Lewis in 1974, I understood instantly what he was on about with A*C*G.

That is the factor that really excites me about the A*C*G map. If there is such a thing as proof, the maps show and declare that we exist in all places at the same time. I think that is the most important thing to remember: We don't exist in our birth horoscope only, and even if we never left our room for our entire life, we can still be alive and dynamic in other parts of the world. The Cartesian subject-object split disappears with A*C*G. We can not only subjectively experience an objective event, but also objectively witness a subjective episode. Astrology deals with subjective qualities of time; one minute is not like any other minute, and our experience of that is accurately quantified by astrology. The quality of any minute in time is delineated by the aspects, signs and houses.

The other prevalent world-view that A*C*G demolishes is that individuality is the *only* reality. This is patently untrue. The cult of individuality is relatively new to consciousness, and to astrology. The only people who were individuated in ancient times were kings, pharaohs, and priests. Today, we all hope to achieve that goal. Two thousand years ago, the king was the only person with a horoscope. Today we all have one. Individuality only exists in the context, that is, faced off against the collective. With A*C*G we join the collective while still retaining our individuality, finding it expressed in as many ways as we are capable. Aspects of our psyche emerge in different place, at different times, and under various conditions. Wherever you go, there you are, but more or less so. It doesn't matter where I go, I still have my natal Sun square Mars/Saturn/Pluto. However, that aspect will manifest in different ways in various parts of the world. It may also be more alive, more strengthened as an observable characteristic. By "strength", I mean either it can be on an angle, such as rising at the Ascendant, or more "quietly placed", as it is natally, in the 9th house – where it will not register on my A*C*G map as angular at my birth location, as we shall see later on.

Moving around may amplify the darker, shadowy side of my Mars/Saturn/Pluto, or it could illuminate the more exalted side, where it becomes a reconstructive, hard-working aspect as opposed to a potential nuclear warhead. One might be able to manifest oneself in a conscious way by drawing on oneself as one appears in different parts of the world, and these maps are basically that simple. A*C*G maps look a bit complicated at first glance, but if you look calmly and sequentially, you shall see it differently.

Seeing the world

Has anyone seen an eclipse path, that is, a drawing of an eclipse path? Raise your hands. Good. Every time there is a total eclipse, the news media present this diagram in the papers. It is now pretty familiar, as it depicts the path on Earth where the eclipse will be visible. Simplistically, an eclipse path shows the path of the eclipse's umbra, its shadow, as it travels along a celestial longitudinal and latitudinal path and curves according to the equivalent Earth coordinates. The path of an eclipse describes an arc where the umbra or shadow of the eclipse travels across a part of the world. There are stories that the Romans used these eclipse paths to march along, setting their armies forth to conquer in war.

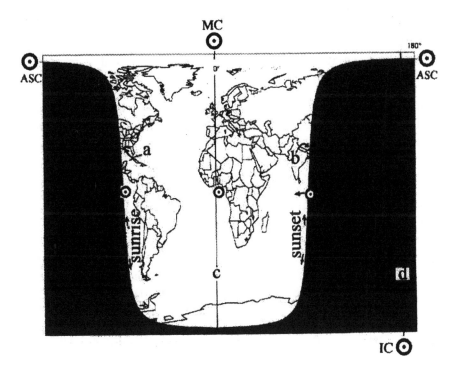

Figure 3

a = NewOrleans b = Tibet c = Prime Meridian
d = International Date Line

Figure 3 is called a Solar Map©4, and it is an offspring of A*C*G. Anyone can run off this diagram from their own PC if they have the software. What this particular picture shows is half of the world in darkness, while the other part of the world is in light. This is a picture showing the perfect division of night and day on planet Earth at the equinox, the period of balance of day and night in the world. Equi-nox: equal night. It is set for 12 September 1997, a couple of weeks ago, so it is pretty close to the equinox, and it is set for London, with a Eurocentric world projection.

Now, you all know that as the Sun is setting somewhere in the world, it is rising simultaneously somewhere else in the world, right? Where the Sun is rising, for example, in New Orleans, USA (**point a**), it is setting in Tibet (**point b**). New Orleans and Tibet are linked, "twinned", by latitude and longitude.

As the Sun rises, it also sets. Since this diagram is set for noon in Greenwich, 12 September 1997, GMT, it is, as I said, fairly close to the equinox date of the 21st. In Greenwich, at the Prime Meridian (0° longitude), and all down that meridian, the Sun (tropically, zodiacally) was at 19° Virgo at the MC – noon. And exactly opposite, at 180° longitude, is the International Date Line (IDL), all down which the Sun at 19° Virgo was at the IC – midnight. The Prime Meridian is at **point c**. The International Date Line is at **point d**. This meridian splits the world in half, into two hemispheres. Please think in terms of spheres or globes, now, not circles. The Prime Meridian and the International Date Line "split" the world into the two date-line hemispheres, calibrating time. The divisions of time and space are illustrated in this way.

Continuing on: see that, at noon along the Prime Meridian, it is midnight at the IDL. The progression of an hour per 15° of longitude works very conveniently in this way: if you telephone somebody in France, it is one hour later on the clock than in London. If it is noon in London, it is 1.00 pm on the clock in Paris. If you ring up

---

4*Solar Maps*©. Program by Esoteric Technologies Pty Ltd, PO Box 159, Stepney, SA 5069 Australia. Published by Astrolabe Inc, 350 Underpass Road, PO Box 1750, Brewster, MA 02631 USA. Email: astrolabe@alabe.com. Website: www.alabe.com. The Solar Map in this example was provided complimentary by Astrolabe, Inc.

somebody in Greece, it's 2.00 pm; somebody in Egypt, then it's 3.00 p.m.; somebody in Baghdad, it's 4.00 pm. We can carry this on until we get to the point where the Sun is setting, and thence to the International Date Line, where it is midnight, becoming the next day from us here in London. (However, we do know this is merely a convenience, and that the Local Mean Time is the solar time in real measurement.)

If we were to pick up this acetate flat solar-map and curl it into a cylinder, we would see that the GMT line (**c**) is directly opposite the IDL line (**d**) , and half the world (**c**) is lit and the other half is in darkness (**d**). In fact, it is noon right now, in England, so this is a graphic picture of what the world looks like relative to night and day. Now, as the Sun rises in the east, this shadow or umbra moves from the east toward the west. (See "sunrise" and directional arrows, and "sunset" and directional arrows). Because the Earth is a sphere and tilted on its axis, the North Pole is still experiencing a full twenty-four-hour day in full light, while in Antarctica, at the south pole, it is still perpetually dark.

As astrologers, that is how we need to see the world. To reiterate, this solar map shows how we are experiencing day and night right now. Simultaneously in the world, some of us are asleep at night, and others are awake and conscious. In some ways, this picture is like our individual consciousness. It also represents our global collective consciousness. Even though we are up and running and intellectually active at this time of day here, other people are at deep levels of unconsciousness, asleep. That is not to say that some of us are not at deep levels of unconsciousness whilst awake!

This demonstrates the path of the Sun and how it works as its light moves across the surface of our globe, bringing dawn and sunset to the world in the same moment. And, metaphorically, it epitomises us as a collective, half awake and half asleep, and us as individuals in our conscious and unconscious states.

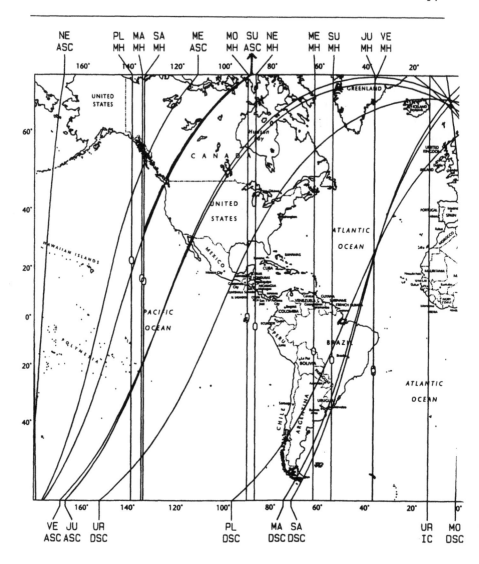

Figure 4: Erin Sullivan

Astro*Carto*Graphy Map

Note: Due to the limitations of page size, this and other A*C*G maps in the book have been split between two pages. The map should be viewed as a single unit, with 0°E/W (Greenwich) at the centre.

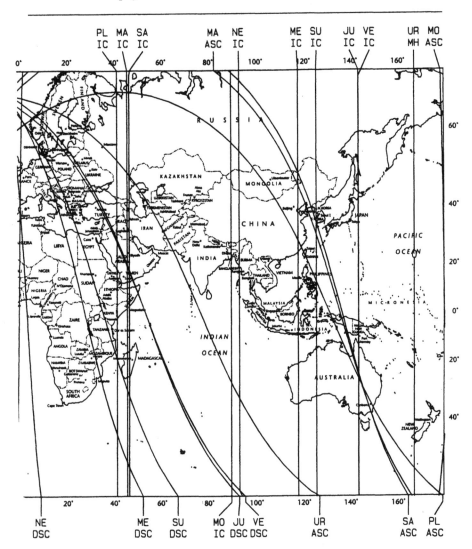

*The SU/ASC line may be seen on the facing page, at the top of the map, marked by an arrow. It curves southwest and on the "other side" of the world appears at the bottom of the map on this page as the SU/DSC line. The SU/MC line may be seen at the top of the map on the facing page (MC=MH), just above Greenland. On the "other side" of the world it appears as the SU/IC line, which may be seen on this page at the top of the map.

Being global, thinking local

Now I am going to use an A*C*G map to demonstrate solar movement in another way (see **Figure 4**). It is difficult to see the cities in these maps as they are projected, but if you look at your own maps, you can see the cities – unless you are over forty, in which case you can't even read the *London A-to-Z,* let alone the A*C*G map. Also, you need fairly good geography to read this map as you see it, so I shall speak the cities as we view them.

I happen to know this particular A*C*G map very well because it is my own, and while it doesn't reveal a whole lot about me as a person, it does show that I was born at a time of day, in a part of the world, where the Sun was actually rising, spot on the Ascendant. I was born with the Sun 24' into the 12th house. I have made the sunrise line, now called the SU/ASC line, thicker in order to demonstrate that fact more clearly. Although I was born in Vancouver, British Columbia as the Sun was rising, it had not yet risen in San Francisco, just slightly to the south. But it was rising just west of San Francisco, in the Pacific Ocean. See the SU/ASC line curving from the Pacific, through Vancouver and on up toward the North Pole? When the Sun was rising in Vancouver, it was noon, so the Sun was at the MC in Newfoundland, Canada, the very furthest eastern point of North America. Thus, my SU/MC line is running all the way down the meridian from pole to pole, through Newfoundland (about 66°W), and so on down that meridian, through Montevideo in South America. On the "other side" of the world, at midnight, the SU/IC line is running down the meridian that passes through Russia, Korea, the Philippines, Indonesia, and so on down the line.

As you already know, while I was born at dawn in Vancouver, the Sun was setting in Berlin. See the SU/ASC line as it curves "upward"? It actually begins to curve downward well above this map, but if you look to the SU/MC line, that is where the SU/ASC line becomes the SU/DSC line at the North Pole. At the intersection of the vertical MC line and the curving ASC/DSC line we find the absolute turning point of night and day. Note also on this map that at the equator, the SU/ASC and the SU/DSC are exactly 180° apart. This further demonstrates the previous example of the global solar map at equinox, but in a personal fashion.

Now, as for Germany, my younger daughter lived in Hamburg for many years, did very well in modelling, and was on the cover of *Birgitte* many times. Now I have a German-born son-in-law, thence a German grandson, and all my books seem to sell very well in the German language translations – better than in any other foreign editions. Interestingly, my mother had an inflation, a negative fixation about "The Germans", and it was part of her projected shadow – some World War II colonial material in there somewhere.

Theoretically, if I am waking up in Vancouver, I am also going to sleep in Berlin, all at the same time. On a subjective level, we could say that my Sun/Ascendant-ness is well received in the land of Sun/Descendant, where the solar purpose and identity is found in the 7th house. On an objective level, the Sun was rising in Vancouver (and simultaneously, all along the SU/ASC line) and it was setting in Berlin (and simultaneously, all along the SU/DSC line).

One of Jung's ideas was that there were periods of time in life when one was more capable, inclined, or disposed to be more of oneself; or when certain aspects of oneself were more alive at a particular age. Astrologically, from infancy until around age two, a child is more "in the Moon", whereas solarism begins to emerge at the Mars return at two years and two months, and so on.

With A*C*G, it is very similar, in that a sleeping characteristic can "wake up" in a particular part of the world because it, or the planet which agents the characteristic, has become angular or powerfully positioned, bringing it to dominance in the personality or in the environmental response. Thus we will experience ourselves in another light. Perhaps a quiescent or suppressed aspect of our self is enlivened in another part of the world.

As another example, using my own A*C*G, remember when I mentioned my natal Mars,/Saturn/Pluto conjunction? It is not angular at birth; it is in the 9th house. But it *is* angular elsewhere in the world. It is angular in coastal Western Canada in the Queen Charlotte Islands and the Alaskan Panhandle (MC lines) at 135°-140° west; and also at the IC lines at 40°-45° east, down through Russia, the Arab countries, and Eastern Africa. It is rising, as you see, up through South America, deviating widely at both polar regions, and then descending from the north polar region down through

Central Russia, Mongolia/Asia, Malaysia, and Western Australia. Note that the crossings of MA/SA/PL occur at 30°N x 40°W and at 30°S x 140°E. That is where Pluto comes to meet Mars and Saturn exactly at the MC and IC respectively, both in declination and zodiacal longitude. This picture of the ascending and descending lines illustrates the eccentricity of Pluto's orbit relative to Saturn's and Mars' orbits.

I have never been to the Great Artesian Basin of Queensland in Australia, where my JU/VE/IC line crosses with the MA/SA/PL/ASC line. Maybe someday, but it looks like a "hot spot" to me. As for the other hemispheric manifestation, I don't think I shall sail from the Bahamas to Morocco any time soon, but I have been to the Canaries, which is on the MC/DSC latitude crossing of all those planets – Venus, Jupiter, Mars, Saturn and Pluto. But I won't tell about that!

Living all over the world

Astro*Carto*Graphy is that straightforward. For basic interpretations, you can use keywords, and become increasingly more elaborate, psychological, spiritual, or mundane as you progress in your facility with the maps. If the Moon is about where feelings from the very earliest, instinctual stages of life emerge and develop over time, then the four lunar lines – MO/ASC, MO/DSC, MO/MC, and MO/IC – will all accent the earliest emotional responses, matters that pertain to nourishment, nurturing, instinctual/gut reactions, the collective mood of the society, mothers, women, home, roots, and origins. However, all the Moon-y experiences will be expressed through the medium of the angle at which it is prominent.

The Moon at the MC brings your feelings and responses to the most noticeable place, and thus you might become high-profile at that location, in politics, business, and creativity. Public issues rise to prominence. Conversely, the Moon at the IC would emphasize home issues and matters of private concern; your inmost feelings would be marked and significant in this place. Domestic matters rise to prominence.

It is because the Earth is round that you see the curved lines for ascending and descending angles for each planet. On the sphere of the Earth, these lines would be circles. Further, you will notice that all the MC/IC lines are perpendicular, running straight up and down the map. Meridians clearly run from top to bottom (meridians divide up our time zones very tidily). These lines also are circles on a spherical globe, but they run through the polar regions, from top to bottom around the Earth. The further north we go, the more distorted our separation and distinction of time and space appears as the meridians converge at the global Poles. Hence the Ascendant/Descendant lines meet at the top of the map somewhere. But at the equator, where 1° of longitude equals 60 miles perfectly, notice that the lines are all balanced or equivalent.

Astrology works differently "up there"

Longitudinal measurements, as they converge at the polar regions, become increasingly distorted. In the zone between 30°N and 30°S latitude, there is quite a lot of similarity in distance and angle. However, by the time we get up to 60°N or S, to the polar circles, you get an increasingly distorted picture of our view of local celestial space. This is where you see the great convergence of all ASC/DSC lines. I call them vortices. It is at this vortex place that everything meets, colliding together. It is as if the whole of your Ascendant/Descendant self is converging in a central point – rather akin to your navel, but an astrological one. It is as if the whole of one's horizonal planetary array meets at this part of the world. A great confusion lies in the vortex region, and individuals who have been there, worked there, or in some way had an experience there have reported very weird things – a short story about this later.

Myself, I had the dubious opportunity to be in that part of the world, right up in Norway, from Oslo to Tromsø. I have been there twice, actually, once at the summer solstice in 1972 for the UN Conference on Anti-Whaling with a group of alternative ecological planners. However, the time I wish to tell you of relates to our work today. Fortunately, I was there with other astrologers, so that we could share the collective madness consciously and have frequent reality checks. In the autumn of 1992 a whole bunch of us, including Jim Lewis, who was dragged, kicking and screaming, went to a conference in Norway. Weirdly, because it was so complicated an itinerary, schedule, and venue arrangement, we all knew it was going to fail. Everyone involved in the scheme began getting superstitious and religious and phoning each other and saying things like, "I saw a black cat out of the window, just as I was speaking to X (the organiser)."

People were having horrid dreams about the trip, which involved four separate cities as venues and a cruise down the fjords. At one point, I was crying down the phone trying get the organiser to explain the schedule, which I didn't understand. We had to fly from Oslo to Tromsø, then take a cruise ship and travel down through the fjords, and do lectures on the boat, ending in Bergen at yet another conference. It was an absolute nightmare.

Anyway, we all went. None of us were stupid – at least intellectually. We were all expert astrologers. But the whole time we were there we were asking ourselves, "What have we done, why are we here?" All of our A*C*G lines were converging in Norway. The poor man who ran it, notwithstanding all the fury we vented on him at various stages of the trip, did very badly in the end. However, as these things usually go, if one survives, it becomes a joke. I called it the Fjord Follies. Indeed, we wormed a lot of good jokes out of it – for instance, "We were bjorn again."

But the actual "conference" itself was a total disaster. There were between twelve and twenty speakers over the entire stretch of the two weeks, but there were only eight of us that were actually on the boat and *in situ* throughout the entire two-week experience. Over those days on the ship, there were only three or four attendees. There were about eight speakers and half as many attendees on the boat. It was an absolute scream. We had all these lectures and workshops set up to do for the hundreds of people who stayed away. I won't tell you some of the things we did to contain and relieve our anxiety, but being troupers and rather self-amusing people, we did manage to entertain ourselves much of the time. In the end, we filled up each other's lectures.

All four possible movements of the boat were happening: listing, yawling, pitching and rolling. One morning, one of the speakers was giving a very serious lecture, and his lectern was sliding across the floor; and we were all listing and yawling. Suddenly a magnificent, full-domed, multiple rainbow appeared at the stern of the ship. Everybody (well, all fifteen or so) got up in a body, and darted away from his lecture toward the stern, looking out the back of the boat, talking about this rainbow. He was still up there attempting to lecture, until he could get his sea-legs and join us. That is what it was like the whole time. It was unbelievable.

By the time we got to the last venue in Oslo, a few other people had arrived. Probably about twelve more attendees came, and by now there were about twenty-one speakers. The ratio, of course, remained the same. As speakers, we were trotting back and forth to each others rooms, saying, "Okay, you've got three people, I've got one. We'll come over to your talk." It actually turned out to be really quite fun. But the catch-phrase for the entire experience was the result of a thinly veiled, hostile meeting between the speakers and the organiser. His explanation was, "Astrology works differently up here." So that's what this means, we said. Aha! But of course astrology works differently "up here".

My advice is, if you want to have a very interesting time, go there – go straight to your vortex and get to work. You will find that at certain times of year and certain times of day, the MC is actually below the Ascendant, because the Sun does not rise above the horizon at all in the winter months. We had the opportunity of doing horoscopes for individuals with this phenomenon – the same sign on the MC, 11th house, 12th house, and Ascendant, but the MC just a few degrees below the Ascendant.

In the same vein, a client of mine, a merchant mariner, found himself on his vortex, just off the coast of the Alaska Panhandle, almost at the Russian border. The ship's boiler broke down. While they were attempting to fix it, the sea started to freeze up – and if it starts to freeze up in the north, that's serious, because it means you could be ice-blocked for the duration of winter. They were trying to get ice-breakers in to aid the ship, and their boiler was broken. Helicopters were flown in, dropping parts which fell into the sea rather than onto the deck. Every attempt to repair the boiler was failing. It took six weeks before the unit was repaired, and in the meantime, the seamen had got bored and thought they would paint the boiler room to kill some time and be productive. However, the paint wouldn't dry because it was too damp, too humid, yet beginning to freeze nightly. This situation went on and on. When they managed to get everything sorted out, six weeks had passed, and a hundred and fifty men had been stuck in their vortices (I assume). Ice was beginning to form all around them, inches of it by the hour, with all that incredible chaos. That is the vortex. Indeed, astrology works differently "up there".

As above, so below

Audience: How do you read a horoscope for 60°N if there is the same sign on the MC and Ascendant and all the intermediate houses in that quadrant? What happens to the person who is born there with such a distorted chart?

Erin: If you set a chart for the dead of winter in Reykjavik, Iceland, let's say for 1 January, you could end up with a horoscope – visualise this – with the MC, the zenith of the ecliptic, under the horizon. The Sun never rises above the horizon in the winter months. It travels a little oval path just below the visible horizon. Now, what is the Ascendant? Don't all speak at once, please.

Audience: Where the Sun rises in the east; it is the point in space where the extended horizon of the birth location intersects the zodiac.

Erin: Good enough. Well done. So where is the Ascendant found?

Audience: In the east, where the Sun would rise, when it does. In the horoscope, it is the left-hand or eastern part of the "line" which bisects the chart, forming the upper heavens and the lower heavens, creating the two halves of the chart. It is the eastern point on the horizon of the chart.

Erin: Perfect. The proper use of the term comes from the Greek, *horoscopos*, which is the actual degree rising over the eastern horizon. Technically, the Ascendant is determined by finding where the eastern point of the horizon intersects the ecliptic at a particular time and place.

At the solstices in the far north (and south), the Sun either never rises or never sets. As I said earlier, the Sun will either describe an oval just above the horizon in the course of twenty-four hours, or just below the horizon over twenty-four hours. This means that the Sun never rises in the winter months and never sets in the summer months. This makes for very odd horoscopes, from our common viewpoint. While in Norway, we set charts for these dates, and found that, indeed, there is the possibility of having the MC below the Ascendant.

One way of dealing with this is to measure an equal house system based on the MC degree. This is a false picture, but it makes it easier for an astrologer to use. Naturally, the planets all have the same aspects as they do in any other chart set for other latitudes at the equivalent time of day, so there is that consistency. Personally, I tend to value aspects more than houses, or signs for that matter.

However, to carry on with the second part of your question, you are right. If you look at my A*C*G map again (Figure 4, pp. 14-15), I have a JU/VE/DSC line in Norway, and I had a pretty good time, regardless. My vortex is just above the UK, but at about 68°N. Everybody else is going to look at their own maps to see where their mess is, their vortex. As we get closer and closer to the equator, we start to get a kind of perfection in angularity, because that is where the Sun rises at dawn and sets at 6.00 pm, always. At the top of the world, at the Poles, it never rises in the winter and it never sets in summer. When we derive the spaces between the angles, that is, create intermediate houses, the closer we get to the equator, the more equal are the angles, and subsequently so are the intermediate houses. Thus, when you set a horoscope for the equator, you always end up with an exact 90° angle between MC and Ascendant.

The problem with the computer age, and new astrologers coming in at that level, is that they have never learned to actually calculate a horoscope, and have never studied the Tables of Houses and experienced – visually and intellectually at least – the elegance and flow between what changing latitudes present at the same sidereal time. Some of you may find it exceptionally hard to visualise this. I do recommend getting a good, basic astronomy book. *Astronomy for Astrologers* by Filby and Filby is an excellent one.[5] As an exercise, you can take a sidereal time, look in a Table of Houses, run your eye down the latitudes, and notice how the MC changes.

Audience: So you can't make a chart for somebody born in Norway?

Erin: Well, we did, and they do. And we looked at them, with the MC below the Ascendant and things like that. What some astrologers have done is try to rationalise ways of dealing with it – as I said earlier, by creating an equal house diagram based on the MC degree. However, as I said at the beginning of the seminar, I do not want to blind you with science. The distortion of houses is a phenomenon that I'm sure you must have run into. Have you not run into it? People born in Scotland, for example, will often have, say, a Sagittarius MC, Sagittarius 11th house, Sagittarius 12th house, and Capricorn rising. It is not unheard of. London can also produce very distorted results. Any northern latitude can; at certain times of season and day, moderate latitudes can have very large 1st/7th houses or 6th/12th houses. That's where the whole concept of intercepted houses came in, which the creation of the equal house system dissolved.

Audience: How do you interpret intercepted signs or houses?

Erin: I don't perceive the horoscope with "intercepted" signs. I just see big houses that involve two or more signs. This is the visually accurate view, using the European wheel. And I don't use equal house system at all. However, I might if I were doing a lot of astrology "up there". Intercepted houses are a result of the old-fashioned 30° divided wheel with the mid-sign squeezed into it. The European wheel does not do this – it is visually accurate with the house represented by its size in degrees. And with houses, "size" is equivalent to "duration" when you consider a transit moving through the house. A transit spends more time, more duration in a larger house. There is

---

[5]*Astronomy for Astrologers*, Chapter 3, "Earth and Sky: Lines, Circles and Projections", *op. cit.*

more emphasis in that house after years of such a habitual experience.

Productive and creative people do live in Iceland and Greenland, and in the Northwest Territories and the far north of Russia, and there are tribes that live on the fringe of the polar cap. However, not many of them have as much in the way of opportunity or latitude for change and choice as the moderate latitudes offer. Houses represent the realms of human experience, and when the houses are either non-existent or very small or exceptionally large, then the opportunities represented in the house realm are relative to size. For instance, if there is a magnified 6th/12th house axis, then symbolically they spend a lot of time in the dark, in their imaginations, and a lot of time working.

Audience: There is a very high suicide rate.

Erin: Indeed, there is a very high suicide rate in all extreme latitudes. In the major cities in the north, life proceeds according to the laws of cultural progress, but there are still limitations of latitude of expression – time, weather, and travel. The more moderate and temperate latitudes have more opportunity, theoretically.

East or west of the line

As I said initially, angularity is extraordinarily important in natal horoscopy, but particularly significant in A*C*G. For instance, if you were born with Mars right at the MC or Saturn at the IC, then you have those planets angular natally. Many of us do not have angularity in the horoscope, but can find it on the A*C*G map. There is an orb allowed, in A*C*G maps as in natal astrology. Let's think natally for a minute to get a grip on the concept. Let's say you have a planet 10° into the 12th house. Then it is an applying aspect – that is, applying to the Ascendant by transit or secondary progression. Now, if that planet is 10° into the 1st house, it is a separating aspect, that is, separating from the Ascendant by transit or progression.

The applying aspect is always more powerful than the separating aspect. This is basic stuff. With respect both to A*C*G and natal horoscopes, a greater orb is allowed for planets behind an angle, that is, in a cadent house. The difference is this: with A*C*G, if the location you are concerned with is east of the line, it is a stronger influence and is allowed a greater orb, whereas a location west of the line is being "left behind" by the line as it transits.

With Astro*Carto*Graphy, the planetary line itself is doing the transiting and progressing toward the eastern location, and by the same reasoning, the line is separating from the western location. The orbs, therefore, are greater when the location being considered is east of the line, and smaller when west of the line.

Audience: If the planet is retrograde in the natal chart, how does that affect its symbolic motion as an A*C*G line?

Erin: If the natal planet is retrograde, and thus the planet line is "retrograde", then it is separating from the angle natally, and is "moving" back to the west. What would be happening in that case, especially if it is Mercury or Venus in their faster retrograde periods, is that the planet line is moving away by secondary progression from the location considered. The inner planets and Mars are symbolically "moved" by progression in Cyclo*Carto*Graphy®, while the planets from Jupiter to Pluto are graphed in transit.

However, if it were Uranus, Neptune, or Pluto we were looking at, I would still consider that the location is stronger if it is east of the line, and less so if west of the line. Even if these outer planets do move station-direct by progression, the apparent motion is virtually nil in a lifetime, so the rule of "east of the line is stronger than west of the line" still prevails. However, the planets from Jupiter to Pluto are "moved" in Cyclo*Carto*Graphy by transit only. Therefore we still would use the standard rule of east of the line being stronger than east of the line.

Has everybody been looking at their map and making sense of it, and noting where they've been or where they're going, or where they've always wanted to go? That plays a huge role. Why do people long to go to Southeast Asia, or the Falklands, or anywhere, for that matter? Look at the world and see where you are aligned through the power of angularity. Angles are the enlivening part of our lives. This is where I move into some basic astrology, and get away from the technical material for a while.

The angles: orientation to life

The angles – MC, IC, Ascendant, and Descendant – are our orientation to life experience. They are the four stations of incarnation, and as such, are the most personal of points in the horoscope.[6] The angles in the natal chart not only demarcate precise places and times in which major turning points occur, but they also give us a chronology in our lives.[7] This is another reason why the angles are so important in the A*C*G map.

We are born with an innate astrolabe which gives us our extreme points on the horizon, toward which we reach and look back upon where we have been. In celestial navigation, the "guiding point" is called meridian passage. In mid-ocean, a navigator will look at the sextant to find the MC or, in nautical terms, meridian passage. The meridian or MC, as you all learned in basic astrology, is a consistent measurement. Every four minutes a new degree crosses the MC, no matter where you are on the planet.

That is not always the case with the Ascendant and Descendant. The Ascendant's relationship with the MC is dependent on the latitude of your birth. In the natal chart we have four angles only. They are derived from the precise time of birth. They "fix" the planetary picture – once the sidereal time is achieved, and the Table of Houses looked at, we find the degrees rising and culminating according to that sidereal time at the latitude of birth. Once done, the intermediate houses are inserted, and then the planets, in accord with that framework. But in your A*C*G map, there are forty angles, or

---

[6]*Incarnation: The Nodes and the Four Angles*, Melanie Reinhart, CPA Press, London, 1997, and *The Twelve Houses*, *op. cit.* Note 3.

[7]*Saturn In Transit: Boundaries of Mind, Body and Soul*, Erin Sullivan, Arkana, Contemporary Astrology Series, 1990, pp. 141-6.

forty-four if you include Chiron – one for every planetary body.[8] Lots of angles: lots of life direction in many places.

If we consider our natal charts, our MC/IC axis is our point of orientation, from the base of the Earth where you stand, to the heavens. Literally, it is your roots and your results. We think in terms of those angles being important for the establishment of security, whereas the Ascendant symbolises our outreach, and the Descendant our receptivity to others and the influences around us. The Descendant is that to which you are both extremely sensitive and visible, and on which you may project your own inner vision or image. A great deal of the Descendant material is projected outward until one becomes conscious of it. It is not necessarily the "partner that you attract", but of course it concerns that too, in that we attract that which is familiar to our soul. Fortunately we know that astrology is as multi-levelled as people are, so the Descendant might well be your marriage partner; but on a deeper level it is what you are most responsive to on an unconscious level. If you are aware of this, then you might gauge some of your responses to life more consciously, even though those responses may be surfacing from deep layers of the unconscious.

Ascendant, Descendant, and MC lines

When I said that I was on my SU/DSC line in Berlin, and I wanted to sleep, well, that's humorous and true. But also, my experience on my SU/DSC line was a deep response to the layers of energy of the place itself. However, remember that wherever you go, there you are. If you are a Libran on your SU/DSC line, you are going to be responding to Libra energy. If you are a Scorpio on your SU/DSC line, you are picking up Scorpio undercurrents.

The Descendant isn't always about, "This is where I am going to meet my life partner." It is about what you are going to pick up in the collective around you. And the Ascendant is going to be what you drive out toward, and what you want, and also how you are received by your environment. The MC/IC meridian is about the deep roots of

[8]*Incarnation:The Nodes and the Four Angles, op.cit.* Note 6.

the self, and the visible presentation of that. All the things that you want or aspire towards at the MC will also be apparent on your maps, only these lines will be straight up and down. Your MC and IC lines run vertically, whereas your Ascendant and Descendant lines curve, because at one part of the world one is rising, as you saw in the Solar Map, and the other is setting. They are really connected, Ascendant/Descendant, in this interesting way. And your MC lines are exactly 180° from the IC lines. The Ascendant and Descendant lines curve, and exactly in the middle is the meridian. See how, right at the apex of the curvature of the Ascendant/Descendant line, one becomes the other, and exactly 180° from the MC is the IC.

Orbs

Audience: Could you tell me how close you have to be to a line for it to be effective?

Erin: You're really asking about orbs. That's what I was saying earlier. If you are east of the line, then the influence is greater, because the once-natal planet, an A*C*G planetary line, will begin its trek from west to east (by transit or progression). We would allow 700 miles east of the line as maximum geographical orb, or about a quarter of an inch on the map. West of the line, the orb is smaller, because if you are west of the line, the line has "separated" already from the location, which means that you would use about one-eighth of an inch of orb of influence. That is quite big – it would be about 400 miles.

Audience: Looking at your A*C*G map, my question is this: if you had been born 30 miles west of Vancouver, where the SU/ASC line is exact, would you have noticed a difference?

Erin: Indeed, I did experience that. I spent eleven very happy years, very productive years, in Victoria, BC, where my SU/ASC line is exact. I lived there from 1978 through 1989, when I moved over here, to London. Victoria is 30-ish miles west of Vancouver, and thus is 1/2° of longitude west of it. And my sun is 24' into the 12th house, so I was born "east of the line" by 1/2° of arc, or 30 miles. Thus, by moving only 30 miles or 1/2° of longitude, I moved smack onto my SU/ASC line. A planet is at its most powerful when it is right on the line. But the further east you go from the line, it remains relatively strong until you leave the orb of influence. Jim Lewis thought you could be as far as 700 miles east of the line and it would still be effective, and about 400 miles maximum orb if the location is west of the line.

Latitude and declination

Audience: Does A*C*G bring in declination?

Erin: A*C*G accounts for declination and latitude in the calculation of the planetary lines. Declination and latitude are implicit in planetary line placement, unlike in a natal chart, which only demonstrates zodiacal longitude based along the ecliptic. You have to look up latitude or declination in a separate table when setting a horoscope. Normally it is not considered when doing horoscopes anyway.

Audience: You mean you can see declination on that map there?

Erin: Well, yes, implicitly. The fact that it is Astro*Carto*Graphy already incorporates all three dimensions. Literally, you have quite a lot of latitude, longitude and declination! Declination and latitude are similar, but different. It is the same measurement north and south, but based relative to different circles. Latitude is measured according to the Ecliptic Circle – the distance a planet is north or south of the ecliptic – while declination is measured relative to the Equatorial Circle – the distance a planet is north or south of the Celestial Equator. The zodiac is a band or belt which extends about 8°-9° on either side of the ecliptic, within which the Sun, Moon and planets are always found, with the exception of the aforementioned Pluto, which is inclined to the ecliptic as much as 17°.

Now, the ecliptic and the equator intersect at the equinoctial or zero points – 0° Aries and 0° Libra – whereas at the solstice points the Sun is at its maximum distances north or south of the Celestial Equator. This is why the Ascendant/Descendant lines of natal planets that are in Libra or Aries are much more vertical than planets that

are in Capricorn and Cancer, which are the most curved on the
A*C*G map. You see, a horoscope "assumes" that all the planets are
in the same plane of the ecliptic, which they are not. Planets are
placed in the horoscope according to their degree along the zodiac.
The A*C*G lines also take latitude into account, which explains the
mysterious position of Pluto.

In A*C*G, the picture is more accurate than a horoscope, in that it
accounts for the fact that all the planets do not revolve around the
Sun on the same plane, nor are they in a consistent declination.
Pluto is about 17° from the plane of the other planetary orbits, and
Venus deviates by about 7°. The A*C*G map shows this graphically.
Horoscopes do not. These planets (Pluto and Venus) operate on
oblique ascension, which means that they are not rising (or setting)
on the horizon, as the other planets are, but are rising (or setting)
obliquely above or below the horizon.

This is the seasonal effect of the ASC/DSC lines as well. At the
equinoxes you will notice that the SU/ASC/DSC lines are not curved
in the fashion of the SU/ASC/DSC lines at the solstices. The Earth's
23° tilt on its axis causes it to "see" various planets on the ecliptic
from a "seasonal" viewpoint and, depending on the season (i.e. if the
planet is in Libra or in Cancer), we see it high or low in the sky. In
mid- to north/south latitudes, we see the Sun higher in the sky in the
summer, and lower in the sky in the winter. That is declination. The
zenith points, the little circles on the MC lines, are where the planet
is at its highest point in the sky from the observer – where on earth
it is directly overhead at the time of birth on the A*C*G map. The
degree of terrestrial latitude at which you find the zenith point is the
exact degree of the declination of that planet.

To get a personal picture in your mind, all of you with Neptune in
Libra, look at your map, and you will see that your NE/ASC/DSC
lines are perpendicular by comparison to, say, your PL/ASC/DSC line
in Leo. If you have any planets in Libra/Aries, check your map's
ASC/DSC lines, and you will see them running more up and down
rather than widely curved around, as other planets are that are nearer
the solstice signs. You can approximate by the "up and down-ness"
of your planetary ASC/DSC lines what sign they are in.

The power of angularity

There are lots more technical questions, but I really want to explain more about the psychological and manifest power of angularity.

Audience: So it doesn't make a difference that I come from Paris, as it is so near to London?

Erin: No, that isn't true, actually. To get to the finer points of the difference between London and Paris, we would do a relocation chart, which we will do in the seminar next weekend. Because Paris is about 49° N and London is 53°N30', the Ascendant will change and so will the MC. Paris is also a whole time-zone east from London. From Paris to London, you are moving slightly west and north, and hence both angles will be affected by this change. This is the fine-tuning. We look at the A*C*G map and see the global location of angular lines, and then set local charts to have the actual horoscope in the new place, replete with aspects and houses. You will see this when I show you Princess Diana's horoscope and her Astro*Carto*Graphy.

There is a level at which all of this is very elastic, but my tendency is to go for precision, and it has to run through the exact place on the map. Jim actually allowed quite a large orb, which is fine, but if you want to rectify a chart or find minutiae, then you need absolute precision and exactitude. Experience from Jim's vast client files, however, shows that this orb of influence – 400 miles if you are west of the line and 700 miles if you are east of the line – works. I have experienced the same thing at my own MO/NE crossing. I have Neptune running right through the dot of London, and the Moon just slightly east of it, because the Moon and Neptune are only 3° apart. But they cross precisely, and so become angular apparent, over Majorca. My experience there brought the MO/NE/DSC line to its absolute possible extreme.

A Moon/Neptune story

Audience: What extreme was that?

Erin: Okay, more stories. I became a perfect screen for a lot of projection and imagination from others. I ceased to be "real", in the sense of making any true contact with others. In December of 1992 I moved to Majorca, thinking it would be the "winter place" while living in London from spring to winter. I was a wandering thing on the limb of the world in the coastland of Robert Graves. I didn't exist, except as a figment of colour in other people's minds. In Deia I became their projicient of the collective Neptune – and it is a Neptunian place. Of course, it was my own MO/NE/DSC, so I must take responsibility for that.

It was the ultimate rootless, expatriate exile's state of being. Many of the people who lived there year round were lost souls, the usual kind of remittance-type individuals – lots of drinking, bad art, and worse writing going on. It was a very romantic and almost surreal time in the foggy *calle* below Deia, the home of one of my favourite poets and persons, Robert Graves, which remains now the base of his family concerns. Ah, yes, Moon and Neptune – I lived in a rock house in a sheltered bay, the Calle de Deia, trying to finish a book which never happened. In the end, I cancelled the contract and dumped the idea, giving back the advance.

I loved Deia, and, still love it in my soul, but my life and mind could not be there. It was there, I think, that I finally realised that I didn't want to be in voluntary exile much longer. But it took me three more years, and yet another Pluto transit, to shift me from the Moon/Neptune experience of eight years "over here" on GMT. While in Majorca, I amused myself by identifying with George Sand, who had spent a miserable winter in Majorca with Chopin, who was ill and dysfunctional his entire time in paradise – a hauntingly beautiful place in which I almost disappeared. I shall write a novel titled *Diabolo en Paradiso,* and dedicate it to Poseidon. And that won't happen, either.

More on the angles

Audience: You were talking about different angles, and didn't mention what the IC was.

Erin: Right. I rely on you to reel me in. Let me go on with this interpretive section. If you have got questions, please write them down and get me in between these interpretive bits, because this rote material will help you settle more into what you are seeing on the maps.

The Descendant is a response to our human environment. Also, it is where other people might perceive you in a way which is more revealing than you would ever dream. Other people will see you through your Descendant and tell you in various ways who you are, whether it is implicit in their behaviour toward you or explicit through words, overt action, or environmental situations. This occurs in a tangible fashion wherever you have a planet or planets descending. A planet on the Descendant is at its greatest potential for external manifestation, so you do see your insides on the outside.

Audience: With the exception of Neptune, you said.

Erin: Gad, back to Neptune again. What I meant was, when living on a Neptune line you can become everyone's fantasy and lose your sense of identity. However, it means that your inner core identity is not terribly strong. If you go to a NE/DSC line when in a state of transition, liminality, or extreme vulnerability, then you are very likely to experience the negative facets of it. Now, "losing" your ego is not always a bad thing. Indeed, it may be necessary in the stages of transition called liminality – when one is in the threshold of change or in transit, and the ego becomes a non-functional deterrent to change. In the *Odyssey,* Odysseus discovered this after his confrontation with the Cyclopes, when he reassumed his ego against the ancient laws of the traveller, and was thence persecuted by Poseidon (Neptune) for the duration of the journey to Ithaca.

The Descendant is not your "personality" in the same way as is the Ascendant. However, it is your personality in the collective sense. In other words, the part of you that others are attracted to is often a dormant characteristic, and not conscious except through projection. It needs someone else, or a group situation, to act as a hook or a screen. Thus, on some deep level, you don't see me at all; you just see the part of you that is like me, or as you imagine it to be. But remember, this is not natal astrology per se. It is a collective, global view of who you are in the world. A*C*G is the big picture – not the local you, but the global you. When you deign to live on a specific planetary line, then that unique part of you rises more fully to consciousness. It is very significant to work with the agency of the planetary line you are living on or have travelled to.

Thus there is a greater magnitude to who you "are", who you could be, if you existed in all places at once. As I started out saying today, you actually do – your psyche is huge, as big as the universe, but your psychology has limits within the confines of the world, those being the power-lines, the angularity of your natal planets. The points of identity, the angles of your natal horoscope, are the fated or karmic aspects of being incarnate here on the planet. No matter where you go, there you are, but how that is demonstrated is terribly more complex. You will have to consider culture, ethos, economics, religious biases, opportunity, and so on. Astrology is not the whole picture, but a very rich framework through which the whole picture is focussed. Your VE/MC line is going to be very differently experienced in Algeria, Mali, or the Gambia than in Paris (all are connected by meridian). Although the archetype and nature of Venus and the MC remain the same, they are experienced through you in your own way and then, within that, they will be contained and bound within the ethos of the culture. Similarly, your SU/IC line will be very differently experienced in New York City than in Lima, Peru. Your solar-ness, your spirit and sense of liveliness, will find appropriate ways to root, to sink into the culture.

IC lines

The MC is how you are seen in the public eye, and the aspirations you might have toward the future of yourself – your ego/Self-future. Thus the MC lines are your global aspiration lines – that is, who you are in a way which attracts attention in that particular place. That is basic astrology right there. The IC is your home, but if we consider the world, if we consider ourselves global citizens of the world, that means that we are at home wherever the IC is. We can transform our interior "family", how we experience our family, and our earliest experiences, even those intrauterine preverbal essences. When an IC line is running down a meridian, it is along that line where we experience the archetype of "home", and we are responsive on the

IC line to what goes on there as if the inhabitants were our family or tribal members.

The planet associated with that IC line will further delineate the more defined aspect of the archetypal "home". For instance, if it is a MO/IC line, it will feel very familiar and very comfortable, but if it is a PL/IC line, there will be deep undercurrents of process that will always nag at you, reminding you that there is "something under the rug" to be cleaned out, or work to be done that involves secret things, private issues. People who live on their Pluto/IC lines seem always to be finding out something new about themselves, something deep and resourceful. It is a place of inexhaustible information, but this can be tiring. Offhand, I know two people who did their medical degrees and internships under Pluto lines, and another woman who did her M.D. under the Pluto progressed line. As Jim Lewis pointed out, John Kennedy, president of the US, was assassinated under a Pluto line, and indeed, it can bring danger and death, or threat of same.

Of the ten or eleven IC lines, all will describe the kind of connection you have to the collective ancestral lineage in that area of the world. In the natal chart, the 4th house cusp is the personal ancestral lineage stemming from the family of origin, but it is extrapolated out into the global family with maps – how your personal family origins relate to other cultural and social origins. In other words, are you "at home" here?

The difficulty with the IC itself is that it is the most mysterious part of the horoscope, and often what lies buried in the IC is not made manifest until a transit activates a memory or an event. The IC is both archival and future. It contains our entire DNA family history and the potential for our own progeny, on every level. Melanie Reinhart and I were discussing the IC one day, and she said to me at one point, "Oh, I get it, it is the 'I don't see!'"

Audience: What about NE/IC?

Erin: We'll get into some specifics later, when I delineate planets and we start looking at maps. Blast Neptune! I wonder why everyone is on about Neptune today? Must be something I ate.

You see what I mean about the IC and it being home in its most root astrological symbolism. Natally, it symbolises our biological and familial origins with Mum and Dad. But with A*C*G it is the archetypal imago of Mother and Father, on back through the ancestral line of humanity. Astro*Carto*Graphy IC lines show in which way you are in touch with the roots, the ancestral and "tribal" lineage, of the lands where the line(s) run down through. You may well be quantally connected to all cultures and peoples along the IC lines, according to the planetary agency/archetype that is that IC line.

Angularity was shown as being very important in Gauquelin's work, wasn't it? When Michel and his wife, Françoise, did all their research on famous or successful individuals, it was seen that angular planets produced strong representations of archetypes – Mars for athletes/warriors, Jupiter for judges, Moon for writers. Naturally the research is limited, because statistics always limit whatever you discover to whatever it was that you were looking for. However, it remains valid for that specific thing, even in that very small and very narrow way.

The Gauquelins did manage to come up with startling statistical and probability theories that demonstrated that planets culminating or rising – less so descending and at the IC – are powerful. Interestingly, he found them to be more powerful when slightly cadent – in other words, just into the 12th or just into the 9th or just after sunset. That is east of the angles or, Astro*Carto*Graphically speaking, east of the line. (Angular "houses" of the planet line are west of the A*C*G line). This figuring gives an orb of about 10° into the 9th and 12th houses, which then gives an "orb" of about 600-700 miles in the moderate latitudes, when the city of your choice is east of the line – and halving that if the city of your choice is west of the line, to about 5° or 300 miles.

We have tried, as astrologers and not statisticians, to figure out why this is so. Basically, it is pretty evident to me that it is because the planet is fixed in time and space and will immediately "turn into" a transit and progression which then heads toward the angle(s). You do get powerful influences just into the 12th and 9th house sides of your lines, which would obviously be east of the line if it is an Ascendant line and east of the line if it is an MC line, because the Sun rises in the east and applies itself around the apparent motion of the world from east to west. East of the line is stronger, west of the line is weakening in effect.

Audience: I guess, if you went to a SU/IC line, you would feel happy.

Erin: If you have a self-realised Sun, and you are happy anyway, and if you are not living in denial, yes, you would "feel happy". Happy is relative. What is happy? Living in a place which has a planet on the IC line would feel "at home" in the sense of the planet, but the planet you see at the IC is the agency, the part of the psyche, through which this feeling of hominess or connectedness moves. The SU/IC line will be different from the JU/IC line because your Sun is still your Sun. Remember, no matter where you go, there you are – it's still you.

The SU/IC line is a band along which your own sense of self and identity will feel rooted, connected, and purposeful in the comfort zone of your home experiences. It's your natal horoscope placed in a global context. Your own experience of home and family and tribal roots and safety and security are emphasized on the IC lines. That SU/IC line would be a good place to work through any anxieties, fears, and insecurities you have about your own solarism, your value and productivity in the ego world. But you are not going to get away with anything by shifting yourself around the world.

Audience: You're not going to turn into Joan Collins.

Erin: No. Good grief, why would you want to "turn into" Joan Collins? She's a bad writer. Someone like Alexander Durrell, or P. D. James/Barbara Vine, or someone like that, would be fabulous. Through shifting a planet to an angular placement, you could, however, actualise something extant within yourself that you suspected was there, deeply felt, but couldn't realise. Not everybody is born with Mars at the Ascendant or Saturn at the MC.

Audience: Thank God!

Erin: Hello, don't want to work, eh? All right, then, how about Moon at the MC? Just trying to be generous. MO/MC brings your soul to the public; you would be a "public servant", so to speak. It would bring out the part of you that would care for, nurture, nurse, support, be responsive to, and responsible for the soul or psyche of the collective or community to which you belong.

Crossings: all across the world

We don't all have angular planets in our natal charts, and although I don't think that planets in succeedent houses are weak, they are not as pronounced. They are not going to be as defined. They are much more on the level of body and inner life. For example, the succedent 2nd house is very subtle – it's about self-worth, self-value, and comfort in the world. The 2nd house pertains to the way you were treated as a small child, almost as an investment. In other words, were you touched, were you handled lovingly, did you feel valued? Your values are reflected in the 2nd house, based on a visceral response to original messages sent to and received by the five senses, and the extra-perceptual senses as well. That's all very subtle stuff which doesn't necessarily demonstrate itself in the public arena. But if 2nd house planets in the natal chart become angular, that is, if in the A*C*G map they are found on a line, then wherever that is, you will bring to consciousness the values that were instilled in the infant-self, and you may be able to work on them in a more conscious way than in another location where the 2nd house planet is not angular.

The same applies to 5th, 8th, and 11th house planets. These are all subtle *loci* compared to the power of angular placement. Traditionally, they are considered to be "weak". Astro*Carto*Graphy is more decisive because it is only dealing with angularity and the locus in which a planet is on an angle. It is not subtle and Ptolemaic, and minor aspects are not considered at all unless in the form of "crossings" or *parantellontae* or parans – mundane squares.

Parans

Parantellontae (parans) occur when you have a crossing of planets – for example, a planet on the IC and a planet on the Ascendant. If you have SU/IC crossing with SA/ASC at a place on your map, it would be at that very spot, should you have been born there, that Saturn would have been on the Ascendant and the Sun on the IC simultaneously. You can practise this by setting charts for the actual places where you see parans or crossings on your own map. When you have trines, squares, and even more minor aspects, you can track them on the map to see where they become angular by paran. See if you can find a Sun/Jupiter paran in your own map.

Audience: Aha! I was born in Greece, I have a Sun/Jupiter trine in my chart, and it is crossing from the SU/ASC line to the JU/MC line in Avignon. And I did a thesis on the Knights Templar at Bristol University, where I have Jupiter in my 9th house. Amazing!

Erin: That is amazing, but not unusual. For us, the usual is amazing and vice versa. Your 9th house Jupiter honed in on the high romance of the Templars and their place of origin – and the 9th house mystery and religious history found its perfect "home" on your JU/MC line at Avignon, France. A good illustration – your 9th house Jupiter is east of the JU/MC line, and therefore, by "moving" west, you move toward it.

Now I will demonstrate that very thing, to show that an "aspect" can change. I will continue to use my map for this, only for the sake of the fact that we have the familiar SU/ASC line variety of aspects that become parans, mundane squares (see **Figure 4**). First, notice where this curving SU/ASC/DSC line is intercepted by a couple of MC lines – the MA/MC and SA/MC lines.

Are you now comfortable enough with the map to notice that there are ten MC lines? And you will notice that there are three MC lines all together – Saturn, Mars, and Pluto all meet there. They will always be clustered together, no matter what I do, because that is the natal stellium. That they happen to be at the MC is because they were in the 9th house, but Saturn was very close to the MC when I was born.

Conversely, see where the SU/DSC line is intercepted by the MA/SA/PL/IC lines? On the opposite side of the world, MC lines become IC lines 180° away, and vice versa, and if there is a crossing between an Ascendant line and an MC line, then 180° away will be a Descendant line intersected by an IC line. Got it? Good. There are going to be places where MC lines and IC lines are going to intercept the Ascendant/Descendant, which is a very special kind of aspect. I have Sun square Pluto in the natal chart, within 2°. Here I am, born in Vancouver, BC. The Sun is on the angle of the Ascendant, as you know. Right here at 20°N, just below the zenith mark (the little circle on the PL/MC line), I have Pluto at the MC and Sun on the Ascendant *precisely*. That is a PL/MC-SU/ASC paran or crossing. They are in mundane square. Repeat that to yourself as a mantra; in this way you learn. Paran, crossing, mundane square, *om*.

Audience: The MC isn't necessarily square by 90° to the Ascendant.

Erin: Exactly. Indeed, rarely is the MC 90° to the Ascendant, except at the equator at all times, as I pointed out earlier. However, it is called a mundane square - *in mundo* (on/from Earth) – and it operates as a traditional 90° square aspect. And it demonstrates the curvature of the Earth, the locus of viewpoint on that curve relative to the ascension of the planets involved.

Audience: Which is Pluto and which is the Sun?

Erin: The PL/MC line is running vertically (MC) and the SU/ASC line is curving along to cross it. When we get further to the west coastline off California, right in the same latitude as Los Angeles, I have Mars/Saturn at the MC crossing the SU/ASC line, so that latitude would be a very powerful latitude all across the world. That is a paran between MA/SA/MC and SU/ASC.

Audience: So that is effective all across the world?

Erin: Yes, though much more subtle and secondary to the actual crossing itself. Wherever you have these angular crossings, put a clear straight-edge or ruler across the map, and find any other crossings that might occur there. The genuine A*C*G maps come supplied with a list of crossings at important latitudes north and south, and major cities that are aligned with these crossings, so you can check them out that way. But to learn, you must familiarise yourself with the mechanics by hand.

I can show a second line crossing my SU/MC/IC line. This latitude PL/IC, SU/IC, and PL/ASC line is at the same latitude as SU/ASC and PL/MC. What that does is connect an energy pattern all around the world at that latitude of Sun/Pluto, Sun/Pluto, Sun/Pluto, Sun/Pluto – four times over, because it is also running here, here, here, and here, at 30-35°N. Phew. And now I live in that latitude range, two degrees below my JU/VE/ASC line.

The SU/MC is a little further down along the ecliptic, because the ecliptic is curved. What we get here is this: planets that are rising and hitting MC lines are hitting on the equator, and then, because the ecliptic is 15° wide (7.5° on either side of the centre), you end up with a kind of "travelling" pattern where the planets will be at any place north or south of the ecliptic centre. The intersection of Sun/Pluto, which I have as a natal square, becomes actual on the horizon and at the MC right at this latitude of 30°N, at the Tropic of Cancer. Then Sun/Pluto occurs as an MC/DSC line at 30°S, at the Tropic of Capricorn. This will be consistent.

Zenith points

Audience: What are the little circles on some of the lines?

Erin: Well spotted. Notice which lines the "little circles" are on.

Audience: The MC lines only.

Erin: Yes. Any idea why that may be?

Audience: Are they to do with the zenith point of a planet?

Erin: Indeed, the little circles are the zenith points, the point at which the planet is directly overhead. As I mentioned a bit earlier, the degree at which the zenith point occurs is the declination of the planet. That is why only the MC lines are marked – MC/zenith – and that is also why the zenith points are located within the band of the ecliptic, which shows us at what declination the planet is. If you connect the circles with a pencil line, they will trace a curved line, which conforms with the curve of the ecliptic band (with the exception of Pluto, who is extremely eccentric). You can see eclipses on this map, too. If you have a close conjunction (2° orb) in your natal chart, find the MC lines for those planets. Look down toward the equator for their individual circles. If they are on top of each other, that means that they are conjunct in zodiacal longitude and celestial latitude, and hence are eclipsing each other.

Audience: Are these the most powerful places on earth for the planets? Would that place be where the planet is at its most effective?

Erin: Theoretically, yes. However, because they tend to fall in the equatorial zone, between the tropics of Cancer and Capricorn, it really is lunatic to contemplate moving yourself to a small sector of the world where these power places fall – unless it is practical for you, and it falls into a place in your life. For example, if you have a Venus or Jupiter zenith point in Jakarta, or Nicaragua, or over Sri Lanka, and you are an adventurer, anthropologist, painter, poet, drop-out, social worker, importer, or business person, you might find those places to be extremely fruitful for you. Even if you don't live there, you can activate the line. Living there could be very good, indeed, and fulfil a spiritual longing, but it may not be wholly practical. Ideally, you can work with the maps in a remote-access fashion. Keep in mind that zenith points are the maximum of MC energy, so it is with that high profile that you are working. I wouldn't advise acting in a secretive fashion on a zenith point!

The only way to learn is to look. You should make numerous colour copies of your maps and draw and write all over them, using them for learning tools.[9] The most important learning I did to teach myself

---

[9]Editor's note: Authorised distributors of A*C*G maps are given in Note 10. Distributors for languages other than English and German may be found by searching the Web. These authorised maps are of very high quality. However, for learning purposes, it should be noted that Astrodienst AG (http://www.astro.com) provides a free on-line chart calculation service including the "AstroMap", similar to the A*C*G map, which also indicates

astrology was to read the ephemeris, read the Table of Houses, and look at material like this and notice what is connected. It's the only way you are ever really going to appreciate your knowledge. I think, by the end of this day, you will be somewhat versed in looking at these maps and understanding them. It takes a while.

Moving right along: Cyclo*Carto*Graphy®[10]

As I have implied throughout the day, you can "move" these lines. They transit and they progress. Just as the natal chart instantly becomes a series of progressions and transits, so do Astro*Carto*Graphy lines. The progressions of the Sun, Moon, Mercury, Venus, and Mars, along with the transits of Jupiter, Saturn, and the outer planets, are drawn onto an acetate overlay to illustrate the symbolic movement of the natal A*C*G in a map called Cyclo*Carto*Graphy.

When I am one year of age, my progressed Sun will have moved along by 1°, and by now, at this age in 1997, my progressed Sun is at 7° Capricorn, which happens to be right on my Moon lines (natal Moon at 7° Libra, hence A*C*G Moon crossing-line). Transiting Saturn is at 7° Aries (C*C*G puts it at the transiting Saturn/Ascendant line in September, 1997). Funnily, I moved here to London when Saturn was 8° Capricorn and Jupiter 8° Cancer, and I am slowly reconnecting back to North America as Saturn is at the same degree of Aries.

---

the planetary lines across the world. These maps may be printed out on a colour printer and are ideal for the student to experiment with.

[10]Registered and authorised distributors of A*C*G and C*C*G: UK: The Astrology Shop, Equinox, Covent Garden, 78 Neal Street, London WC2H 9PA, http://www.equinox.com. Tel: London: 0171-4997-1001. Europe: AstroData, Chilenholzstrasse 8, CH-8907 Wettswil, Switzerland. North America: Astro Numeric Service, Box 336-R, Ashland, OR 97520. In the US call: 1-800-MAPPING. [All maps used in the CPA seminars from which this book derives were provided complimentary from Equinox Books. All the maps actually used in this book were provided complimentary by and printed with permission of Astro Numeric Service.]

Audience: How do you calculate the progressed and transit chart of the map? What is it called, again?

Erin: It is called Cyclo*Carto*Graphy (C*C*G from now on). You can order it from licensed A*C*G outlets. As for calculating it yourself, I would give it a miss. Or if you become terribly familiar with A*C*G, then you can do it roughly for a few years, once having a C*C*G done for you.

"Real" movement

To create the C*C*G map acetate overlay, the inner planets are moved by secondary progression – Sun, Moon, Mercury, Venus, and Mars – and the other, slower moving planets, Jupiter, Saturn, Uranus, Neptune, and Pluto are placed in by transits for the year. (These transits and progressions are set for the mid-point of the year you select, *i.e.,* for the period of January through December of a given year, the set date for C*C*G would be in July. You can have Cyclo*Carto*Graphy done for yourself each year. Or, after a while, once you are used to working with it, you can roughly figure out yourself, by the progressions and transits, where the lines will be.

However, beware! It is in this realm of "real" movement where things get odd, because two of our planets' orbits, those of Pluto and Venus, have a greater tilt to the plane of the ecliptic. Pluto inclines 17° off the plane of the ecliptic, and Venus is 7° off the plane. Thus, by declination, even though the given planet in transit or Venus progression is exactly conjunct a planet in your natal chart, it may not be conjoined by declination. In other words, the transiting planet may be at the same zodiacal degree along the ecliptic, but it might be much higher or lower in latitude because of oblique ascension, as mentioned earlier.

Audience: So the effects of the transit might be viewed very differently. This adds a new dimension to progressions and transits! It would seem that there is a level of involvement that is more to do with activity and contact.

Erin: Thank you! Exactly – another dimension, literally. That is what A*C*G is – three-dimensional astrology. It takes into account time, space, and relationship. We are not looking at a flat chart. In viewing astrology in such a global fashion, we are opening our brains to accept that fact – that the obvious is only the gross manifestation, while the invisible might offer a more subtle nuance to a situation.

Having mentioned this, I want to tell you about a perfect example of this phenomenon. I have an exact conjunction of Jupiter and Venus at 3° Sagittarius. My JU/VE/ASC line runs right through the Pacific Ocean off the coast of Baja, California, up through Phoenix, Arizona, the Midwest, on up into Canada, through Winnipeg, Manitoba,and on up to the now famous vortex.

This conjunction is at 3° Sagittarius longitudinally in the zodiac (and at birth both planets were within 1° of declination of latitude). Now, as we speak, I have a Pluto transit over my Jupiter/Venus conjunction at 3° Sagittarius – zodiacally conjunct. However, when I looked at my Cyclo*Carto*Graphy overlay, Pluto is at 3° Sagittarius in the zodiac, but its latitude puts its place off the western coast, almost on the dot of San Francisco. Hundreds of miles away, and it never even comes close to the natal lines of Jupiter and Venus, which are in the same zodiacal longitude! In fact, the PL/ASC line by transit, as seen in the C*C*G overlay, runs from 140°W (south latitude), "enters" North America at San Francisco, as said, and then runs on up to only 130°W at the top of the map. It is practically a vertical line, certainly not the curved ASC line we think of normally. Pluto in Sagittarius is looking very different in declination than it did in Leo! The strange thing about the Pluto C*C*G line running through San Francisco is that it is where Jim Lewis lived in the same flat since the 1960's. That is where he died, and it is from that place we contracted to write his book, and, of course, he was a brother to me. He had Pluto at the Ascendant in his natal chart.

Changes in latitude, changes in attitude

What I then see is the reality of the transit. Yes, it is in line with the 3° Sagittarius longitude, but the transit of Pluto is much higher in latitude than my natal Jupiter and Venus (which are very close in latitude in the birth chart). As a result, the actual transit of Pluto is not eclipsing or occulting the JU/VE conjunction. It is implicating the conjunction in profound transformation, but not devastating it totally.

My theory about this kind of differentiation is: if Pluto were exactly crossing over the JU/VE line at its precise crossing in the same longitude and latitude, rather than in a more distant declination as it is, then the results of the transit would have been much more malignant than they are or have been. As it is, it has resulted in my choosing not to live abroad any longer – with some attendant "events", not all at the cheerful end of the feeling spectrum – and to return to my roots and change my travel life completely. There has been stress, of course, but it hasn't, and likely won't, kill me. Indeed, it will give me a new lease on life when the final direct pass occurs, Pluto being in its final stage of the eighteen-month retrograde cycle of transiting the third longitudinal degree of Sagittarius.

I differentiate the longitudinal zodiacal transit from the declination position thus. The zodiacal conjunction of the transiting planet (in this case) brought in the manifestation of the sign, planets, and house. The fact that the transiting planet (Pluto) was doing its "thing" out on the coast in declination, and nowhere near the declination of the natally placed Jupiter/Venus line, brought a sense of latitude, of freedom of choice – a more diverse manifestation, with numerous horizons upon which to enact the transit's effects. Maybe longitude is Fate and latitude is Choice? Longitude is fixed and latitude is flexible in the horoscope wheel, as the Midheaven and Ascendant demonstrate.

Audience: Are you different "over there"? I mean, are you really affected by this move? Can you tell what part of you is more alive, as you put it?

Erin: Oh, yes, and immediately. Both are still "me", but the part of me that is Jupiter/Venus has changed, wanting new ways of living it out, while the part of me that is Moon/Neptune has become, once again, less dominant as a persona, but still integrative as an innate characteristic. In fact, having been immersed in the experience of the line, it is no longer the blurry issue it once was. The natal horoscope remains fixed always, but the experience of the Self is obviously much more fluid and demonstrates itself in its global sense. I feel that my Moon/Neptune experienced a full life on the angle of the Descendant, and is now more available and conscious. I just want to plant in your mind that these technical realities are there, and they are interesting and highly thought-provoking, and reveal truths. You don't necessarily have to know them in order to be able to interpret and work with people's Astro*Carto*Graphy maps, but to know them deepens your wisdom of the subject. I have always felt that a picture and a thorough understanding of the solar system and its movements is always better – for me. *Physis* – nature – is the root of physics, and the nature of things is the truth of things.

Audience: Which way do the transits and progressions go?

Erin: Transits and progressions move in zodiacal order from Aries to Taurus, and so on. They appear to move from west to east when moved along the zodiac of a fixed natal chart; and on the A*C*G map, you see the planets (lines) more visually as they also move from west to east. This is the key difference in perspective between horoscopes and A*C*G maps. When we look at our A*C*G maps we are looking down on the Earth, whereas with the horoscope we are looking up (or out) at the sky. Remember, the A*C*G map is your natal view of the global picture.

As the world turns: the planetary lines

Having talked about angles and their significance in the map, I would like to go into the planets as agents of our worldview, and some potential experiences that are associated with each planet. At this stage we can speak about specifics – the planets and their placements on the map according to the north-south, east-west picture that we have of the angles. This delineative section of the seminar will be approached from a basic, archetypal viewpoint. In *The Psychology of Astro*Carto*Graphy* there is a cookbook section which covers every possible combination you can get with all the lines. But my experience, when we look at it from a more depth analytic psychological viewpoint, is that when we experience planets on angles, we experience that aspect of ourselves in a more clearly alive way.

As I pointed out, we don't all have planets on angles in our charts natally, but in parts of the world we do, and we might like to travel to those parts of the world to enliven something – or we might not, depending on the planet and angle. For instance, in Thailand you may have a Jupiter line, which would express your ability to relate to that culture on a deep, systemic, tribal level. It might be a place where you could instigate a business of importing, publishing, travelling, or study. That's very practical.

Sun lines

A*C*G maps not only portray how you exist in the world, but also where you exist more intensely – more archetypally, if you will. Sun lines are not only fame lines, as we may have assumed. Solar lines are where you feel your life force, your libido, your fire, the fuel that you burn – and where, with the earlier character codicil in mind, the inherent qualities and nature of your Sun are more dominant. You will find that you affect those around you more powerfully because you are more in tune with the component of your solar self, and hence, with any explorative, pioneering and leadership qualities that you contain. The animus, the spirit within, is strong on Sun lines, and courageous acts and adventurous schemes are more attractive. The qualities of heroism and achievement are enhanced, and you may well find that you are at your most social and attract more attention.

Again, this depends on the inherent quality of your Sun in the chart. The need for attention under Sun lines is also present, and you may find yourself drawing attention to yourself in ways which are not good – so be aware that a solar line is not always a positive thing. If you are working on secret projects, then secrecy is harder to maintain. If you are trying to live a monastic or monkish existence, then you will grapple with the temptations of the world of achievement, striving, and success.

"Know Thyself" and "Nothing Too Much": the Apollonian *dicta* from the Delphic monument apply here, in that the truth of your deepest urges and desires to be and become are strong on Sun lines. Ego and inflation are part and parcel of individuation, as well as indulgence and perfection. Thus, your Sun lines are your greatest test and your most open place for understanding your self as it actualises through the ego – through your behaviour, accomplishments, longings for success, and your social reception.

Moon lines

Lunar lines will run through areas in the world in which we are most likely to have recall of intrauterine, infantile, and childhood experiences. Thus, on a Moon line you may have feelings that you can't articulate. Very often it takes time for a line to activate or come to experience in consciousness. In other words, you could go to a Moon line and not have a strong experience if you are on holiday; but if you were to move there, it would become increasingly more dominant the longer you stay and become immersed in the environment.

Inarticulate, non-rational, feeling-tone responses – gut responses – arise on Moon lines, often stemming from preverbal experiences. We often recall the past in ways which are shocking to the "adult" perception of self. Moon lines illuminate one's sense of personal security, and exacerbate one's sense of insecurity as well. On a Moon line, we are more aware of our need for safety, containment, nourishment, and nurturing, which is why the lines are associated with "home". There are people who are not generally responsive in a lunar sense, but if they go to a Moon line, they find themselves doing things and behaving in ways which they might not normally do because they feel free to be more feeling.

One English client cannot resist having past-life regressions, full submersion rebirthing, and healing massage when on her MO/IC line, which happens to run through Santa Fe, New Mexico, mecca of New Age philosophies and practices. This is not her London persona, but her natal Moon is in the 12th house in Virgo, and not inclined to acknowledge her feeling levels in general. But on the MO/IC, well, it is all about food and comfort and psychic, back-to-the-womb treats. It is not just about Santa Fe; it is her MO/IC line precisely on Santa Fe. A*C*G is unusual in that it involves both place and relationship. For her, Moon, IC, and Santa Fe combined are all about getting in touch with her infantile self, and needing to know things that other great Mummies or Daddies know. The coincidence of the agency, the planet, with the location, the culture, is the function of A*C*G – time, place, and relationship. Hence, guru-seeking is not just the domain of Neptune lines, but falls into the category of parental issues as well.

Moon lines are about family background and how one was raised, and these things will often be perceived in more profoundly feeling ways when one goes to Moon line locations. One is more in touch with what one's family did, what Mother and Father were like, and what one's family pattern and domestic lineage are. You may find that a MO/ASC line somehow "allows" you to demonstrate your feelings more, and that a MO/IC line will put you in touch with the part of your feeling self which you cannot access normally. High feelings and emotional responses are highlighted along Moon lines.

Mercury lines

Mercury lines are not always about communication *per se*. The function of Mercury is multiplex. Mercury not only symbolises one's own perceptions, but also is the agent of one's receptivity to the perceptions of others. It is the subtle response to the collective, ethnic interaction. Say that you go to a Mercury line that is located along an isolated part of the world, where the aboriginal energy and peoples are still deeply connected to their ancestral roots. That you have a Mercury line running through there literally *means* that you are connected to that place through inherent understanding of their tribal and ancestral links – the common link of humanity becomes personal along Mercury lines. In that place you may even "recall" lost or hidden aspects of your own primitive and undeveloped unconscious – that is, your mind will be awakened to an archetypal recognition of the link between all peoples, but particularly those people in that place.

Audience: I have a ME/IC line running right through Darwin, and it is the zenith point, too. I had a profound experience in the outback, on a trek that originated in Darwin and was led by aborigines. I was actually able to speak rudimentary words and communicate in their tongue after two weeks of this astoundingly memorable experience.

Erin: Perfect! Also, on Mercury lines, you would be much more responsive and less resistant to whims and the ebb and flow of serendipity. Mercury is a trickster figure, so you may find that you feel and act more spontaneously and quickly to interruptions, delays, difficulties, and strange experiences. In itself, Mercury has no fixed persona, and often is absorbed into the mood of another planet or takes on the quality of a strong contact. Hermes will emerge in his multifarious natures, taking you to the recesses of lost civilisations in the psyche, as psychopompos. He will also agent the serendipitous events that are magical and lead you along a thread to a place of mystery in yourself. By this I mean you just might find yourself with ideas you never realised you had.

Thus, for example, if you find yourself on a Mercury/Pluto paran (crossing), you would be more likely to "see" or perceive the hidden or deeply psychological aspects of life in that place. Too, Mercury lines will bring up the trickster aspect of your own psyche, and your puer-ness, your eternally youthful self, is let loose. You will be less rigid, and more excited by change and new horizons, either mentally or geographically. Your movement and your responsiveness to your environment are much more flexible under Mercury lines. Of course, on the mundane level it is a great place for teaching, for learning, for studying languages, and for working in Mercury occupations.

Venus lines

You are all sophisticated enough in keywords, I think, to interpret these lines from that perspective, but there is always another slant to planet lines. For instance, Venus isn't always about romantic love. On a deep, visceral, non-verbal level it is about self-love, and the ability to appreciate one's own values and insist that those values be upheld. If they are violated in any way, there is a physical reaction to this. Venus lines enhance the side of you that is more responsive to the environment as an aesthetic. You may also find that Venus lines are about the things that are beautiful to you, and everyone's concept of beauty is totally different. What's beautiful to me may not be beautiful to you.

Venus will represent, to some extent, the "other" in your life. What I love within myself is more readily seen outside myself, and thus I will be projecting it to some degree, and receiving that projection back. Our subtle responses to "beauty" are totally personal – beauty is relative to the interior light of beauty. It will only shine on that object or thing or person or idea which is lit from within. It is very possible that, wherever Venus lines are, ideal types of relationships are formed. Also, you are more responsive to people who come from that area, because they fall into the muse of your more poetic, aesthetic self.

You don't have to go to lines on your map; you can access them in many other ways. For example, you could meet somebody very significant who was born on a Venus line of yours. That's not uncommon. The idea I have about being everywhere at the same time works with relationship and A*C*G. For instance, somebody born on my Venus line might come into my life as significant person who exemplifies my values, my ideals, my desires for love and emotional well-being.

When you are doing synastry or comparison of maps, you will notice that friends, associates, lovers, and children will have lines running through the same places. But they are different lines. It shows that these people may have a different "fate" or destiny or feeling about the same place. People are connected by common degrees in the zodiac, directly or indirectly, and thus experience the same things for different personal reasons. It reminds me of a couple who came for a full natal and A*C*G consultation, and wanted to "retire" and create a retreat for healing. They consulted me about places and timing. Their maps showed that they had two places in common, and one of the places was perfect for such a venture. But the lines each of them had running through this "best" place were very different planetary agencies. Those planets described the personal, individual needs and motives for the common venture. They wanted to do the same thing for different personal evolutionary reasons, and it fell in the same location in the world. The project has been a success.

If your Venus is shadowed, then it is hard to feel connected to the beauty in life. In fact, a woman in Berlin said she felt she had never been in touch with her Venus. I said, "Well, where is it in your chart?" She replied, "It is in Aquarius in the 12th house, retrograde." Indeed, this description does feel bereft of feeling or aesthetic sensuality. This is a classic configuration for Aphrodite Urania, a picture of the observant, cold, removed, Platonic Venus who decries the common love, the common element of humanity – that of the flesh and the body.[11]

Everything else was very "out front", angular, a 1st house/7th house kind of thing. I thought, "Of course, that would be an unborn aspect of herself." Aquarius isn't known for its emotional connectedness. The 12th house is known for its womblike or embryonic qualities, and to have Venus there does say that there may have been times when the woman was completely unaware of what her own quality of values were. She may not have had good, warm, loving experiences within her infant body, and thus in her adult life it manifests as a feeling of non-attachment to Venusian life.

A Venus family line

A friend and colleague of Jim Lewis' and mine submits this story about Venus lines. Glennys is a Sagittarius and Brian is a Libra. Glennys has her Venus at 22° 08' Capricorn, and Brian's Jupiter is at 22° 23' Capricorn. When they were married, there was a Sun/Venus/Descendant conjunction between 21° and 23° Capricorn. Glennys met Brian in New York, where she was on her VE/ASC line. In fact, the line curved close to Brian's birth place in Canada. Her relocated Ascendant in New York is 21° 13', and at the time she met Brian her progressed Sun was in orb of conjoining her natal Venus. When Glennys and Brian decided to marry eighteen months later,

---

[11] *Venus and Jupiter: Bridging the Ideal and the Real*, Erin Sullivan, CPA Press, London, 1986. Part One of this book illuminates the "split" of the archetypes of Venus/Aphrodite in love and creativity.

Glennys' progressed Sun was 23° 30' Capricorn and her progressed Moon was 21° 06' Capricorn, a few months before the exact progressed New Moon on her natal Venus and Brian's natal Jupiter.

When Brian met Glennys, his progressed Moon was 25° 11' Capricorn, just past his Jupiter in the 8th house. He was already planning his trip to Australia the next year, and already had his date of departure – 14 January, the day the Sun was at 23° to 24° Capricorn. He was already invited to attend the conference in Melbourne, Glennys' home town, where his relocated Ascendant is 21° 51', his JU/ASC line. Brian went back and forth to Australia during this period of his third Jupiter return. Brian and Glennys bought a house for holidays and retreats in Stanley, Tasmania, a place they both fell in love with. Glennys' father's name was Stanley, and he was born on 14 January – so the degree of his Sun was that same degree. In Stanley, Brian is on his JU/ASC line again – the relocated Ascendant being 23° 44'. Brian's stepson Cameron, Glennys' son, has his natal Ascendant at 24° 28', so wherever Cameron goes in the world, he has the same Ascendant as Brian. When he went to Ottawa and Toronto with Brian, they both shared Brian's natal Ascendant. Both Brian's stepdaughters have been to Canada and the US, where they both have Venus lines.

Brian and Glennys created and work together at the Chiron Centre in Melbourne, Australia, with three other practitioners, so it is not surprising that one has 23° Capricorn on the Ascendant and the other two have 23° Capricorn on the Descendant. That's how the Jupiter of the Libra man and the Venus of the Sagittarius woman found each other.

Mars lines

When we move beyond the Earth's orbit to Mars, we travel outside our deepest personal selves into the outer environment. The Sun, Moon, Venus, and Mercury are our personal identity planets. They are less shakeable, those planets, because we identify with them viscerally. They are super-personal.

But Mars shows how we push our inner world out into the environment, and how our environs receive our extraversion. Under Mars lines, we become more self-externalised and effective in the environment. Mars line are hard work. They all require as much conscious civilisation as possible. Our own evolution from infancy through to effective adulthood is exemplified by the evolution of the Ares/Mars archetypal expression, from his Greek to his Roman persona. Mars' mythical evolution from the infantile Greek Ares of strife and war, through to the founder of Rome and protector of the cultivated fields, is rather like our journey from infancy to adulthood. By his own lights, Jim Lewis had a rather weak Mars – in his own words, a "shadowed" Mars. His Mars was succeedent in the 8th house in Pisces, and remember, he first became interested in mapping as a result of his "flat tire zone" on his MA/MC line, Salt Lake City.

Audience: I just noticed that my MA/MC line goes through Kingston, Jamaica. I was en route there when a violent hurricane blew it to smithereens. We never actually got there. We ended up sitting in the airport.

Erin: So you were on your way to your Mars line in Jamaica, where there was a big hurricane, but you never actually got there.

Audience: We missed it by half an hour.

Erin: Amazing. Well, you'll have to go again, won't you? Just don't go between the middle of August and the early part of October – that's hurricane season. I would say that, if you are going to go to a place under a Mars line, be aware that there is likely to be a hostile atmosphere at some point. That could be just a strong wind, or it could be a mugger; it could be an infection or it could be a *coup d'état*! Mars is about acute things, sharp things, revolutions, and so on – very yang energy. Too, our Mars lines are about our own rage, lust, desire, anger, and animus side. It also is a place that you would find to be very hard work, if you stayed on. Holidays don't always bring up the lines in such dramatic ways, but they can activate instantly.

Audience: If you don't like someone, you could send them to their Mars lines!

Erin: "Go to this Mars/Pluto crossing, it's fabulous!" One could do really nasty things with this, I suppose. But ideally, you want people to go to their JU/VE lines and Moon lines and Sun lines – all the pleasant lines, right?

Audience: Let's talk about the Pluto lines.

Erin: We are going to talk about the Pluto lines soon enough.

Audience: My Mars line goes right through Ecuador. The only time in my life I have ever had anything stolen was in Ecuador. I twisted my ankle and had all sorts of painful things happen, including a relationship bustup. The end result was an acute awareness of my own anger and rage "out there" in the world, coming back at me.

Erin: We have Susie's map and chart, which we are going to talk about later in the day, when we are looking at personal stories. A Mars line can be a violent attack.

Audience: And it was hard work.

Audience: Can I just say something? My Mars line goes through Bali, and I also have a Venus/Uranus conjunction that goes through Bali. They cross right over it.

Erin: So you have got a Mars/Venus/Uranus paran in Bali. Okay, what happened?

Audience: I went to Bali, and my partner and I had a horrible breakup while there. It was probably one of the worst times of my life. I thought Bali was beautiful, just a beautiful, gentle place, and yet it was painful and difficult for me there.

Erin: You see, this is where we have got to get over the idea that what you see is what there is. It simply isn't true. It is all a vast hallucination, and the only way you are actually going to see anything of personal meaning is through your own eyes. This shows you how you see the world through your own eyes. You do not have to go to these places to be able to visualise the world through that lens, but going there, and having experiences like you describe, is peculiar to your A*C*G view of Bali.

Audience: I sort of liked it, in my own weird way. I thought it was interesting, but it was hard work.

Erin: I see your experience there as an indication that Mars is a shadowed planet for you – you didn't have the courage to dump your partner in another part of the world. This is how synastry can work intra-dimensionally. In using A*C*G for synastry, you can see that a couple might do very well in a particular part of the world. But if you shift them, if they move, suddenly the sleeping side or the dormant, unaware side of the relationship might start to emerge. You can shift yourself around and see what your relationships will do in various parts of the world.

Audience: If you have Mars on the Ascendant or on the Descendant, is it also a difficult line?

Erin: Yes. What I am doing here is defining the planetary agency, and then, with the very brief bit of knowledge we did on the angles, putting it together. If you have your MA/DSC line running through London, then your experience here will be quite martial, filled with energy, thrust, force, action, drama, and animus. You will likely have to fight your way through, and work very hard, and experience your own rage. If it hasn't ever been brought to the fore in other parts of your life, then you will find yourself "getting in touch", to use the common parlance of the day. It can also be very healthy, very healing.

On a psychological level, what one might do is go to a specific place to unlock an aspect of oneself that is buried and needs to be brought forth and civilised. People do that instinctively – they go to places without knowing astrology, A*C*G, or anything mythological or psychological, and they live out the needs that are repressed. I did that upon coming to London. At midlife I moved from my SU/ASC line to my MO/NE/DSC line, and I did it because opportunities arose. But I also came knowing, with conscious intent, that it was what I was to do – to explore my "opposite" and make more conscious an inner mechanism that needed to be made angular in my life. And it has worked. I can only give you positive ways of utilising these lines, which may sometimes seem devastating, difficult, hard work.

Audience: So if you worked on your Mars, then your experience of Mars would change.

Erin: Yes. You are speaking about individuation, and earlier I began with the idea that at different ages in our lives there are different levels of awareness of ourselves. Certain lines could become less and less perilous, and more and more civilised. We can, perhaps, learn to articulate more aspects of our sleeping self by being aware of the map of the world, and also through travel. You were asking about "working on your Mars", and going to a Mars line – and whether you would be less likely to experience the violent, attacking side of it if you did so. Maybe you can now go to Jamaica, if you have worked on your Mars, and not have a hurricane! It's not actually so bad. There's nothing like the elements out of control if you want to be excited. Mars is good for excitement.

Audience: I know two people who live on their MA/MC lines, and they have both done a lot of work on themselves, and a lot of therapy. And they still had a very difficult time there, even after three years.

Erin: It is an ideal that we can somehow cure ourselves of ourselves. I am not sure that it is wholly possible, but I think that we can modify some of the more destructive aspects of ourselves. I know personally one of the people you are speaking of, and indeed, I don't think there is any escape from ourselves. My own recommendation would be to avoid lines that were potentially dangerous. I wouldn't want to go to my Sun/Mars/Saturn/Pluto crossing. I just wouldn't want to do that. It's not because I am altogether psychologically unrealised – although I am psychologically unrealised to a great degree, obviously, as everybody is – but I wouldn't bother to do that one. After all, how much can you take? I would leave a place of suffering, based on my knowledge of the map and myself, no matter how much energy it took to make the change. Sometimes – indeed, often – it takes more life-energy from you not to change than to change.

Audience: Could you say more about a shadowed Mars?

Erin: An unrealised Mars can be a dangerous thing. It is the first "social" planet, and it first returns to its own place at the age of two years and two months. This is our first step outside of the world of Mummy and into the world of assertion and aggression. Mars is a planet which I believe is the most potentially suppressed planet, because anger is something that very few people know how to cope with or deal with properly.

The declaration of war in appropriate ways, times, and places is important, and as a two-year old – in the so-called "Terrible Two's" – the child is experiencing the results of a complete transit of Mars around the entire horoscope to its first Mars return. Suddenly the child has Mars come home, after having made every possible aspect in the chart, and as soon as Mars returns to itself the first time, and moves onward, the child starts to say, "No!" and "I want!" and "Mine!" and "Me!" He or she is running out of the yard, wanting to drink whatever is in that bottle under the sink, striving to do everything within his or her grasp, and the parents are running around half out of their minds, trying to figure out how to keep this child from falling out of a tree, cutting himself or herself, getting into a car with strangers, biting others, climbing on the chairs, and endangering himself or herself in myriad ways. Hopefully, they are trying to prevent damage without killing the child's spirit.

Children try everything at the Mars return period. They push the envelope, and test their limits and their boundaries. In that very important time, a civilisation process begins. You might look at your Mars line as if you were reacting from a time period in your life ranging anywhere from the age of two to about five. If you were seriously punished, repressed, or violated, or your spirit was damaged or under-appreciated in a Mars way, then a good feeling about assertiveness will be lacking. After all, we cannot let children run into the street and over cliffs, or drive cars. We cannot let them do certain things to hurt self and others. You have to save their life and limbs, but you can't crush their spirit and you can't crush their aggression and assertion, their need to defend, and their animal instincts of possession and territorialism.

Mars is possibly the most difficult of the classical planets to civilise healthfully, and it is probably also the planet that is most likely to be shadowed because of its primal survival cutting characteristic. Also, it is the planet I associate with the first stage of individuation. This initial stage of individuation does require a sharp and clear cut of the umbilicus, and often it is painful for both mother and child. Often our first Mars memories are difficult. If your Mars was not well received and handled in accord with your needs for learning how to get what you wanted, then you might have buried it. Then it will fly out at some unexpected time when something arises that reminds you of it. There is that aspect of repression.

Audience: If our earliest aggressions were shamed, or beaten out of us, or we didn't experience natural anger in a healthy way at two, would this assist in repressing and creating a "shadowed" Mars? Could this occur with any planet?

Erin: Yes, to both questions. Also, the first Mars return at two years old is when the child begins to understand the anger of others – the anger of the parents. I would see this age as the most sensitive time for a child to experience his or her parents' rage. As Mars is expressed by one or other parent, it acts as an example for the two-year-old. Hence, some of our irrational fears of anger are embedded in our two-year-old self, in the self that was traumatised by specific types of anger expressed by mother or father – or, in the case of the "family secret", appropriate rage reactions that were not expressed.

Audience: Which is more important – natal lines or progressed lines?

Erin: Oh, natal, just the same as in a natal horoscope. In other words, if you are asking what I use for significance and weight, choosing between Cyclo*Carto*Graphy and Astro*Carto*Graphy, it is the A*C*G map and the natal lines that are you. But it is just like a natal horoscope; I consider the progressions as they approach the natal planet and make a perfect aspect. To my mind, secondary progressions are "promised" growth waiting to happen, and when a progressed planet actually makes a precise contact, then a shift is made evident. And when progressed lines make contact with natal lines, we have a shift in the working of the line. (Solar Arc doesn't work for this, by the way.) When a secondary progressed planet makes a contact to a natal planet, the natal planet comes alive. The progressed Moon is very important because it has such a steady monthly motion. Transits, too, are very important, as they are with natal charts. Transits activate lines, and often people are drawn to a place on a line that is being enlivened and awakened by a transit (or progression) to it.

Audience: I see in my chart that almost all the Mars and Venus lines are in the open ocean.

Erin: That brings up another important philosophical point. This is where the map is fate. For instance, I can't get rid of Uranus in the 8th house – that is where it is in my natal horoscope. I can't get rid of my SU/ASC line where it is. It is to be accepted. The fact that there are big spaces where there are no lines is natural, as natural as it is to have empty houses in your chart.

In the same way, some people – and they find this disappointing – don't have positive lines running through habitable places. I look at their map and have to say to them, "You do not have strong lines running through metropolitan centres such as London or Paris or Hamburg or Teheran or Delhi or Vancouver or Los Angeles, or any other big places." You don't have any lines going through highly civilised places. Civilised? What am I saying? Los Angeles? Teheran? Hardly civilised, but you know what I mean – buildings and cars, running water and elevators and telephones and fax machines and shopping. Obviously, commodities don't always denote civilisation per se, but are necessary for industry. Some people who are thinking, "I want to relocate and build my career," but whose SU/MC runs right through the mid-Atlantic or the Galapagos, have to reconsider their purpose in life and really look at what it is they want to do. Not everyone is burning with ambition, passion, or compulsion, or the need (or destiny, in fact) for fame or great challenges to achieve in the world.

One of the most enlightened things to do is to accept one's own mundaneness – to really love one's own self and dimensions. Not everyone is significant in the big picture of things. That is life. A great life achievement is to be as small as you are and as great as you can be in that small way. People who have no lines in important places are simply meant to be happy with what is.

Audience: I know a person like that. All his Sun lines go through the ocean. All his JU/MA lines run through the land. He has been trying to succeed as a writer for many, many years now, and he just can't.

Erin: Has he ever thought of being an investigative reporter, or a political commentator? Or a mystery writer? Horoscopes and maps do not always deny what someone longs to be, but will describe what kind of actor, writer, painter, or astrologer they could be.

Audience: He does write about this stuff. However, he's ended up living in Greece, which is his NE/DSC line, and he has lived there for the past fifteen years. He has allowed his passport to expire, and has no status in Greece, either.

Erin: He doesn't exist. That's what I mean – Neptune lines can rob you of a strong sense of personal identity. But this is literal – no passport, living on his NE/DSC line. You know, he may not have come to terms with his deeper self's desire for obscurity, or the part of his deeper self that will not take the challenge of the Mars/Jupiter task of hard work and success at his chosen vocation.

Audience: When he tried to go to Los Angeles with a script, the only line that goes right through there is Pluto/MC, and he had no passport.

Erin: And?

Audience: He found a way, without a passport, to go there and get a new one. He's Canadian, not American – he went to Canada, and then, after clearing up the identity problem, went down to Los Angeles, but there was no sale on his script.

Erin: That is the type of story that an Astro*Carto*Graphy map would produce. Travelling from NE/DSC to PL/MC: a lack of identity (NE/DSC) toward the place in which a strong identity is needed to survive (PL/MC). Also, PL/MC is a place in which one is caught out if hiding something, whether it is just one's own self, or something more illegal. The part of you that is secret or unknown, Pluto, is more public at the MC angle. A*C*G is as effective a guidance and counselling tool as is the natal horoscope, if you approach it that way. You see yourself spread all over the map.

When we say that as a kind of jokey phrase – "Oh, I'm all over the map!" – it's true. Those are the kinds of stories we hear.

Audience: Could you just repeat what you said about when there are no strong lines through habitable places?

Erin: One would need to consider very seriously, "What is my purpose in life? Maybe I am not really meant to live out angular experiences. Maybe my life isn't about making a huge impact in the world. Maybe it's about finding something deep inside myself which doesn't have to register in any kind of externalised, forced, or dramatic way." Western society is particularly geared toward extroversion and science, and these two functions are, by and large, exclusive to a minority of the population. We have not been encouraged as a western collective to take value in the more contemplative and interior aspects of our lives. A huge segment of America is medicated – either by prescription or by self-medication – and they are medicated in such a way as to flatline personality. Many individuals are taking Prozac or some faddish drug that gives everybody an edge of extroversion and a lack of feeling tone and a performance-orientated persona. This is because it is not acceptable to be melancholy or eccentric or deviant from the popular norm. This is where a person might need to reconsider their investment in life, and where they truly belong, rather than measuring themselves against some kind of constructed norm. As R.D. Laing said, "How can a society declare a person insane and itself sane?"

Be heretical. Value the inner life. In the examples that we will look at today, and the examples in the book, *The Astro*Carto*Graphy Book of Maps,* you will see the drama that is played out.[12] By the way, if you do find a used copy of that book, then buy it, because it is now out of print. Not all of us want to be that dramatic. John Kennedy had a date with destiny. He went to his Pluto line and got blown away. Not everybody wants to do that.

Audience: I think, if you had asked him, he would have declined.

---

[12]*The Astro*Carto*Graphy Book of Maps,* Jim Lewis and Ariel Guttman, Llewellyn, 1989. Currently out of print.

Erin: He probably would have said, "No, thank you." I think we had better take our lunch break now. Then we'll continue with the planets from Jupiter outward.

Shadowed planets, sleeping self

In *The Psychology of Astro*Carto*Graphy,* Jim Lewis gives a list of possible indications of a shadowed planet in this order:

> 1. In a cadent house, particularly the 12th
>
> 2. Stressful aspects, especially from outer planets
>
> 3. Square or opposite the Lights
>
> 4. On the western hemisphere of the chart, especially from the 6th to 8th houses, where they are more easily projected
>
> 5. Debilitated through sign placement – an old but effective measure of power
>
> 6. Totally unaspected (Ptolemaic)
>
> 7. Singleton, especially if singleton and retrograde, which it would be if it is any planet from Mars outward
>
> 8. Combust - within 1° of the Sun

Audience: Can you realise a planet consciously, to the degree that you could transform its action? Could Kennedy have avoided his assassination?

Erin: Yes and no. I don't know if Kennedy could have "avoided" his assassination, as he had a date with destiny. But, yes, he could have integrated his Pluto more with consciousness. For John Kennedy, Pluto in the 8th house acted out through his sexual compulsiveness and risk-taking. But it served in other ways, too. He was a hero in the armed services, a pioneer in politics, and a hound against organised crime. His family destiny was very Plutonian, with many tragedies locked in the ancestors and in his immediate family. However, there are certain aspects of ourselves that are so deeply buried that we can't always self-realise them to the point that they won't act out in a projected fashion.

That was one of Jung's important ideas. If an interior experience or aspect of oneself isn't brought to consciousness, it will externalise itself in the form of fate. If you have a planet that is shadowed, it simply means that it is not in its full function. It is part of the self that one doesn't like or can't really come to terms with, or one has not found a way to work with it that is pleasing to the rest of the psyche. The main gestalt of the horoscope may in fact alienate or ostracise a planet or configuration, which sometimes manifests as a complex. A complex can be extremely productive if it is at the core of creativity, but if it isn't a productive complex – in other words, a gathering of energy in such a way that the constellation of that energy produces art or music or good ideas or social acts or something that is really excellent – then it will remain buried.

Sometimes, going to a place where that planet is angular, it will erupt into the environment or within yourself, so that you experience it in a more personal or more actualised way. The planet that is most likely to be considered shadowed would be a planet without any Ptolemaic aspects, or located in the 12th house, 8th house, or 4th house. Sometimes squares to Saturn will "shadow" a planet, where its fullness of expression is swallowed by the devouring, insecure, starved Kronian component of Saturn. Then the creative impulse is swallowed and unborn.

Audience: Even if it is the Sun?

Erin: Especially if it is the Sun. Planets can be shadowed if they are singleton, as well. Any planet (except the Moon or Sun) that is isolated by hemisphere, or found in opposition to the gestalt of the planets, is going to be retrograde. You can consider that as potential shadowing as well. Remember how I said it doesn't matter where you are, because wherever you are, there you are. You might think, "Oh, I'll go to my Venus line because it is lovely and beautiful, and Venus means birthday parties and lovely people and aesthetically exquisite things." But when you have a Venus-Pluto opposition, you are taking it with you. You are going to a VE/PL line, not just a Venus line. So consider that. All is not always joyful on what appear to be joyful lines, because some things have to be lived out regardless.

Latest degree planet as a "shadowed" planet

I have discovered something interesting about the latest degree planet in the horoscope. It acts as a "reservoir" of life's experiences. It does so by being the last planet to receive all aspects by transit (and progression). As planets transit to the natal chart, they apply to various planets, make the aspect, and separate. But the planet which is in the latest degree in your chart is the terminus for all transits. That planet holds the richest store of experience and memory in your chart, and thus in your psyche and environmental experience of self. That is an extremely powerful planet, because technically, all your other planets in the chart are earlier than that degree. Thus, the latest degree planet receives the final task assigned by any transit. It then becomes the repository for every externalisation of your life.

A shadowed planet could also be the planet which occupies the latest degree in your horoscope. That planet can become shadowed and buried as a container for all of the stuff that occurred in the course of, say, a monthly lunar transit or a yearly solar transit or a two-year Mars transit. The transit always terminates with that planet, and it then holds the sum total of your experience. That planet can be an extremely explosive place. It can be also the most powerful, talented, resourceful, intelligent, and useful planet in the horoscope. If the planet is in the last degree of a sign, it also leaves you very little in the way of "void time" in your life, because there is always a planet applying to it by transit. Thus it is so alive that it could be bristling with all sorts of unexperienced parts of its own energy.

These latest degree planets can be incredibly surprising if you encounter them on angular places (lines) in unactualised ways. Also, I find that planets in water signs tend to be more deeply buried. There is a womblike quality to water signs. The 12th house is also a weak-ish kind of place. That is also a Vedic concept, but truly, it is a place where one of your planets may remain unborn; and if you bring it to an angle, it will give birth to itself in a new way. If you take yourself to a place where an unborn or shadowed planet (especially 12th house) is on an angle, it can be a shock. It may mean moving a few miles west if you are going to bring this 12th house planet into the Ascendant place.

Unaspected planets as shadowed forces

Unaspected planets can act in a similar way to latest degree planets, but with less in the way of coherent or linked parts. When there is no "conversation" between a planet and its cohorts, then there is a withdrawing of the agency of the planet from diplomatic or even confrontational relations with the other planets. An unaspected planet is a maverick, and can often be the introvert in the family of planets. Think of a room of ten family members, one of whom is withdrawn and has his or her back to the rest, receives no messages or challenges, and delivers no messages or challenges. This can be the function of an unaspected planet. It will develop its characteristics outside the demands of the other planets, and can be brilliant and unusual in its autonomy, producing something remarkable. Or it can be autistic, having a lack of tone to it. "Aspect" means to regard, discuss, lean on, look at. "Unaspected" denies this communion. The unaspected planet can be the autistic planet, full of unrealised and undifferentiated forces, waiting for birth. I have also found that an unaspected planet is available for whatever comes along. It is rather like a stark singleton – the handle of a bucket formation – where the planet is a repository for early conditioning and is a hook for others' projections, developing no cohesive characteristics of its own until a major transit and life experience come along to activate its volition.

Let's move on to the rest of the planets.

Planetary lines continued

Jupiter lines

Getting to Jupiter and its influence on angles, we move toward something that is simultaneously socially responsive and dependent.

Among other characteristics, Jupiter carries our tribal instincts, our need to group, clan, and gather together under a common aegis, whether that is family, religion, social protocol, or ethnic origins. In these days of shifting globalism, our tribal leagues tend to run more along ideological paths; and the ideological path and Jupiter work very nicely together, but so does hunting and gathering. Fundamentally, we can still divide ourselves into the archaic hunter-gatherer tribal instincts.

The myths and stories I relate about Jupiter/Zeus, both in *Retrograde Planets* and *Venus and Jupiter*, lead to a conclusion that Jupiter has something to do with morality. Jupiter conditions our capacity to love that which we don't know, and one of Zeus' epithets was Xeinios, which means the "guardian of strangers". In this guise, Zeus created a law – a guest/host law – wherein the stranger was considered to be sacred and under the protection of the gods (unless, of course, the traveller violated the code by raping the host's daughter or stealing his food or running off with the sacred chalice, treasure, secret, or whatever). The concept that strangers are inviolate is one side of the coin, while the other side of the coin is xenophobia, a fear of strangers, of anything different – anything that is a different race, creed, colour, ideology, or origin than one's own self. Thus, Jupiter is about learning tolerance and how one can extend oneself beyond one's own boundaries into other realms of awareness.

This is why Jupiterian, Sagittarian, and 9th house people have an insatiable desire to explore other cultures, religions, histories, and languages. They love to test their own limits. Jupiter lines have to do with your ability to find the side of you that exists in the stranger. If you go to a Jupiter line, it will be exciting, because you will be finding familiarity in strangeness. Jupiter lines run through places where people are spiritually, mystically, mysteriously drawn toward, and may even adopt, the religion or philosophy of that particular region. Or they find they have more spiritual consciousness and desire to become more linguistically or culturally involved, whether it is through business, trade, importing or teaching, or through meeting someone there, or someone from a Jupiter line of yours who offers an advantage. The Jupiter line experience introduces you to a part of yourself that you didn't know – the stranger within.

The word "hypocrite" comes from the ancient Greek *hupocrites*, which translates into "actor". The *hupocrites* were the stage actors of the theatre of Dionysus. We can find our hypocrite within on our Jupiter lines, just as we can find the dramatist, the actor, and the grandiloquent benefactor within ourselves. Also, Jupiter is good for exploring your opportunities for being successful in full-blown expansion of yourself, bearing in mind your natal Jupiter aspects. A Jupiter line, like a Venus line, isn't going to turn into sugar and spice if it has challenging or difficult aspects from other planets, like a Saturn opposition, which is a social issue. You may be drawn to Jupiter lines for education, religious teachings, adventure, and indulgent, playful reasons as well. Not that all of those activities cannot run together! Indeed, the pleasure of a Jupiter line can be about work – keeping in mind what Jupiter is about in the natal chart.

In Shakespearean days, Jupiter was the second-to-last stage of life, where one arrived self-satisfied and full of one's own wisdom:

> And then, is Justice,
> In faire round belly, with good Capon lin'd,
> With eyes severe and beard of formal cut,
> Full of wise saws and modern instances;
> And so he plays his part.[13]

Saturn lines

For those born before he advent of the outer planets, Saturn brought to the classical past the

> Last scene of all,
> That ends this strange eventful history,
> Is second childishness and mere oblivion,
> Sans teeth, sans eyes, sans taste, sans every thing.[14]

People still worry about Saturn lines because of the usual old saws, thinking in terms of being old, boring, difficult, depressing, sad, or

---

[13]*As You Like It*, William Shakespeare, Act II.
[14]*Ibid.*

limited. Saturn isn't a planet which is shadowed so much as it is so very easily projected. It is also a planet that we encounter in growth stages in our lives in specific seven-year cycles. With every seven-year cycle we have an opportunity to gather increasing personal *gravitas*. We become increasingly authentic, and our authority should be decreasingly projected outward as we march on through the sequential Saturn squares, oppositions, and returns.

When one is between the ages of one and seven, Saturn is obviously not going to have a whole lot to do with your going out and getting a car and a flat and a good job and being successful. It will have more to do with the family environment and how it treats material acquisitions and success, feelings of authority, security, and status in the community. We not only have an inherent Saturn, but also an imposed Saturn. Thus, feelings of self-confidence begin at the root, at the base of life, in the home, and from that origin we develop according to the transits of Saturn and recall the aspects to (and from) Saturn in the natal chart.

Saturn is another one of those planets that, depending on your age, may or may not manifest in a way that is important in your own personal authority or success. Anyone over the age of thirty, past the first Saturn return, is more likely to encounter a Saturn line with a little more grace and a little more knowledge than somebody who is in their early twenties. The younger person is more likely to encounter the external forms of Saturn through the status quo – what is socially right, what is correct, what is proper, what is authoritative, what has weight. If you go to a Saturn line, it may be more difficult to change. Saturn rules the homeostatic principle, which operates not just physically, by rigorously maintaining one's own shape, but also psychologically, by holding fast to old, outmoded beliefs.

Just as when you experience a Jupiter line you are more likely to open up, here you are more likely to seize up and be more contained. The tendency under Saturn lines – to have to work exceptionally hard on breaking old patterns – is a very good thing to do under this illuminated aspect of your own self. You will be more aware of your inner and social restrictions; but this can lead to success through the process of eliminating more fantastical ideas and focusing on realistic ideas about success and personal gain.

Occasionally people go to Saturn lines during times of crisis and
chaos in their lives, because instinctively they know that they have
got to be more in contact with their sense of solidity. I see the Saturn
lines not as a "hard labour" kind of place, but more as a place where
one might be able to withdraw, with effort, projections of one's own
authority onto other people, things, or accomplishments. If life
circumstances have led one to live on or work on a Saturn line, it is a
good place for recognising one's own power and shape and form. A
Saturn line, observed and experienced in a conscious way, could begin
to work to loosen a lot of fear, anxiety, repression, and historical
attitudes.

The root of such words as authority, author, and authenticity is the
Latin *auctor,* which simply means "author". Though it is always
work, becoming the author of one's own fate and life is the ultimate
achievement of Saturn. It can come in the form of seeing how others
have accomplished something admirable, and taking on some of
those characteristics. Or it can come in the form of realising that
one's parents are simply a vehicle for one's own self-growth and
maturation process, rather than being watch-dogs.

Saturn lines are places where we find life to be serious, but not
necessarily miserable. Serious study, hard work, self-actualisation,
stillness – all require discipline and drawing on inner resources. If we
are victimised by others, projecting our own authority and
authenticity out into society, we will encounter great difficulties with
such figures in the world around us. One is more likely to have this
experience directly on a Saturn line. We can find ourselves more in
tune with the ancient part of the land or society on a Saturn line, and
enjoy the history, the beauty of austerity, the wonder of success
through effort, solid achievement, and awards for time put toward a
goal. But people have still told me about Saturn lines being pretty
hard news, really, and the tremendous efforts they had to exert to be
happy there.

Moving beyond the boundaries of ego

When we get out into Uranus, Neptune, and Pluto land, we are
looking at options and consciousness, just as we are in natal

astrology. We are more likely to fall into the more deeply unconscious realms of each of these planets. When one is on or near a crossing of an outer planet and an inner or social planet, it can be the most exciting place in the world. You will find that you are required to stretch, to grow in unexpected ways, but in ways which the outer planet will dictate.

Uranus lines

Uranus lines are opportunities to observe the world from a distance, and be objective and clear. On occasion, a Uranus line will allow you to witness your own behaviour. By that I mean seeing one's own self clearly within the collective environment. Where Mars is the first step outside the self, Uranus is the first step outside the proscribed values of the social order. A new level of individuation is required to work with Uranus. We can not only find our special gift under Uranus; we might also be required to share that gift with a larger collective, and perhaps even to change the collective ideology or mind-set.

A Uranus line can allow you to govern yourself, and instigate new order within your group-mind. Sometimes we can be very critical of ourselves under Uranus, because Uranus is a perfectionist, like his eponymous celestial presence, Ouranos. Ouranos did not like the monsters he created with Gaia, and refused their birth. In the same way, Uranus can refuse our instinctual nature to surface. Uranus has been associated with revolution, and indeed, the separation of Gaia and Ouranos in the ancient myth, and the castration of Ouranos by his Titan son, Kronos, resulted in one of two major epic revolutions in the history of the ancient gods. The revolution of Kronos and the Titans resulted in a new status quo called the Golden Age – the age of idealism. Hence, idealism and fanaticism can arise under Uranus lines. Either you become so, or you witness it.

You might be caught up in idealistic, revolutionary action, or you may become a victim of it. Depending on where the Uranus lines fall in the A*C*G map, the likelihood of waltzing into a major revolution can be determined (generally) by the current ethos of the place of destination. Indeed, you might do well under transiting

Uranus lines, if they are crossing or conjoining with Mercury or Venus or Jupiter lines. We can witness ourselves in ways which are very objective, and we can allow the "monsters" – as metaphors for the deep instinctual, animal, primal nature – to emerge. We will find that we can have most unorthodox experiences under Uranus lines, for that very reason.

Neptune lines

I think I have covered a lot of Neptune's characteristics already in the course of the day, and can only add some delineative material. Neptune's a funny one, because it is the planet which can act rather more like a multifaceted lens than a focus. Using vision as a metaphor, if we were looking through the eyes of Neptune, we might see everything refracted and iridescent, rather like the descriptions of mescaline and psilocybin experiences. The "eyes" of Neptune-vision would be multifaceted, rather like flies' eyes. Images can be so fractured and refracted and deflected that you are not really seeing the thing, whatever it is you are observing, but seeing it particled and prismatic. By seeing, I mean perceiving, as well as visually observing. There is a romantic quality to that which we gaze upon when Neptune is the force behind the perception. Neptunian lines fall along places on your map which evoke a romantic vision. A sense of unreality may permeate the place, or your perception of the place.

One's experience under Neptune lines can be deceptive and shape-shifting. Neptune is the old Poseidon, the god of the sea, horses, earthquakes, and freshwater tributaries found under the land. All his progeny are slippery, underwater types, and they are usually shape-shifters, like Proteus. Neptune can actually eliminate or refract, or in some way shatter a lot of what you have always thought to be the truth. It can be spiritual and it can be enlightening. This is the spiritual side of Neptune's performance. But it can also be deceptive. That's the shape-shifting, mind-bending side of Neptune.

Jim Lewis did not like Neptune much at all, and it shows in his interpretations. He had a real problem with it. Maybe it was a shadowed planet. Certainly, his Mars in Pisces would add to his annoyance with the vicissitudes of Neptune. He and I talked about this quite a bit. I do think that his fear of Neptune was quite profound. If you read about his concept of Neptune in the little booklet, it's pretty dire. It's all about being deluded and ripped off and misunderstood and going mad – all of which are an aspect of Neptune on angles. However, mystics, messiahs, and martyrs, escape artists and fools, all apply to Neptune for inspiration, plugged into the same cosmic circuit. These are the subtleties of difference. Reality? What is reality? Being caught up in something you don't understand – that is Neptune reality.

There is the sacrificial and redemptive theme of Neptune, and under its lines you may well feel both sacrificed and redeemed. If you are going to sacrifice something, it may as well be for a good cause. We use the word martyr far too loosely. Martyrs die for good causes, not because Mummy wanted you to eat your dinner and you didn't, so she became long-suffering and sad about it – after which experience you run to the analyst or astrologer with your Moon/Neptune square, and say, "My mother was a martyr."

That's not martyrdom; that is manipulation and hysteria. Martyrdom is Joan of Arc material, and actions of that nature – big stuff, activities that bring the highest motive to bear upon (usually) appalling circumstances, resulting in the sacrifice of self for the collective. Neptune could be the point of real crucifixion or real sacrifice for the sake of the collective. A Neptune line might take you to the thing that you believe in most and would sacrifice something for, and everything is well and good because it's true, clean, and spiritually sound. But in that case you would need to be terribly conscious of what you were doing, and as pure in your motives as one can be. Or you might meet someone who was born on your Neptune line, and they might make a great spiritual teacher or a good drug dealer, or someone who deludes you into thinking you are something that you are not, depending on what Neptune pulls you to.

Pluto lines

We'll move on to Pluto. Pluto lines are places where we meet that which is unseen. The name Hades in Greek closely translates into our word "unseen". Hades himself was the "unseen one". And his domain of the same name, the underworld, was a very lively place in the Greek world. It wasn't the Christian Hell, all fire and brimstone and perpetually stoking up the Aga. It was more the place whitherto one went exactly as one died, including full costume, wound, etc., and stayed that way and hung around waiting for your next hop onto the wheel of incarnation. Once that took place you were then woven, spun, and cut into another lifetime.

Hades appears to have been a rather lively, social place where the shades retired between incarnations. Returned heroes had their spot; the bad guys, like Tantalus, went to Tartarus, wherein he was in a perpetual torment of thirst and hunger – with water rising that he could never drink, and food just out of reach that he couldn't eat. Sisyphus, too, was there, endlessly rolling the stone uphill. There were very specific laws and activities in Hades, depending on your incarnate state at the time of your death. I imagine it wasn't totally dark, but rather shadowy. At some stage most heroes went there, either to talk to their mothers and resolve something before they went on to the next battle, or to retrieve information from a dead leader. There was always a mission about going into Hades in order to get some information which was not available anywhere else. And the guide into Hades was always Hermes, our astrological Mercury. Only he was allowed free transit between the shady underworld and the bright, upper air.

Pluto lines are akin to Hades, in that they run along places in the world where you might go to get specific and mysterious information that you would otherwise never be able to acquire. Remember when I told you earlier about the three people I knew who did medical degrees under Pluto lines? And usually it is information about how to live better, or succeed, or find the treasure, or other such mythic stuff. This is what people forget: the reason that any of these heroes went to Hades, even though it was perilous, as Virgil says in the *Aeneid* when Aeneas descends to the underworld and receives instructions from the Sibyl. She tells Aeneas that he can get to Hades easily because the doors are always open, but returning is very difficult. The descent into Hades is easy, she says; the return to the upper air is the hard work, the hard labour. *Hic labor, hoc labor est.*

You can go and do your business down there but at all costs, you must remember how to get back. If you go there to find out something important that will either bring the boon to mankind, start a new civilisation, bring intelligence to the masses or, at least for us more mortal types, make us less afraid of ourselves from the inside out, then you are assisted by the gods.

Pluto is the planet most difficult to consciously work with. It is the last known planet out in the solar system – "known" being the operative word.   As such, it the last planet we "grow into". To individuate toward Pluto, one has to survive many trials, and in the survival, to be conscious of the gift of life. Whether we like it or not, Thanatos – death – has an attraction. To succumb to that power early in life renders the Pluto function destructive. Pluto isn't so much a shadowed planet as it is vastly unconscious, until bits of it begin to operate in the context of the whole of the self and thus in the personality in a core-power way. Pluto doesn't become a truly workable psychic function until well after midlife, and even then, it remains surprising.

We meet death in many ways, not always and not often corporeal. Most times we encounter our own mortality in psychological ways, or in ways which the intellect processes. However, on Pluto lines we can meet death literally, through hauntings, through ghosts, through work, through grief and loss, and through collective suffering. A descent into the labyrinth of the psyche is well met under Pluto lines, as are bringing up latent talents and abilities, studying, and working very hard. These are the healthy, mundane activities we do well with under the Pluto lines. I wouldn't think of it as a relaxing line, or one to take lightly. Clearly, a two-week holiday might not produce an encounter with a vampire unless you were off to Romany or Transylvania, but there are "vampires" of sorts in all places.

However, some people have gone to Pluto lines for a holiday, and have been accosted, assaulted, arrested, or caught up in collective chaos such as *coups d'état,* revolutions, or sudden weather eruptions like hurricanes. Also, I have had people tell me they have gone to Pluto lines, or to places where transiting Pluto is marked, and nothing happens – but they feel a constant dread, and there's something deeply creepy about their experience. They are picking up all the unseen, unheard material that lurks in the collective Hades, in a place of waiting. It is not necessarily a bad thing, and if you are aware of what it is, then you can snoop around a bit. Granted, whatever it is one is feeling, it can remain unseen, but that shouldn't stop an investigation. It is like having a penlight in a mine shaft. You are only going to be able to see a little bit of it at one time, but at least some illumination will come.

Real lives, real lines

Pluto down under: hauntings of the Antipodes

Audience: Erin, when you were speaking about Pluto lines, I remembered something. When I was in Australia last year, which is where I have my PL/ASC line exactly running through Sydney, I was staying in an incredibly haunted house. The whole time I was in that house, I fought with a feeling that I was going to see "them" any minute. I felt if I relaxed and dropped my guard, I was going to start seeing the ghosts. A lot of people who have been in that house have seen them. It was quite known that it was very haunted, and it was absolutely terrifying. Actually, it was an overwhelming experience.

Erin: Knowing you and your chart, I know that you are not inclined to Victorian vapours and visitations. Isn't that where a friend of yours saw someone sitting on the bed who wasn't really there?

Audience: Recently, after I left Sydney, yes. It was an old woman sitting in the midst of a pile of books on the bed, reading out of a book. In he middle of the night my friend went to the loo, looked in this room on the way, and saw her. Then, when he came out of the loo on the way back to his room, he looked in again for some reason, and she looked up and growled at him like a dog. That's the kind of thing that happens in that house. When I was there I was overwhelmed by it, and very, very frightened.

Audience: Did you leave or did you stay there?

Audience: I stayed there for three nights. On the first night I stayed awake all night, planning to leave. It was my friend's house and I was invited to stay, and when I told them in the morning how disturbed I had been, they were so upset about it. Of course, they are quite happy with these ghosts – they are used to them. But I couldn't bring myself to check into a hotel. My friends would have been mortified that I had left. I actually stayed for another two nights.

Audience: And was that difficult?

Audience: The second night was a bit better because I did loads of visualisation and prayer and mantras and things, and it staved them off a bit. But the third night it was back to being as bad as the first night. It was the whole time – it wasn't just at night. Any time of day in the house I could feel it and hear them walking past the room. Extraordinary. That's the second time I've been to Sydney. The first time I went to Sydney, I went with a friend. His mother was dying, and that was the reason I was in Sydney – death again. So I'm very interested to see what happens when I go back again next year.

Erin: Me, too. That's very interesting. Here's where I think fatedness comes in. Myself, I believe that, had you left, you would have felt really dreadful for leaving. You see, it's as though you are damned if you do and damned if you don't. As the Romans said, *saxa inter unda* – "between the rocks and the waves" – because you would have felt guilty, apprehensive, and frightened because you had been frightened. You would have been scared away from something. It is better to stand and face it. It is a metaphor for all fears.

Audience: Sometimes in the night I would think, "It is all right to think, 'I'm not going to deal with this.'" I have come across this kind of thing before, so it is interesting that in this situation I wasn't all right with them. It was far more than I could cope with. Maybe they were disturbed.

Audience: When you came upon them before, was it on a Pluto line?

Audience: No.

Erin: Perhaps you have pretty and pleasant ghosts on a Venus line, or Romeo-and-Juliet visions under Mars/Venus crossings. But under a Pluto line, I think it would be very frightening to the psychic integrity. Why bother, as you say? I am a great believer in, "Look, there are times to bang your head against a brick wall and times not to, and if it is going to work, great, do it." But you say you had three days when you just prayed a lot.

Audience: And it worked.

Audience: I'm looking at my Pluto now!

Audience: It was my PL/ASC line which runs up through Sydney, Shanghai, and Beijing. I have been to those two cities as well, but I didn't have those kinds of experiences there. I was only in Beijing for three days as well. There were no ghosts, but I felt as if I had been plugged into an electric current. You were talking about connecting with somebody else's dark tribal collective. That's what happened there. It was an extraordinarily powerful experience.

Erin: When you are getting into places which have layers of dynasties which have collapsed and then been reconstructed one upon the other, you are getting into a kind of Hades place. It is compartmentalised, and there are different levels of culture. None of them ever die. I had a similar experience when I was in Zululand, where I was horrified by the burying of the Zulu culture. I could not stay ten minutes in a particular village that had been reconstructed. It was as if something really dreadful was saying, "I will not sleep here." Whitney Houston was playing in Durban, which meant that every hotel was booked. We had to drive up to Pietermaritzburg, 100 miles from the coast, to try to find a motel, because there was nowhere to stay. But I refused to stay in this Zulu place, because you could feel the restlessness of the destruction of a culture that was perfectly fine until it was destroyed – only in its death has it become terrifying. And it is still there, haunting. Pluto will resurrect things like dead cultures, returned heroes, and people who have been important in the growth of the world but have been killed off. Certainly it could be ghosts. You should find out who these folks were.

Audience: You mean you didn't?

Audience: Well, actually, this particular house was in the Temple Gardens in Sydney, and was very old. The Temple Gardens are right next to the rocks where the convicts were brought. The person who lives in the house says, "We know that such and such a convict – we even know his name – died next to that tree over there, a hundred yards from the house." I felt that the house had become a repository for a lot of very disturbed souls. There must have been some horrible deaths in that small area two hundred years ago. Somehow that house was a magnet to them. That was my theory about it.

Erin: It is a very sound theory, because Pluto rules the disenfranchised, the disaffected, the submerged, the marginalised – people who are forced underground to live in areas of society that nobody wants to know about. We can't see these people. We don't know that they're sleeping in the road. England shipped off all of its "nasty" types, its living shadow, down to Australia. Well, they couldn't see them there, could they? They were down under, so to speak – the Antipodean shadow.

Audience: As well as that, I have shared my home for eighteen years with somebody who was born in Sydney. He's from my PL/ASC line. You were getting around to speaking about knowing people from your lines. Now I'm wondering about how we experience our life through somebody else.

Audience: So you experience him as Pluto/Ascendant?

Audience: Yes. He can be an unconscious agent for unrealised contents in my own unconscious. He may, periodically, bring forth the "demons" for me to conquer and civilise.

Audience: Not everyone can move from one country to another for obvious reasons. But it is interesting that I have my PL/ASC in my house, in my life, and in part of my "non-relocated" self.

Erin: When considering relocation, we have to be practical in working with clients. People will ring up and say, "I want to emigrate to the States/Europe/Australia, and I want to look at my Astro*Carto*Graphy map." My first question is, "Is it viable? Is it actually possible for you to do that?" If it is not realistic, it is simply not possible. There are times an individual can relocate in accord with A*C*G. But unless all practical systems are in order, I wouldn't encourage people to uproot and move based purely on A*C*G lines. If the viability of a major move is good, then I encourage them to work with proper transits to the lines, because transits activate the lines. That's where Cyclo*Carto*Graphy comes in.

Transits to lines

Audience: When you say transits to the lines, what do you mean? A planet which is transiting over what?

Erin: Planet to planet, hence implicating planetary lines. Let's say you have Mercury at 5° Gemini, and transiting Pluto opposite your natal Mercury by zodiacal degree.

Audience: When you look at transits to lines, how does that work?

Erin: As an illustration, Saturn in your natal chart looks like it is in one fixed place, because it is in one place as seen from your birthplace. But, as we now know, it is actually rising and setting and culminating and also at the IC, all at the same time. That means there are actually four Saturn lines. They are where Saturn is around the whole world, but it is in exactly the same place in the zodiac. If you have transiting Pluto conjunct your natal Saturn at 5° Sagittarius, it is hitting your MC/IC lines exactly, but is obliquely ascending, and thus not on your A*C*G SA/ASC/DSC.

Think back to the earlier part on latitude and declination. The "transiting" line, C*C*G, may not be exactly on the Ascendant or Descendant lines, but it will be exactly on the Midheaven and IC lines.

Audience: What is the ecliptic line?

Erin: When you got up this morning, did you notice where the Sun was?

Audience: Behind the clouds.

Erin: Right. Then, to be more precise: somewhere behind the clouds was the Sun, which then rose as "high" as it will get. Then it began its downward movement toward its setting, which is in a couple of hours – right now, the Sun is moving from the 9th to the 8th house, it being about 3.30 pm now. That path of the Sun as it "transits" across the sky is the ecliptic. Every planet stays within that place called the ecliptic, and it is also the path of the zodiac. In other words, it is the place where the band of the signs runs from Aries, Taurus, Gemini, and so on. It is the path in the sky that the planets are confined within, as we see them from Earth. It is their "satellite" path.

Andrew Cunanan: Mars on the loose

Figure 5 is the natal horoscope of Andrew Cunanan, who recently shot and killed Gianni Versace in Miami. **Figure 5a** is his A*C*G map.

I just want to make a very quick statement about this one. This is his MA/DSC line (see *Note under **Figure 5a**). Now look again at his natal horoscope. Where's his Mars? It's in the 8th house in Sagittarius, square Pluto. He has a very volatile Mars. He also has a Moon/Saturn conjunction on the Ascendant, which we are not going to worry about right now. I just wanted to quickly show you the natal Mars content, and then the path of Mars, which he followed to his destruction.

Cunanan was born in a southern suburb of San Diego, which is exactly his MO/ASC line. The SA/ASC line is running off the coast of the Galapagos in the middle of the Pacific, but the planets, Moon and Saturn, are only separated by 1° of zodiacal orb. What we have here is a clear picture of an angular-type horoscope – with an angular Moon/Saturn on the Ascendant. Cunanan's natal Mars is in the 8th house. It is not particularly obvious and overt – indeed, it is shadowed. It is interior and mysterious, and it squares Pluto. In the light of recent events, I think it is safe to say that Cunanan's Mars was not realised. It was shadowed, because he was not aware of his desires, aggression, and longings, to the degree that they achieved the level of violence that they did. Now, locked into his MA/DSC line is the "unspoken" aspect, the natal square to Pluto.

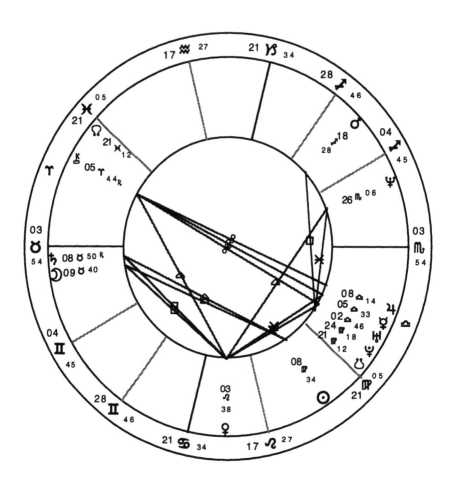

Figure 5: Andrew Cunanan
31 August 1969
9.41 PM PDT (04.41.00 GMT)
National City, California, USA (32N30, 117W06)
Placidus cusps

Cunanan's shooting spree started when he first went to Milwaukee, one of the cities on his MA/DSC line. We can follow the MA/DSC line from Chicago to Milwaukee and Minneapolis, and then south to Miami. He first travelled from his birth place, San Diego, to Milwaukee because one of his lovers was living there. He shot this lover. He then went up to Minneapolis, where he then shot another of his lovers. He then when back down to Chicago and shot somebody else. Then he went down to Florida, where he shot Gianni Versace, and then himself. That's what *he* did on his MA/DSC line.

Audience: Is that an example of a badly realised Mars?

Erin: I think it is what we would call a shadowed Mars. You are quite right, this is not a self-realised Mars. Very good!

Audience: When was this?

Erin: The shootings all occurred in a fairly short space of time. Gianni Versace was murdered last. He had shot the other men in the spring, in May, following down his Mars line. Now, the main transits as he was hotting up were: Saturn coming up to station-retrograde trine his natal Mars, from 18° Aries to Sagittarius; transiting Jupiter at 21° Pisces station-retrograde; and transiting Uranus at 8° Aquarius. He had transiting Uranus in the 10th house, station-retrograde at 8° Aquarius in the middle of May, squaring his Moon in the 1st house by 1° of orb, and exactly squaring his natal Saturn.

The Uranus stationary square to his Saturn singleton retrograde, conjunct the Moon, is a scary aspect, given the other transits and his psychopathology. At some point in his lonely, isolated life, he would have to act out the Saturn/Moon conjunction through his relationships with people. That he was gay might well be part of the starvation diet of feeling and emotional nurturing that Saturn/Moon aspects can play out. Indeed, Saturn singleton retrograde in itself is an "ivory tower" aspect, one in which the relationship with the collective agreement on who is "in charge" is an huge insult to him. With Saturn retrograde and rising, his own internal authority could be inflated – whether they are insane or not, people who murder other people have an inflation of their authority, even if only momentarily at the time of the murder.

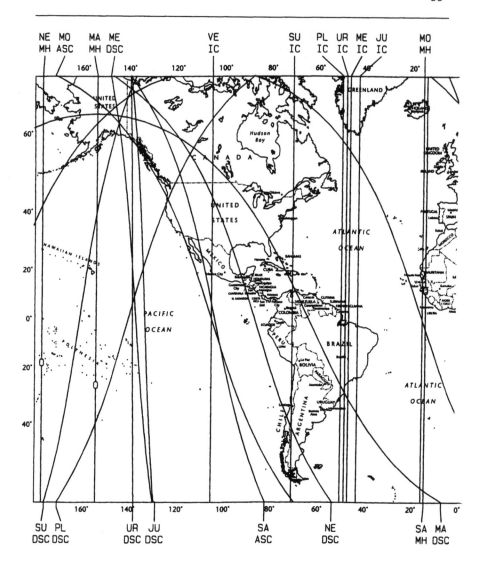

Figure 5a: Andrew Cunanan

Astro*Carto*Graphy Map reprinted with permission of Astro Numeric Service

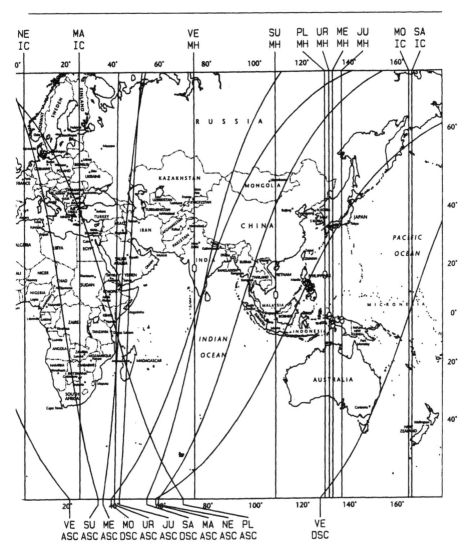

| NE | MA | | VE | | SU | PL | UR | ME | JU | | MO | SA |
| IC | IC | | MH | | MH | MH | MH | MH | MH | | IC | IC |

VE SU ME MO UR JU SA MA NE PL   VE
ASC ASC ASC DSC ASC ASC DSC ASC ASC ASC   DSC

*Note: The MA/DSC line may be seen entering the upper left-hand corner of the map on the facing page, at around 60°N. It curves downward through Miami, leaves the map in the lower right-hand corner, and may be seen re-entering the map (as MA/ASC) on this page at the centre bottom, curving upward through Japan and leaving the map at the upper right-hand corner at 60°N.

Moon and Saturn conjunct (retrograde singleton simply amplifies this) show a real lack of feeling reciprocity. Cunanan likely felt he was doing all the loving and feeling, and getting none. His parental image here is one of a collusion between both mother and father to place this man out on his own, with no family support at all, though he does have Venus in the 4th square this. I would think that the feminine side of Cunanan's psychic background was malnourished, virtually swallowed, by his mother. His chart shows a sad and lonely background, with no family support-system, and this looks like it runs down through the family line – Venus in the 4th house. And with Mars in the shadowed 8th house, his rage, his fury at this lack of supportive background, became the fabric of his emotional and sexual life.

Audience: Didn't he shoot himself?

Erin: Yes, he did, in the end. He finalised his MA/DSC spree by turning his gun on himself. Suicide, especially with a gun, is an episode of introjected Mars.

Audience: Did he go to these places in order to shoot them, or did he shoot them because they were there?

Erin: From what the evidence and statements have revealed, initially he didn't go intending to kill anyone. However, after he shot his lover in Milwaukee, it released the demons, and on he rolled. That it all occurred along the Mars line is remarkable, but to me it shows the degree of unconsciousness operating within him, driving him on along that line, as if it were an army marching along an eclipse path. And the fatedness of it all – that all these men lived along his Mars line, and were there for his Mars spree! However, he did intend to murder Versace. The most horrible aspect of his resultant suicide is that there is now no way of knowing what was going on in and around him, and what his true motive was for killing Versace. But remember what Sun lines do? Especially the SU/ASC?

Audience: High profile, fame, finding one's purpose in life.

Erin: Quite. Now, look at Rome – capital city of Italy, the home of Versace fashion. There is Cunanan's SU/ASC line. And his natal Sun is largely a quiet one, located in the 5th house, trine Moon and

Saturn. Seems passive and nice enough, but under the surface is the act which made him infamous. Was this his purpose in life?

Rectification with A*C*G

I think A*C*G is an excellent rectification tool. Jim Lewis used it to illustrate the two given times of Martin Luther King, the civil rights activist, preacher, and Nobel Peace Prize recipient. Two birth times were given for King. The recognised time was given by his mother for "noon", but another time has emerged through A*C*G rectification for 11.21 am, just thirty-nine minutes earlier. As Jim pointed out in his certification seminar in 1993, King was born in Atlanta on 15 January 1929. He was assassinated in Memphis, Tennessee, which, if we use the 12.00 pm time, has no line, nor is there any line in Washington, nor any strongly characteristic lines based on the "noon" birth recollected by his mother. Jim started playing with Martin Luther King's A*C*G map, and noted that, if the time was shifted back thirty-nine minutes, it showed the following dramatic planetary line activity:

> 1. PL/IC in Memphis – assassination in 1968
>
> 2. SU/MC in Washington, DC, where a holiday was named for him, and now many streets are named for him in the US
>
> 3. JU/ASC runs through Atlanta, where he was born, became a Baptist minister, and began his politically active career as a liberation spokesman (Jupiter rules "freedom", which was the cry of the civil rights workers)
>
> 4. JU/MC runs through Stockholm, where he received his Nobel Peace Prize in 1964

The case for A*C*G as a tool for rectification continues now with the chart of Princess Diana.

Diana Spencer, Princess of Wales

What I want to show you enlivens the continuing speculation about Diana Spencer's true birth time. I find A*C*G to be a valuable and valid tool for working with speculative birth data, especially when there are several possible times given. There are several ways that birth times have come about for Diana Spencer. I have the two maps and the two horoscopes that are commonly used for her. The material I will present this afternoon via her Astro*Carto*Graphy and her natal map(s) leans strongly toward the earlier birth time, giving her Libra rising. When you see her relationship with France, Alexandria, Florida, Italy, Angola, Somalia, and Romania – indeed, all the various places with which she is strongly affiliated – you may think a bit differently about her chart. The Sagittarius rising chart may not be the final answer.

Diana: Sagittarius rising

Here is the most commonly accepted chart, with Sagittarius rising (**Figure 6**). In Geoffrey Cornelius' book, *The Moment of Astrology*, he writes about the difficulty of conflicting times and reading the wrong chart.[15] Because of Diana Spencer's unique situation being married to Prince Charles, coupled with the fact that she sought guidance and advice from astrologers and psychics and various alternative healers, there have been several times that have been given for her birth. Both of the times I am going to work with this afternoon were given by her to both the media and to astrologers. For some reason everybody seems very fond of the Sagittarius rising chart, set for 7.45 pm. This time was quoted by her in the press. Yet another time, given at some other stage to another astrologer in confidence, was issued. Thus there are two primary contenders for the horoscope of Diana. We will look at the Libra rising chart, set for 2.15 pm, after discussing the Sagittarius rising chart.

---

[15]*The Moment of Astrology*, Geoffrey Cornelius, Arkana, Contemporary Astrology Series, London, 1995. Currently out of print.

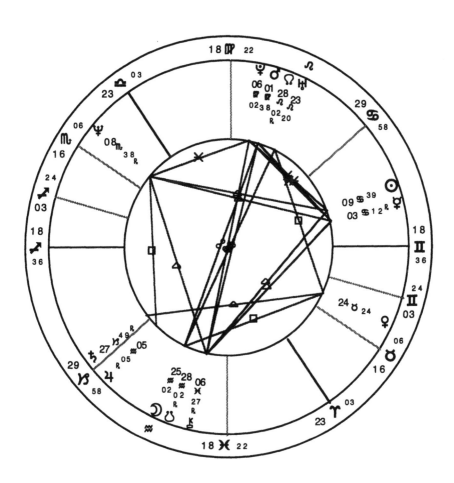

Figure 6: Princess Diana
1 July 1961
7.45 pm BST (18.45.00 GMT)
Sandringham, GB (52N39, 0E30)
Placidus cusps

To me this chart is not particularly strong. We have no angularity, nor any weight in the family sections of the horoscope. There are no indicators here of anything particularly outstanding that would indicate the degree of power that lived within and around this young woman. There really wasn't anything about her that made me consider her as Sagittarius rising – none of the exuberance, forthrightness, clumsiness, spontaneity, carelessness, and puella-ness that Sagittarius ascending presents. Arguments for Sagittarius rising are many. One is that, because Uranus, Mars, and Pluto are in the 8th, she would die "a violent death". This is not a valid delineation – it has no merit and insults us, as sensible people, to think along those lines. Other arguments run like this: she is athletic, interested in travel, has an international reputation, is naive. I don't see the Ascendant in the same light, however.

We can read into the house positions for her aspects in the Sagittarius rising chart. Sun and Mercury are in the 7th – married to royalty, a strong husband who carries her own projected solarism. The Moon is in the 2nd, opposite to Uranus in the 8th – wide mood swings, thoughts of death and destruction, feelings widely separated from her experiences, a sense of isolation as a child, a cold, unloving background leading to cold, unloving family surroundings. Venus is in the 5th – a great love for her children, a "beautiful" person, a feminine icon. Neptune is in the 10th – everyone's princess, a screen for the fantasies of the public. Astrology in retrospect is brilliant – it can fit anything – but there are the practical realities to attend to here, and they are precise measurements of time and space.

The strongest focus in the planetary array for Diana is her T-cross from Venus to the Moon/Uranus opposition. This T-cross exists in both charts, obviously. But I would expect to see it more prominent in her life, not only by looking at the houses in which it is found natally, but also in her A*C*G maps, by finding living examples of what that T-cross symbolises. Firstly, it is a fixed cross with the sign of Scorpio in the "empty" part of the cross. Passion and obsession are the "shadow" function of this T-cross. The Moon/Venus split is the confusion of the feminine roles within herself, as well as the confusion of the mother/lover unity within each woman. Diana was a Venusian figure with a strong lunar content, but her marriage forced the split. She became "wife" to Charles, and "mother", while he retained "lover" in the form of Camilla Parker-Bowles. Diana herself was a lover too, but a spurned one. It would have been virtually impossible for her to marry the two aspects of the feminine, the lover and the wife, in her marriage to Charles.

The Uranian involvement in the T-cross shows her rebellion, her need to individuate through the process of unveiling her multi-faceted feminine faces. And this she did, to the delight of the paparazzi who fed the prurient appetites of the common British (and the world's, it seems) person. This powerful configuration exists in the Sagittarius rising chart in the 2nd, 5th, and 8th houses. These are all succeedent houses, locked into the weakest parts of the chart. But in the Libra rising chart, the T-cross spans the two family houses (4th and 10th), and Venus is in the 8th in Taurus – all speaking of a family inheritance and family issues. And I think we have to admit that all of Diana's short life was bound up with family. Every curse and every blessing for her was family-originated.

Audience: Yes, that is right. She had to move through her own family, and then to the most powerful family in England, in order to come into her own sense of self. How interesting. She never escaped the family issues while alive. And I have the feeling that, had she married into the Fayed family, her situation might not have been that much improved – from a family standpoint, that is!

Erin: That also crossed my mind. From the frying pan into the fire, so to speak – the Fayed family would have been a tremendous burden after a while, wouldn't it? More of the same, really, only of another culture. Anyway, those are the aspects in the chart. Now let's see where the planet lines lie in the Sagittarius rising map.

Diana's A*C*G map for Sagittarius rising

Figure 6a is her Astro*Carto*Graphy map for the Sagittarius rising time. First of all, I am presenting a case for Sagittarius rising, as we will see a number of significant lines running through important places in Diana's life. I have to give credit where it is due, and there are some pretty lively things in the Sagittarius rising map.

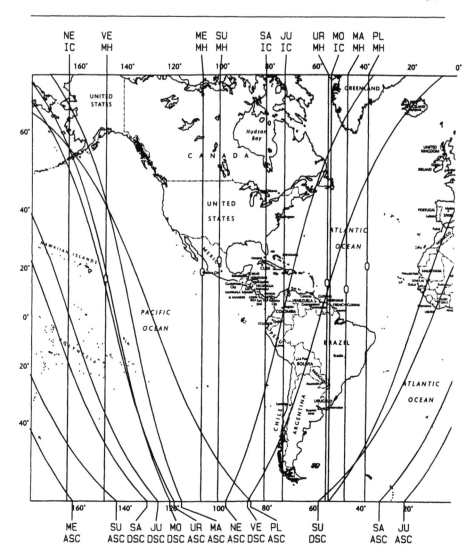

Figure 6a: Princess Diana

Astro*Carto*Graphy Map for Sagittarius Ascendant reprinted with permission
of Astro Numeric Service

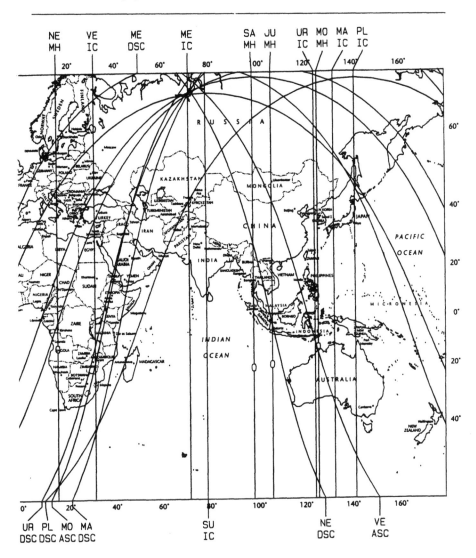

*Note: The SA/IC line may be seen running from the centre top of the map on the facing page at around 80°W, down through Hudson Bay, the tip of Florida, and just touching the west coast of South America.

I've focused on several places where we know for certain she had invested energy, time, and love. One of them is England (where there are no lines at all in the Sagittarius rising map), one of them is France (where she has ME/DSC through Paris), and another of them is Angola (where there is a NE/MC zenith point). Then there is Egypt, where her VE/IC line passes directly through Cairo; Somalia, where MA/DSC and CH/ASC run through; yet another is India (ME/IC through Bombay, and SU/IC through Madras and Sri Lanka); and yet another one, very recently, is Florida, where her SA/IC line passes through the southernmost tip.

Now, those are all pretty strong lines, and interesting, to say the least. We can read a lot into those, especially the Venus/IC line, where her lover, Dodi, was born (in Alexandria), and where it was rumoured she was to marry him in the near future. However, apparently she and Dodi Fayed were looking for a "dream home" in Florida, and I thought that was kind of weird, because I would not expect someone to look for a dream home under a SA/IC line, especially since transiting Saturn is about to pass over her natal IC according to the Sagittarius rising chart (and therefore transiting the SA/IC line in A*C*G). Although Saturn transiting the IC could mean "the end of the life", it isn't exact enough, and not really alive.

It seems odd to pick a place for a love-nest under a SA/IC line, although one could muse that they never did get it, and the idea was terminated. Now, transiting Neptune is currently about to turn stationary-retrograde conjunct her natal Saturn, which could have "dissolved the plan". The Neptune transit means that every SA/IC and SA/MC line is experiencing the transit of Neptune – both precisely along the MC/IC lines, and crossing the ASC/DSC lines in key places. There is also Sarajevo, and her concern over the war-torn starving populace, especially the children.

She went to Angola as well, as a peace diplomat, showing concern for the lost and disaffected. Now, the lines running through Somalia – of land-mine fame – are Mars/Descendant and North Node/Descendant, both of which are closely aligned with her Chiron/Ascendant line. Running right through the dot of Paris, in this map, is her Mercury/Descendant line. A lot of people said that it made sense that Mercury was on the Descendant in Paris, because she was killed in a taxi or a chauffeured limousine, ruled by Mercury. That's a bit weak, given the whole of her life and experiences – and Mercury rules many things other than taxicabs! In this chart, she has ME/IC and SU/IC lines running through India. India was very important because she had a strong affinity with Mother Theresa, real or otherwise.

But remember, there are likely to be lines running through part of any country for all of us. This does not mean we are "there", but it is important to see the number of accurately described lines that make exact contact with places that have real significance.

Audience: There is also that photo of her outside the Taj Mahal.

Erin: Yes, sitting alone – a very well-framed photo, redolent with the image of her aloneness, isolation, and interiority. Then there's also the recent photo of her out in the September 1997 issue of *Vanity Fair,* where she is at the opening of the Indian Temple in north London. She has the traditional stain on her forehead, wearing the beautiful flower necklaces, looking lovely and natural as usual. Now, as I mentioned, Dodi was born in Egypt, in Alexandria, which is where she has her VE/IC line passing through in this chart. To me this is the strongest point for the Sagittarius rising time, but it is the only really strong indicator. That is a classic contact, isn't it? Remember the story about Brian and Glennys, where lovers may come from a place through which one's Venus lines are found?

Then there is Cape Town, South Africa, where Charles Spencer, her brother, now resides. We are still resonating to his funeral eulogy, wherein he promises to foster her spirit, her essence, her soul, her wishes, her dreams – and particularly her children. Hmm. All of those are Neptune-like attributes. Essentially, the Earl's promise to nurture and nourish her sons as she would have wanted, the cry from his heart about her "blood family" seeing to her wishes – this could be from the Neptune/MC line. It could be the spiritual call, the wish fulfilled, the brother continuing the dream, since Neptune rules her 3rd house of siblings in the Sagittarius rising chart. I really don't know. There is acceptable and workable action around important places with this time of 7.45 pm. It's possible that this is the right time, but something doesn't quite click – it is not a revelation.

Diana: Libra rising

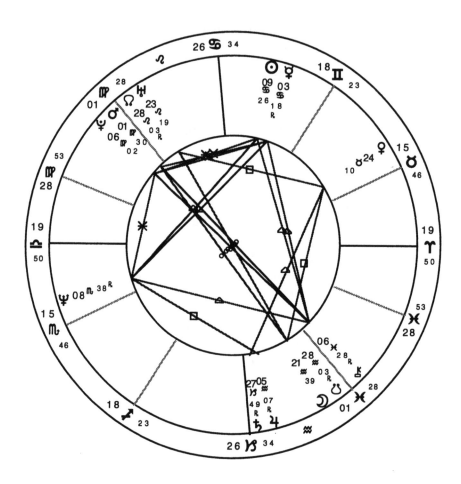

Figure 7: Princess Diana
1 July 1961
2.15 pm BST (13.15.00 GMT)
Sandringham, GB (52N39, 0E30)
Placidus cusps

Let's look at the Libra rising chart, set for 2.15 pm at Sandringham (**Figure 7**), and also at the A*C*G map based on that time (**Figure 7a**). Now, this A*C*G map is considerably different from the previous one. It shows a great deal more evidence of her personal contacts to locations, as well as her global affiliations and attraction in significant places in the world. However, let's look at the natal horoscope first, and then correlate it to the A*C*G map.

This horoscope has a considerable amount of weight, which portrays more of Diana's presence than the Sagittarius ascending chart. It places 4th house Saturn 1° from the IC, and Jupiter and the Moon are in the 4th house as well. That explains a lot to me about the family and dynastic lineage. She comes from an aristocratic family, one which antedates the royal family itself – indeed, it is a more aristocratic family than the one from which her husband, the Prince of Wales, originates. Those three planets in her 4th house are carrying a large responsibility, not only for the family of origin and for the dynastic line, but also for the collective family as it is seen in the public.

The Moon is a repository for the maternal legacy, the long line of women in her genetic origins, and it is why she stands today as an exemplar of women in the collective. Her own mother is a rebel, leaving the home and children to marry her lover. The Moon is opposite Uranus in the 10th house – an absent, cut-off relationship to the mother, and feelings of being "alone" in the home. For all the criticism of Charles' inability to "get in touch" with his feelings, I cannot say that Diana's Moon is a particularly warm one. She is a Cancer woman, and thus has the nurturing and managerial capacities of that sign, but the Moon-Uranus, especially from Aquarius to Leo, and compounded by the square from Venus in the 8th, really denotes a woman in a quandary about her own feelings. She may well have thought she could actually put up with the archaic arrangements of her new royal family and her husband-to-be-king, but she couldn't.

The unorthodoxy contained within the Moon/Uranus/Venus symbolism externalised dramatically through a social channel, using the base of the "family" as the root (4th house/IC), and the 10th house/MC as her expression of originality and social reform. Divorcing the prince is not an everyday act. Were this just a hundred years ago, she would likely have been shut up in the proverbial Tower, or beheaded if it were a hundred and fifty years ago. Such a troublesome woman! Such an iconoclast, but with a good, strong conservative streak – Cancer to the rescue of her mad Moon. In time, Diana became a spokeswoman for undervalued women all over the globe. Her main thrust, once she gained a sense of self, became focused on her role as a mother, and as a woman of influence in the caring professions – from volunteer work in hospitals and hospices to global interest in protecting children, women, the disaffected, ill, persons with AIDS, and the starving.

She confessed to an eating disorder – the Moon – and this eating disorder stemmed from family dysfunction. Her manner of "curing" bulimia was to go to the centre of her created and adopted family and slay the Minotaur that was repressing feeling. The lack of feeling she experienced in her family of origin was writ large in her marriage family, the House of Windsor. The Moon opposite Uranus in the chart, especially from the 4th to the 10th house, exemplifies the split between home and social position in the families – both the family of origin and the family by marriage. Her deepest needs for love and nurture were famously ignored, and her mother left her and her siblings with the father when Diana was very young. This led into her selection of a chosen family, which also demonstrated a split-off, dysfunctional emotional tone.

Her husband Charles, the Prince of Wales, has a singleton Uranus retrograde, and in tune with that, a distinct difficulty in both connecting to his feelings and demonstrating them. But it is now apparent, with hindsight, that Charles did not love Diana at all. Indeed, he fulfils the long line of royal patriarchy, marrying politically and loving extramaritally. An echo of the ancient story of Jason and Medea lies here in the House of Windsor.

What better expresses a lonely and sad childhood home life, leading into a loveless but socially powerful, formal, and highly influential marriage (as an extension of that family of origin) than her Saturn/IC with the Moon and Jupiter in the 4th? Saturn in the 4th house, near the IC in this chart, speaks about her feelings of guilt, apprehension, invalidity, insecurity, and fear – all family-based. Saturn devoured his creations, his children. I have associated this with eating disorders also – the hunger within, and the revulsion toward the body and its ordinary functions. With Venus in Taurus in the 8th house, her sexual dissatisfaction and betrayal fed the Minotaur, and obsessive-compulsive behaviour, food issues, and nurturing issues all rose to the foreground of her personality.

Carrying the responsibility of breaking down the system of traditional aloofness and lack of emotional display – and indeed, the complete lack of feeling-tone displayed by the royal family – almost destroyed her. But her lunar power rose to save herself and her children. In a sense, she fulfilled her destiny, which now seems to be simple. She was imported into the royal family for the purpose of deconstructing it from the inside. She was both circuit-breaker and scapegoat, and using those hard tools, she worked magic. That Saturn in the 4th house in England will find itself precisely on the IC in Paris! Is that where she completed her task? Let's progress.

In this chart, her natal Moon in the 4th exactly squares her natal Venus in the 8th. The aspect itself – which in the Sagittarius rising chart is from the 2nd to the 5th house – is a hard one to carry. When the Moon and Venus are square to each other, the feminine function is powerfully split or polarised (it's the same with the opposition). The split between the exotic, erotic, beautiful, and independent Venusian goddess figure and the nurturing, caring, Mummy-lunar side of the feminine is in some way creating a dichotomy. Inherently there is a difficulty with that aspect. From the 4th house of family of origin to the 8th house of the personal ancestors, it speaks of her own contemporary experience being linked to and nourished by her female ancestral legacy.

Her mother did leave the family at an early age (4th house). Thus she was abandoned by her mother, and suffered hugely each time she and her little brother Charles went to visit and then returned to the father's home. She became her brother's *mater soror*, mother-sister, and she took on a tremendous amount of family responsibility. She loathed – as did the other siblings – their stepmother, whom they nicknamed Acid Raine. Her representative feminine archetypes in childhood and adolescence were pretty dire. And the little princess-ballerina, who was far too tall and gawky to be a real ballerina, continued to incubate within, destined to flower as a real princess with a very large pea under the mattress.

In retrospect, although I was convinced before her death, her entire purpose in life, her fate, was to be fed to the royal family to revitalise and circuit-break a family system that was virtually lumbering towards extinction. Like the virgins to the Cretan Minotaur, she sailed to the centre of the labyrinthine head family of Britain. It is interesting that Queen Elizabeth is a Taurus, with Saturn singleton retrograde at the MC, right in the empty arm of Diana's T-cross, opposing Diana's Venus. A devourer of creative issue? A very convenient cast was set for this passion-play to dramatise itself on the world stage.

The sign of Libra rising is more the presentation that she gives to the world than Sagittarius – graceful, pastel, gentle, politically savvy, very strong, concerned about being loved both personally and collectively, anxious to please. Her political savvy is due to Libra's association as the sign of the "generals" as well as the peacekeeper. She demonstrated very focused cardinal behaviour. When she was at the edge, she marshalled her forces and made calculated, strategic moves to disarm her "enemy" and take them on in the public arena, the *Panorama* interview being the most outstanding of these actions.

There is nothing flaky about this woman. She did not dart off at a moment's notice without making it safe for her family. She was Cancerian about looking after the children. She did not crack in a "loose" way; she did not blow it; in short, she possessed a control and a presence that a cardinal air sign rising evolves into in maturity. She made sure that she worked through her psychological problems, took responsibility for herself and her family, and, in the end, as much as was possible, created a new, more balanced life. This is not Sagittarius rising behaviour. There were no careless, tossed-off, spontaneous flights or activity. Indeed, there was a massive control over self and image, as well as a great longing for privacy and dignity. Her sad love-affairs, resulting from her pain of rejection in marriage, are simply that – the sad affairs of a lonely woman, any lonely woman. All the archetypal and mythic action in her life had to do with self-worth, presentation, issues with the maternal, the madonna/whore complex, relationships, beauty, harmony, peace, matters of the heart, love, diplomacy – she actually declared that she would like to be an ambassador of love, of the heart. Libra, Libra, Libra.

The A*C*G map for Libra rising

Let's look more closely at the A*C*G map set for the same time (**Figure 7a**). What I am seeing is that Saturn in the 4th house in London becomes SA/IC in Paris, precisely. Royalty are not Uranus, Neptune, or Pluto; they are Saturn. They are the highest that exist in the social hierarchy. On the Astro*Carto*Graphy map, the 1° difference between her natal Saturn and the IC of her chart is shifted to become an exact SA/IC line over in Paris, 2° east of London. The SA/IC line is smack through the dot of Paris.

Her MO/IC line runs right through Greece, where they spent some time – indeed, their last trip together. She loved Greece and was always boating around there, and told a journalist friend she would love to be able to live in Greece. The PL/MC line runs right through Somalia, which was part of her campaign over land mines. The VE/DSC line in Angola marks another very important place, where she was known as the peace-maker, the peace-keeper, the spokesperson for harmony.

The SU/DSC is the heroic aspect of oneself, sensing collective needs and meeting them, being a spokesperson for the underdog and the common people, identifying with one's surroundings and being received well by the populace. Diana has been portrayed as being involved with India's concerns via her public persona with Mother Theresa. In the Libra rising map, Diana has NE/ASC running through Albania, where Mother Theresa was born. The two of them are linked, if mythically, but there has been a lot of projection by the media and the public on Diana's and Mother Theresa's similarities. With Neptune located in Diana's 1st house natally, her persona is a shape-shifting thing, a perfect screen for others' fantasy images. And Diana may well have perceived Mother Theresa as the feminine goddess, the ideal of her own spiritual goals.

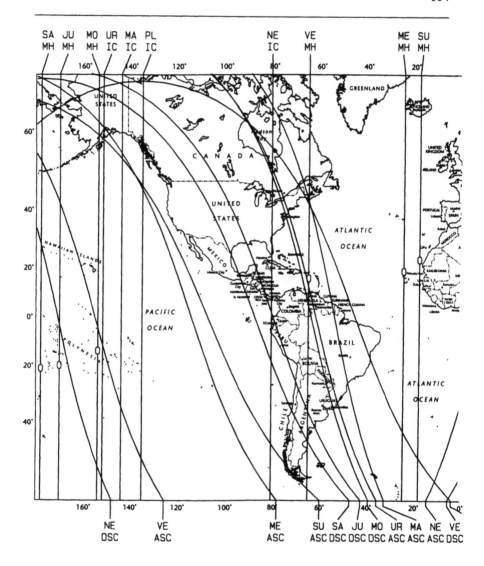

Figure 7a: Princess Diana

Astro*Carto*Graphy Map for Libra Ascendant reprinted with permission of
Astro Numeric Service

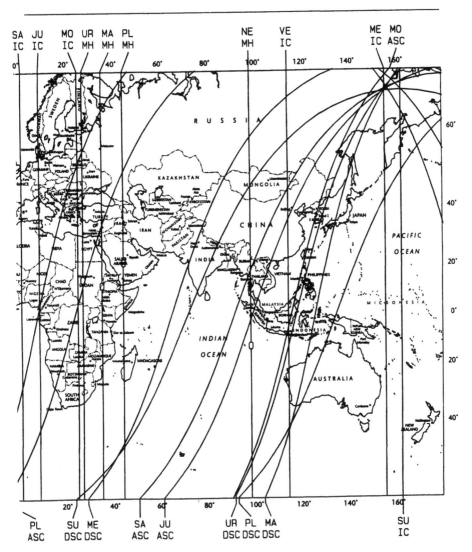

*Note: The SA/IC line may be seen at the top left of the map on this page, just touching the east coast of Britain and running down through Paris.

The world has drawn a fantastic parallel between these two very different women. They are a fantasy in the minds of the world, a romanticised projection. The media loved to photograph them together, so very different in appearance, background, and status, but sharing a common concern for world issues. There was a considerable amount of media management that focused on the two of them as paradoxical cohorts. Their deaths occurring so remarkably close together really serves the Crone and the Princess – the Kore and Demeter myth. Mother Theresa and Princess Diana did have a strong affinity, a natural one, and there is a lovely photograph of them – Diana towering above her, elegant, leggy – embracing.

Here is where astrology can be very tricky, as this example will illustrate. In the Sagittarius rising map, Diana's ME/IC line runs through Bombay, whereas in the Libra rising map, her ME/DSC line is smack through Bombay. It strikes me that Descendant lines speak more about a relationship with the public, being a spokesperson for the masses and reaching out to the world, than do IC lines. Indeed, in India, her Sun and Mercury lines are descending in the Libra chart, whereas they are both IC lines in the Sagittarius rising chart. She never wanted to live in India, nor was she in any way associated with family or property there, so IC lines don't seem appropriate. Similarly, through Madras and Sri Lanka, in the Sagittarius rising chart, is the SU/IC, but in the Libra chart it is the SU/DSC. What do we make of that?

Her PL/MC line through Somalia is where she strove to bring public attention to the land mine problem. I can certainly see that making sense – fighting, making a cause to remove old, undetonated land mines and prevent the future use of land mines that risk all the inhabitants. This is now becoming an important cause, and one which likely will bear her name.

Diana - creating the future

Let's move to the C*C*G and some of the transits and progressions, to see if we can find some more clarity. Her progressed Venus/Descendant line now passes right through the dot of Bombay and up through New Delhi, and crosses the ME/IC line. Do you recall that, in the Sagittarius rising chart, her SA/IC line ran through the tip of Florida:? And there was talk of her and Dodi buying a "dream house" there? Well, in the Libra rising map, her NE/IC line is just seconds to the west of Miami, and her C*C*G shows her conjoined progressed SU/ASC and ME/ASC lines intersecting with her transiting JU/DSC line. Her Sun/Mercury progressions and Jupiter transits over the NE/IC line are more descriptive of a "dream home" than SA/IC with a Neptune transit, which is what the Sagittarius rising chart presents. I see the transiting JU/DSC line crossing the progressed SU/ME/ASC line right over Miami as alive with a progression of events leading to the possible discussion of purchasing some property of value in a foreign country. Certainly it would not have been a thatched-roof shack, but a home of substantial means.

Now, do you recall that in the Sagittarius rising A*C*G, Diana's VE/IC line ran through Alexandria, where Dodi was born?

Audience: Yes, and in this one...Oh! The Descendant makes much more sense than the IC line, as she may have had to live part-time there, but this is much stronger by suggestion. Yes, the VE/DSC line runs through Egypt.

Erin: Right! The VE/DSC line runs through Alexandria. That is much more descriptive of a lover, a beloved, a fiancé – Venus on the Descendant in Dodi Fayed's birthplace.

Okay, let us look at another key location in the world and compare the maps again. Her brother Charles, who now lives in Cape Town, South Africa, gave an emotional and electrifying speech *cum* eulogy at her funeral – and it seems to me he spoke directly from her Moon/IC line. When her brother said, "Your blood family will protect your sons," does that sound like the Moon? Does that sound like the IC? There we have got it. Cape Town is flanked by Venus/Descendant and Moon/IC lines – and which is stronger?

Audience: East of the line...Venus is, I guess, but the MO/IC is near Port Elizabeth, and they have property in that whole southern tip, so they are all there.

Erin: Oh, I didn't realise that. And it happens that her transiting JU/IC and progressed SU/MC lines both run right through Cape

Town, very close to the natal map line of the MO/IC. The speech sounded to me like tribalism; it sounds like a call to war, really. Her sibling house is ruled by Jupiter, too. There was a resounding cheer from the people outside the cathedral at the funeral – first a stunned silence, then a rousing response from the people. It sounds like her brother felt compelled, in the middle of the night before the speech, to have written that emotional eulogy, coming all the way from Cape Town, so close to her MO/IC and UR/MC lines (because she has a Moon/Uranus opposition). Many critics of the eulogy said it was a "call to revolution", a family war.

Audience: Saturn/IC lines feel like responsibility to do with family.

Erin: You are right. In horary it is called "the end of the matter". In classical astrology Saturn was Death. He was the Grim Reaper, remember? Her family obligations begin with Saturn in her 4th house, conjunct the IC natally, and end in Paris, where the SA/IC line is exact.

Audience: Did Mohammed Fayed buy the possessions of Wallis Simpson from their house in Paris? I think he did, and that is very, very curious, isn't it?

Erin: I didn't know that. If so, then it is absolutely hair-raising to see her Saturn in the 4th perfected at the IC in Paris. Though Diana herself may not have been the recipient of these possessions, it shows a strange attraction between the Fayeds and the royals. Also, Muhammed Fayed has still been denied citizenship to the UK, even though he owns Harrod's.

A woman's work is never done

But that brings to mind something else about Wallis Simpson's chart and A*C*G, which I don't have here. She was the first woman to begin the deconstruction of the royal family as a closed, sacrosanct unit, and live through it. On her A*C*G map, she had JU/IC running through Ireland, close enough to England to evoke the image of joining an influential family in a foreign country (she was an American divorcee, remember, and a commoner). Jupiter is about mobility – marrying the King of England is a fairly upwardly mobile move. Her natal Jupiter in the 6th house was at 8° Leo, and thus, with that in mind, we have a good symbol for royal self-image.

Too, Wallis had loads of Ascendant lines through England – right over London are the precise crossings of Neptune, Venus, and Pluto, with the SU/ASC and ME/ASC passing right through Scotland and along the eastern coast of England, crossing together a hair into the English channel. With all those planets in her 4th house natally, by transferring her "home" and "family" to England she gained tremendous notoriety (in the Ascendant in England). By shifting 4th house planets, which are not natally placed in a notoriety house, to the Ascendant, she elevated her profile considerably.

Her natal Sun is in the 5th house, at 29° Gemini, and thus is her latest degree planet and, as such, the repository for her life experiences. The 5th house has to do with love-affairs, no? Certainly for her it was not children, but the abiding love she had for her exiled husband through all the losses and public censure. Her total life and subsequent lonely death (Sun/Pluto) were dedicated to her love – given at great risk. In *The Astro*Carto*Graphy Book of Maps,* Jim Lewis writes: "The couple often visited Germany (her SU/ASC-PL/ASC), where it was rumoured that they were Nazi sympathizers, but during the German occupation of France, they vacated their residency in Cannes to temporarily settle in Spain, where JU is on the IC and VE occupies the ASC. It was here where they reportedly had their early romantic encounters."[16]

About the clothes you mention – funnily, all her Ascendant lines I mentioned, which are natally 4th house planets, run right through the dot of Paris. More significantly, she spent her last years alone, after the Duke of Windsor died, in France – where all five of Wallis' Ascendant lines pass through the whole of the country.

Audience: So Wallis Simpson was destined to instigate the abdication of the King. That is what it appears from what you say.

Erin: Evidently. But in the light of what has happened with the most recent woman to throw the royal family into chaos, I think we

---

[16]*The Astro*Carto*Graphy Book of Maps, op. cit.* Note 11, p. 246-7.

might say that Wallis began the revolution. Her persona, her Ascendant in England, was far, far too powerful and destructive.

Manifestation of an archetype

Let's get back to Diana's Saturn in Paris, then. I am adamant about Saturn being the "reason" she died. I do think she died for a reason, albeit deeply unconscious – both collectively and personally. Diana "lost" her individuality to the collective. This is dangerous – very, very dangerous. She was both the circuit-breaker and scapegoat for the family – all her families, but more importantly, for the royal family. It still, for England, remains the foundation, or, should I say, top of the hierarchy, of the culture itself. I think she was born into this world and died the way she has done in order to break down the old system and shatter the homeostasis of a family which was slouching towards extinction. Basically, it is a family in dire need of rejuvenation, and unfortunately it occurred in a sacrificial way – her natal Jupiter in the 4th squaring her natal Neptune in the 1st describes a personal, social, political, and familial sacrifice.

Her family dynamic, which passes through her family of origin into herself, represented by Jupiter and Saturn in the 4th, portrays an old aristocracy, with all its bills, dramas, deaths, divorces, drugs, and troubles. Charles Spencer had a drug habit which caused him no end of trouble, and he married a woman who, like his *mater soror,* has eating disorders. They are currently separated and divorcing. Her brother has gone into old-style British reaction – voluntary exile in the colonies. That's Moon in Aquarius opposite Uranus, exemplified through her brother.

Audience: It seems to me that Saturn in the 4th house for England in the Libra chart means that the royal family did not support her own thing. Saturn comes with an obstacle, a spoke in the wheel, but it doesn't necessarily indicate death to me, which would be more Mars/Uranus, as I see it.

Erin: Well, first of all, Mars and Uranus don't have to do with death in and of themselves, neither in contemporary nor in classical astrology. They may have to do with the manner of death. If you are thinking of them in the 8th house of the Sagittarius rising chart, then, yes, it could indeed mean that she died a violent death in a car accident. Both Mars and Uranus do have to do with sudden danger and accidents. But you are confusing the two charts. In the Libra chart, Mars, Uranus, and Pluto are in the 10th and 11th houses. And that is public violence – and with Pluto in the 11th house, it is assured that she couldn't trust her closest friends, in the end.

Keep in mind that Saturn is the classical death figure, and Pluto is the contemporary death image. Now, we have to be careful about projection – myself included. You may be projecting your own feelings on the matter, and translating that into a formula for this example. Forgive me, but you are not Princess Diana, and thus your own death might not be so archetypal and dramatic in the eyes of the world. Certainly I can accept that my life and my death are not so celebrated. Therefore, in that way you have a lot less in the way of global exposure. You are not a living symbol, whereas she became that. I am not trying to undermine your value in the world, but merely making a point of relative "fame" and social impact.

On some profound level, Diana's fate required her to abdicated her personal life to be absorbed by an archetype, a voice of the collective. This happens often to people who become ultra-famous. They transcend the personal to become an exemplar, an archetype, a symbol. It takes amazing strength, courage, and personal work to keep one's shape, to retain one's interiority when one becomes a screen for collective projection. Many highly sensitive people who become screens for collective projections do die from it. Of course, many don't, but they are very earthed people who have been able to keep their deepest self safe from contamination by the lowest common denominator. However, her fame was more profound than that; it was no ordinary rise to stardom. This affects a millennia-old dynasty; this is no rock-star or television presenter. Here, we have a world-changing *daemon* at work.

Audience: What you have said is exactly what she has done. All these responsibilities and family burdens – you have to put aside things that you might do yourself to structure your life, because your life structure is in some way family-orientated anyway. But what

Diana had to do was superhuman. Most of us women do not have to die for our family or for our fate in the role of a dying age.

Audience: Why would it happen just then? Why at that particular time? It looks as if she was about to get married again.

Erin: Well, it depends on how you view these things. They did die together, which is a form of *coniunctio,* an alchemical wedding, isn't it?

Audience: Right, it's the alchemical marriage of the King and Queen, who submerge themselves in the bath and cease to exist as separate entities.

Erin: Yes, there are many mythic stories about this sacrificial type of death. In Tristan and Isolde, there is a conflict of family and fate, where the passion of the lovers might not have withstood the reality of an ordinary life. It is far too transcendent to survive the "slings and arrows of outrageous fortune". It is the *liebestod,* the love-death, wherein the lovers die together in a transcendent orgasmic fusion. In alchemical symbolism, when the King and the Queen submerge in the alembic bath, they transmutate into the hermaphrodite, the homunculus. This symbolises the loss of differentiated identity of the couple – and sadly, these two mortals did just that!

Audience: I'm still wondering why this happened.

Erin: That's probably the most significant question in the world right now.

Audience: The fact that she sold all those clothes at auction not long ago seems so suggestive. Doing that, she let go of the past and was ready for a completely new beginning.

Erin: People's deeper selves always know. A dear friend of mine in Victoria, BC, who in 1981 won a Fellow's scholarship to Oxford to paint, went round to see several of her friends just before she left, and gave each of them very significant drawings and paintings. She gave me one with a skull upon a stack of very old philosophy books, with lots of Saturnian imagery, called "The Alchemist's Library". She flew off to Oxford on her birthday, and six days later was run over on her bicycle by a truck in St Giles, across from the Ashmolean

Museum (around the corner from where I subsequently lived for two years in 1993-95). She had made sure that everything was in absolutely perfect order before she left. Just at her departure, she had Saturn transiting her IC and progressed Moon opposite Uranus, and I had told her that her relationship with the world and with her loved ones, her "home" – her mother in particular – would change forever. And sadly, it did. I don't know the answer to those questions, and neither does astrology.

Audience: Do you think the stories about a conspiracy are true? Do you think the royal family had anything to do with her death?

Erin: I was packing to come here on the Sunday night, and it came over on CNN about ten minutes after the accident happened. Actually, I knew about it before most of you did. There were three Americans who were on the overpass at the time, and they all said there was a bang and then a crash. I have never seen these witnesses on telly since that first interview. They were normal average Americans. They really didn't know anything, and least of all who it was, and they were just telling what they heard. No one's seen them since.

That's all I know. Who knows? There are suspicions. Conspiracy theory rumours go around after something of this magnitude. I guess we will never know, but they will dig at it for years. Personally, I find it difficult to entertain the notion that the royal family needs to, would do, or in any way could do something of this kind. It hardly seems necessary, unless we are back in medieval days.

Audience: With the 8th house emphasis on violence in the Sagittarius rising chart, it is very plausible. But the Libra rising chart lacks that kind of 8th house emphasis, doesn't it?

Erin: What is interesting about that 8th house in the Libra chart is that she has Venus therein squaring the Moon in the 4th and Uranus in the 10th.

Audience: A glamorous death.

Audience: Yes, they went out on a high – the best food, drink, and lodging, along with the love that was being professed by each of them for the other.

Audience: Her 8th house ruler is in the 8th in its own sign.

Erin: Venus was a shadowed planet for Diana, and only emerged out from the umbra recently. The implication is that the fullness of integration of the Moon and Venus was not going to be possible for her.

Audience: How was it shadowed?

Erin: With the Libra rising chart, Venus is the ruling planet. Venus in the 8th house of rites, ritual, and symbol was enacted through the cyclic ritual of bulimia – self-loathing, bingeing and purging, alternately polluting and purging her body (Taurus). In one of her speeches, she herself inferred that she suffered from a terrible lack of self-worth, and that eating disorders were a symptom of self-loathing. And her Venus aspects showed rejection – her husband having a lover, and all those painful things she could not bear.

These are mysterious, sad, frightening things to happen to a woman in that position, and so her Venus was malefic toward her at various times. And, it being in Taurus, it presented itself as having a great starving monster inside her. Taurus, Saturn, and Venus are associated with food and eating disorders. It is akin to the mythical Minotaur devouring the virgins, and Kronos eating his children and swallowing his creative issue. She enacted those myths. She was the princess in the tower with the great monster both within and without. I feel that she had shone light on her shadowed Venus just recently, and had brought it back into herself. But perhaps her fate and the style of life would not have let it truly come out of the shadows.

Audience: Does it make sense to make a composite for her and Dodi?

Erin: It would make absolute sense, but I'm not going to use speculative data. I don't have Dodi's birth data. I have a date, but not the time. You do need a verifiable time of birth with Astro*Carto*Graphy.

Audience: Do you have Dodi's birth date?

Audience: 15 April 1955.

Audience: Well, I spoke to an astrologer yesterday, and she said the family said 7.00 am. She was working with the time of 7.00 am, which gives, I think, about 5° Aquarius on the MC.

Erin: So the date of Dodi's birth is 15 April 1955, and the time is as yet unknown. But the speculative time from Astrologer X is 7.00 am in Alexandria. In Alexandria Diana has got a VE/DSC-MA/MC line crossing. Now, that describes the archetypal lovers. Remember the myth from the Odyssey about Ares and Aphrodite caught in the golden net of Hephaistos? Ah! Well, the story is thus: Aphrodite and Ares developed a huge passion for each other, but Aphrodite was married to the lame smith-god, Hephaistos. When Hephaistos was going out of town, she set up a meeting with Ares, and they were entrapped in a net of spun gold by her not-so-stupid husband. Venus and Mars are the archetypal lovers, caught *in flagrante delicto* as the entire pantheon looked on, amused and horrified. The re-enactment of myth occurs daily.

Audience: Can you say anything about the photographers that plagued her? It is being said by everyone, including her brother, that she was "hounded to death". Do they show up somewhere?

Erin: Oh, yes, the media and the paparazzi could well be epitomised by Neptune transiting her IC and Saturn. Neptune rules photographs, and it's transiting angular in the Libra rising chart – thus transiting right through Paris for her. Another of the inferences that Charles Spencer made in his eulogy was the hounds of Diana, the huntress, and, in this case, the hunted. In myth Diana is Artemis, goddess of the hunt, nature, and the great stag of the forest, who had her personal hunting hounds. It is as if Diana's "hounds" turned on her and attacked their own goddess.

Audience: Can you use the north and south Nodes in relation to Astro*Carto*Graphy?

Erin: People are now using the nodes, but they are not actual bodies with mass, but rather, are points in space. Jim would not have included them for that reason, and I agree with this totally. Chiron is different – it is a real thing, a body with mass, longitude, declination, and latitude. However, you can see that Diana has the north Node in there with her Mars and Uranus.

Sans everything

What a story, what a life. I would like to note here, at the end, that the Libra rising chart has transiting Saturn right on her Descendant now (19° Aries), and was 9' from the Descendant at the time of her death. At the time of the accident, the Moon was in Leo in her 10th house; transiting Uranus was in 5° Aquarius, retrograde right on her natal Jupiter in the 4th house; and transiting Neptune was only 12' of arc from her Saturn in the 4th house, right on the IC. The angles are all highlighted by strong transits, and the transits are keyword-accurate – and this, to me, leads back to my original premise, that Diana is Libra rising.

Just to recapitulate the very briefest evidence for Libra rising, here are some of the most important factors. The Sagittarius rising chart does not have anything highlighting the angles, and according to astrologers, that is not a good sign for a radical chart. All the angles are involved with the Libra rising chart, and especially the transit of Saturn to her Descendant.

1. Saturn transiting the Descendant: call to return; end of a relationship with the past; "bringing the boon to mankind".[17] In the heroic round, this is the place where the hero(ine) must bring her subjective gifts to the objective world. In the words of Joseph Campbell:

> The final work is that of the return. If the powers have blessed the hero, he now sets forth under their protection (emissary), if not, he flees and is pursued (transformation flight, obstacle flight). At the return threshold [7th house cusp] the transcendental powers must

---

[17]*Saturn in Transit: Boundaries of Mind, Body and Soul., op. cit.* Note 7. In specific, read "The Heroic Round" and "The Personal Heroic Journey" – Saturn crossing the Descendant.

remain behind; the hero re-emerges from the kingdom of dread (return, resurrection). The boon that he brings restores the world.[18]

I will let those words stand for themselves, as they graphically depict Diana's last hour as Saturn was about to cross the threshold into the 7th house. Indeed, we don't know the final outcome of all this, and she may yet have "brought the boon to mankind" – perhaps through her sons.

2. Uranus on Jupiter in 4th: accident in a foreign country, glamorous, tragic ending. Sudden journey, shattering of all worldly growth and social status in the material world.

3. Neptune exactly on IC (and Saturn): origins dissolved; mystery around family myths; dissolution of "shape", or boundaries blurred, dissolved. Death in mysterious circumstances, sacrifice, transcendence of incarnation.

Stories from the group

Christopher: ships ahoy!

The reason I asked Christopher to take part in this seminar is because of the astounding things that have happened along powerful lines in his Astro*Carto*Graphy map. First, there are some interesting aspects in Christopher's natal horoscope to look at, to establish the quality of the chart and any outstanding configurations that will be dramatised in various parts of the world (**Figure 8**). When you get conjunctions such as the Saturn-Uranus in this chart, you will want to watch for it at all the angle lines in the A*C*G map (**Figure 8a**). Although Christopher has this conjunction in the 10th house, and thus it is strongly apparent in his social "arena", it will be further amplified in specific parts of the world, especially the MC and ASC lines.

---

[18]*The Hero With a Thousand Faces,* Joseph Campbell, Princeton University Press, Bollingen Series, 1968, p. 246.

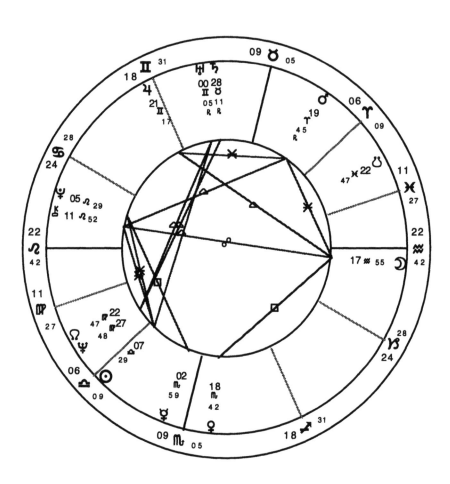

Figure 8: Christopher

(Data withheld for purposes of confidentiality)

When you get a conjunction, a close opposition, or a full Moon in the horoscope, then you need to keep that in mind when looking around the A*C*G. For example, wherever you look on the map, the Saturn/Uranus conjunction will always run together – up and down the IC/MC meridians and curving together, to cross at some point along the ASC/DSC lines. In this case, we see Saturn/Uranus conjunct in the 10th house. By shifting over to the east in the A*C*G map, we will find where that Saturn/Uranus conjunction was directly at the MC when he was born. Do you see? There they are, the SA/UR/MC lines, running down 20° east longitude, through Sweden, Eastern Europe, Central Africa, to run right through Cape Town.

Audience: So by looking at the map, one can see where the "houses" are in the chart.

Erin: Yes, but you are really moving ahead of us. That is great, that you have seen that. What you are saying is this: Christopher has SA/UR in the 10th house in England, and where we see the SA/UR conjunction at the MC in the map is his 10th house in the world.

Continuing on with Saturn/Uranus: if we want to see where it was rising when he was born, then we look to the SA/UR/ASC line (which will become the SA/UR/DSC line precisely on the "other side" of the world map). Saturn and Uranus on the Ascendant (SA/UR/ASC line) runs all the way through Uruguay, Paraguay, and South America, crossing right on Cuba and forming a paran with the MO/MC at the Cuba/Haiti meeting place; through Florida up to the Great Lakes and on up to where astrology "works differently".

Then we have that same conjunction involved as a Descendant line where Saturn and Uranus are descending (SA/UR/DSC) and running up all through this fuzzy part of the map – in other words, up through Indonesia and China and into Russia and connecting at the Russia/US border in the far Northern Pacific. Then there would be the Saturn/Uranus/MC lines and Saturn/Uranus/IC lines together, running down vertically. Now, I would always be curious, when looking at someone's map, as to what might have happened if the person had ever gone to those places. Christopher also has quite stupendous crossings (parans) – for instance, his PL/ASC-MO/DSC-SA/UR/MC crossing running through Cape Town.

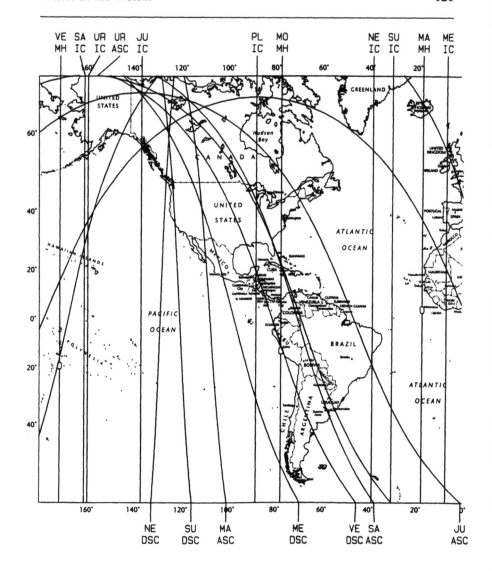

Figure 8a: Christopher

Astro*Carto*Graphy Map reprinted with permission of Astro Numeric Service

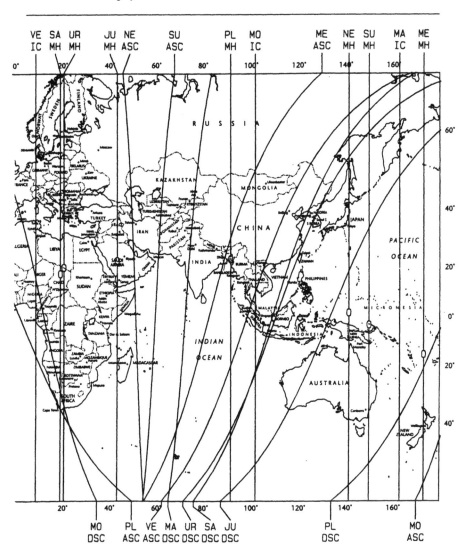

*Note: the SA/UR/MC line appears as a "double" line at the top left hand corner of the map on this page, beginning in Norway and running down through the tip of South Africa where it crosses MO/DSC and PL/ASC.

Natally, there is a wide square from the Moon to Saturn/Uranus, so we would expect a strong paran somewhere. As an example, please do keep in mind that you must look for natal aspects such as trines and wide-ish squares as crossings. This is where a "weak" aspect becomes "strong", as they are then truly angular. The expected crossing is over Cape Town. I think that looks like a fairly powerful place where events may have taken place. Because Saturn/Uranus is in the 10th house in the natal chart, it may well have something to do with officials, job, career, work and so forth.

Do you want to tell us what happened, Christopher?

Pluto/Descendant - mutiny

Christopher: Concerning the Cape Town episode, I must make it clear that at the time that this happened, I knew very little about astrology – in fact, nothing. This is just events happening. In this particular incarnation, I was in the Merchant Navy. I was a Senior Officer. I was responsible for the discipline of the ship and most of the seaman navigation duties. We were on a voyage beyond the West Coast of Africa, shaping up towards Cape Town, in fact straight down the Pluto-Ascendant line. That was more or less our course.

For some time previous to arrival, bearing in mind the speed of the ship being what it is, it was all quite a slow process. I was having some very heavy-duty experiences aboard this ship, bordering on mutiny. The problem was that it was not a British ship. It was of an unmentionable Middle Eastern power. It had European officers and their crew on board. So there was a language problem. I was hoping to use my Junior Officers to assist me in keeping the crew in line and to translate. Right. But they weren't helping at all. In fact, what they were doing was undermining me. They were turning the crew against me, in their own language. These events started to get so serious that I knew my life was in danger. I was either expecting to get to the Deep Six, as we sailors say, or something else nasty.

Erin: Keel-hauled, perhaps.

Christopher: Our destination was the Persian Gulf, right up the other side of Africa. As we approached Cape Town, which was not our destination, things got very alarming.

Erin: So you were actually going to go around the Cape.

Christopher: Yes. It was a time when the Suez Canal was blocked. In the end, in desperation, I said, "I must get off this ship, and now." It was that serious. I persuaded the Captain, who was also a friend, to stand off Cape Town at a distance of about five or six miles. I could have gone off by helicopter, but we ordered a boat. The thing about off Cape Town is this: There are two major world currents meeting in confluence off Cape Town, the Boomas current and the Benguala Current, which give very bad sea conditions down there. Forty-foot waves are not unusual. Ships disappear like the Flying Dutchman.

I had to get off this ship in appalling sea conditions about five miles off. I nearly got killed there because the boat I was trying to get into was ranging up against the side of the ship at least a dozen feet, and I had to time it to do a jump. This I managed, but I was not prepared for the reception committee that awaited me when I reached Cape Town – where I was treated not as some long lost friend but a hostile invader.

Erin: The inner hostile invader.

Christopher: Obviously this was before the Mandela days, during the full Afrikaner bit. I was treated as some kind of criminal. Big Afrikaner policeman with a reception committee shook me down looking for weapons, and all this sort of thing. I had intended to go on my holidays to Durban. I had this fond idea that they would like me and let me stay, but no such thing. They ordered me out of the country inside of twenty-four hours, and made sure of this by getting the airport captain at Cape Town to get somebody off a plane to put me on it, and I was flown up to Johannesburg to get the flight to London.

Erin: Johannesburg is just east of the SA/UR/MC line.

Christopher: It is my parachute. Uranus is always my parachute. This was a Saturnian situation, this sort of confrontation with the forces of law. But what happened on takeoff from Johannesburg was that the aircraft blew out on number four, and it was an abortive takeoff. We nearly didn't make that either. I think Erin will explain what's going on there.

Erin: Well, mechanical breakdowns and this crazy-seeming behaviour of your crew are not paranoia. Your fears for your life were real. As you drew closer and closer to Cape Town, where the major parans of Moon, Pluto, Saturn, and Uranus are situated, the circumstances you were being drawn toward were arising in your consciousness. These lines going through Cape Town are potentially lethal. You could have been murdered, easily. Now, note that the MO/DSC-PL/ASC brings out the angularity – in the horoscope we have a wide opposition between Moon in the 6th and Pluto in the 12th, but it is "opposite" by angle at Cape Town and crosses the SA/UR/MC.

Moon/Pluto *in mundo* at sea

You don't really have a Moon/Pluto opposition in your natal horoscope. But in your map, the PL/ASC and MO/DSC lines cross, creating a mundane opposition, emphasising *in mundo* that you have a Moon/Pluto opposition. It is mutiny and it is potential violation; it describes the complete destruction of your autonomy and authority. That it should intercept your Saturn/Uranus conjunction at your MC talks about the mutiny – an undermining and destruction of the hierarchy on ship. That's the decision of people to overthrow the power of authority. But you wanted to be free, didn't you? And by nature, you are an uncomfortable "leader", and certainly not a real team person.

Christopher: And I have got Saturn in 29° Taurus, collecting this. When you said that earlier about the latest degree planet, it really struck home! I had never really considered that way of looking at the latest degree planet. It is even more significant.

Erin: Yes, Saturn is the most loaded planet in the chart. Then, too, in Cape Town you were on your exact Uranus line, free of everything else, even though it is influenced by Saturn and all this mechanical breakdown takes place. Then what happened?

Christopher: Then we were detained for another twenty-four hours, during which I had too much luggage and I wanted to give it to one of the local boys. More trouble. He was so terrified of accepting a gift from me, in case he got in trouble with the authorities, that I then had to write a letter to the airport Captain in Johannesburg, Jan Smuts.

Erin: That you had "too much luggage" can be taken in many ways. Then you are into Uranus – off-loading, parachuting, as you said earlier.

Christopher: I got out of there very light. And light of money, too.

Erin: I'll bet. Now, that SA/UR/MC line, and your astounding story with that – does that connect in any way to your SA/ASC-UR/ASC line that runs through South America, crossing to be a "perfect" conjunction at Cuba/Haiti? Let's see. You have UR/ASC right over Buenos Aires, and SA/ASC through Montevideo. Had you gone there, I would expect a kind of "continuation" of the experience, though much more personal rather than professional.

Christopher: Yes. A completely different episode took place some years later. In fact, it was my last very big voyage. I undertook a voyage from Gdynia in Poland, right on the SA/UR/MC line there in the Baltic. This was in the good old days before liberation, and there was some heavy-duty stuff going on in Gdynia. The Chief Engineer of the ship and myself had gone to shore, and he was German, and they don't like the Poles that much. He was complaining to me about them in English, hoping it was not understood. I know it was stupid. On my left, sitting at the bar, was a secret policeman who understood every word. He said to me, "You had better tell your friend to shut up now. Otherwise both of you will be coming with me for a long time."

We got away from Poland and journeyed across the Atlantic. Our destination was Colombia in South America. But interestingly enough, we are into Saturn again here, right on the SA/UR/ASC. On this particular voyage, I was once again the Chief Officer, but the Captain was Saturn and he was a workaholic. He couldn't understand why I didn't want to work on deck with the crew. That's all right on a yacht, but on a big ship, Chief Officers don't do that.

He really wanted me to get out there and shift rust with the boys and all the rest of it, and I didn't want to do that. So we were at loggerheads the whole trip. A lot of it was dragging out, big work, big tasks which had to be done aboard the ship, which had no purpose. We had to break out some heavy equipment which hadn't been used in years and was all rusted. He wanted me to fix it, and when we got there we didn't use it anyway, so it was all to no avail. It was all very Saturnian, work for work's sake.

Anyway, upon arrival, he decided that I was far too rebellious for his line, and he decided that, really, I should go home, which is where my troubles started again. The first thing that happened was that Air Bianca, the airline of Colombia, didn't fly to England in those days. They only flew internally in South America, but they did go to America, to Florida.

Erin: Aha. Perfect – right smack through the MO/MC-SA/UR/ASC crossing.

Christopher: They also found that my papers weren't in order. I was standing at the airport checkout and they said, "You're not going anywhere, because we don't like your papers and you don't have any onward tickets from Miami." So they were going to lock me up in Colombia. I don't need to spell out what that means. They were in the habit, in those days, of arresting foreigners, particularly scientists working in oil, shaking them down for everything they had got, and throwing them out on the street to beg. That was their technique in those days. They then went into drugs. Anyway, as we were leaving the checkout, a Texan gentleman said, "Well, it's all right, I've got a plane out on the apron there, my own plane." He said, "If you can just quietly walk over, I'll take you up to Houston."

Erin: Houston. All right. Now we are looking at a place very close to your VE/DSC line.

Christopher: He was nice to me. He was the only one who was nice to me.

Erin: Isn't that great? Your VE/DSC line is the one that brought you out – in luxury, in a private plane. Isn't it amazing that somebody would do that?

Christopher: Eventually I had to get back to Miami to get the London flight. At that time Miami was not an international airport, so they didn't like me either. I had no US papers, so I came under close arrest again while I waited for the London flight. That wasn't so bad, I was just with a security guard. I didn't have to pay anybody. Very strange. I knew nothing about all this astrologically. If I had, I wouldn't have been there.

Erin: That is so incredibly brilliant, that story. I thank you very much.

Audience: In Cape Town, they didn't really care for you.

Christopher: They wanted to care for me big time! But not quite as comfortably as I would have liked.

Erin: Remember, I said that the MO/DSC line is where you are going to be picking up on the collective ethos. That doesn't always mean that you are going to be nurtured, fed, cared for, pampered, bathed, oiled, and otherwise propitiated. PL/ASC-MO/DSC – this brings in danger if it is about – and both Moon and Pluto have to do with the political climate in an area. It is like the story of the ghosts in Sydney – likely the ghosts of convicts, of maltreated souls. The ghosts are there, hanging about the Pluto lines. Not everyone can see them. But when on a Pluto line, you do see them, and you can hear them.

Christopher: The paranoia that was building up as we sailed down the Pluto line was absolutely magnificent.

Erin: It is a fabulous story, Christopher, very helpful and explicit. Thank you. I really appreciate it.

Jackie: healing the family lines

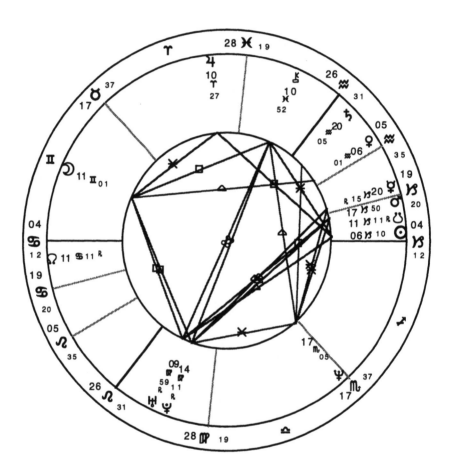

Figure 9: Jackie

(Data withheld for purposes of confidentiality)

I am going to put up another example. This is the most important part of the seminar – the real-life material that is going on. What I am going to do now is a little more subtle, in a sense. I am going to ask Jackie and her *in absentia* son if we can share their information, because it is quite interesting as well. It is not that long a story, and is something that hasn't yet happened, but is about to. I am sorry to be so abrupt with your longing to interpret everything deeply, because I like to do the same thing. But what I need to do today is establish first principles. Next week is a continuation, so some of the material that you want to know more about, that didn't get covered today, will get covered next week.[19]

In Jackie's natal chart we have a Uranus/Pluto conjunction (**Figure 9**). Now, I would be alert to that right away, because it is in the 4th house of the natal chart. That has to do with carrying something over from the family of origin, something unseen, hidden, different, challenging, and potentially secret – Uranus/Pluto – a repository of the merger of the two family lines. Uranus and Pluto are very close together in the natal chart – 5° apart.

Here's an example which clearly illustrates latitude and longitude differences (**Figure 9a**). Those two planets are not far apart in zodiacal longitude, yet are very distant by latitude. If they are 5° apart zodiacally, then they are only about quarter of an inch apart on the map at the meridians (IC/MC). The latitude of Pluto, however, is far separated from Uranus, so that what looks like a Uranus/Pluto conjunction in longitude is seen as being far apart when you look at the ASC and DSC lines.

See where they cross at 40° north and south latitudes? It is from that Earth view that Uranus' and Pluto's paths converge, both in celestial longitude and latitude. Thus, 40° north or south, all along that latitude, is a powerful location for Jackie. Naturally, it is not as powerful as the actual crossing, or a line itself, but it is a backdrop to that latitudinal experience.

---

[19]This is dealt with in Part Two of this book, "The Astrology of Relocation – Finding your Place".

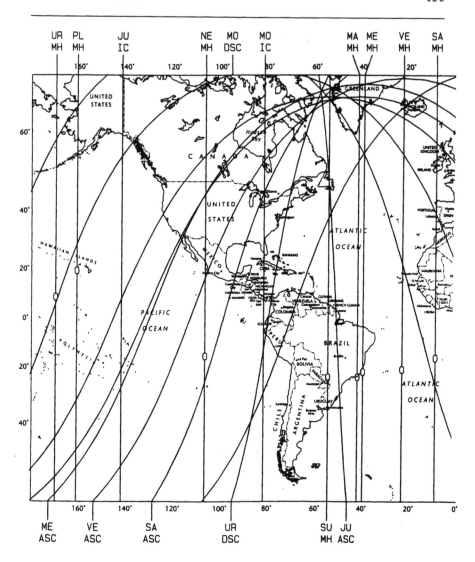

Figure 9a: Jackie

Astro*Carto*Graphy Map reprinted with permission of Astro Numeric Service

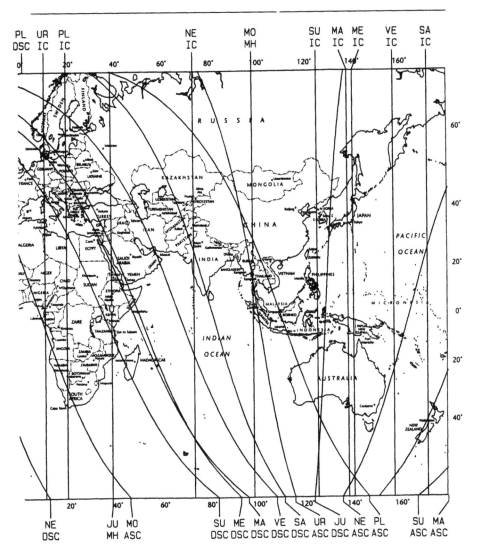

*Note: the PL/DSC line may be seen crossing the UR/DSC line off the coast of Chile, South America at 40°S on the map on the facing page. The PL/ASC line may be seen crossing the UR/ASC line in central China at 40°N on the map on this page.

The PL/IC line runs down through Libya and Chad, through Botswana, and then through Cape Town; and the MO/ASC line crosses PL/IC over Cape Town. That is a true paran. The Moon and Pluto are angular just north of Cape Town – the natal Moon in the 12th and Pluto in the 4th become a mundane square (paran) in that location. If she were born there, Jackie would have the Moon rising, with Pluto on the IC.

Another paran near there is JU/MC-SU/DSC, in the north of Mozambique. That is where Jupiter was at the MC and the Sun was setting when she was born. Now, Johannesburg is flanked by all this angular and linear action. Johannesburg has a kind of "central power", and by the time she was about one year old, the Moon line had progressed to pass through Johannesburg. Jackie has JU/MC and PL/IC running through South Africa, both of which flank the city of Johannesburg, with her UR/IC running right down west of Cape Town and Johannesburg. Remember, east of the line is more powerful because the transit/progression will move toward the location. So the Pluto line is the stronger, and Uranus second in power. We are focusing primarily on that area in South Africa. Why don't you carry on from here, Jackie, and tell the story of those lines?

Roots - black and white

Jackie: The story is that I am the product of a mixed relationship. My mother is white and my father is from Africa and is black. My mother was outcast from her family for having me.

Erin: Those were the days of miscegenation.

Jackie: Yes. That white family – my mother's – then emigrated in 1970 to Johannesburg, leaving me and my Mum in England. Obviously I grew up as a mixed-race child. There was this whole sense of having a white, displaced family in my black country, and my black family in my white country. Curious. I had not seen that family since they emigrated to South Africa. I had seen my grandmother – she had been over here to England to visit – but the rest of the family I have never seen. I am about to go there in February 1998. After having heard the previous story, I am disinclined to go there.

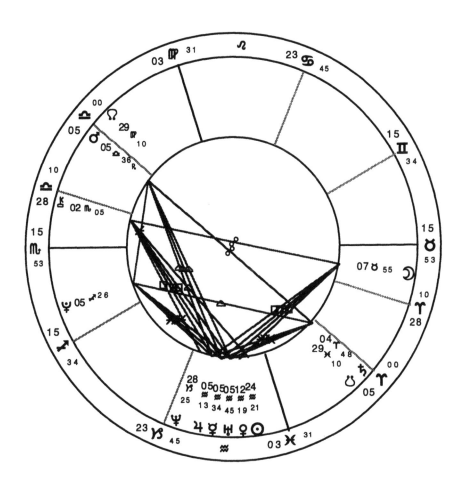

Figure 10: Jordan

(Data withheld for purposes of confidentiality)

Erin: I can understand that, but your purpose is different, and there is conscious intent. It also exemplifies the planetary lines. This makes a big difference. You are making the trip consciously, with intent, and the intent is aligned with the family history and the planets – both natally and Astro*Carto*Graphically. Your Uranus/Pluto in the 4th house needs to be activated consciously, and in that way I should think you will have an entirely different experience than did Christopher, who found himself in a situation which he had not created, but fell into.

What I would like to do now is include little Jordan's chart at this time, as it is his story too. Jordan is Jackie's newborn son (**Figure 10**). And we will also look at his A*C*G map (**Figure 10a**). I think the idea is to take the baby, your son (whose father is a black American from Atlanta, Georgia), down to the family in South Africa, right? Jordan has such an interesting family! His Mum is mixed black and white, living in England, where the black family of origin resides, and his father is a black American. All three of these cultures, from a black person's perspective, are vastly different – they are "worlds apart", so to speak. And Jordan is the integration of all three cultures.

Jackie: For me, Atlanta is on the MO/IC line in A*C*G.

Erin: There's Atlanta, Georgia. That's your SA/ASC line, and that is your MO/IC. Those lines cross up in the Great Lakes area. Atlanta is flanked by MO/IC and SA/ASC. At the crossing, where the two lines intersect, is where your Moon and Saturn are in mundane square, in paran, even though you have Moon trine to Saturn in your natal chart.

Jackie: Yes, I see that. Would that mean that Atlanta, where the two lines are flanking and converging, is where I would experience the Moon and Saturn as "square"?

Erin: Well, sort of, although the most significant indicator of this paran is that it is where the IC and the Ascendant are trine, marked by planets on the IC and Ascendant. This would be where the Ascendant is exactly trine the MC. If we go down the line from where the crossing is exact, to Atlanta, where Jordan's father is, we see that as being an important point, taking into consideration the whole personal story. Now, Jordan's father is a particular kind of black American, one who is exceptionally isolated and insular, southern Baptist, rigorously religious. There is a high level of bigotry still in the US, and Atlanta is the seat of civil rights unrest. To this day it is the symbol of black oppression and hopeful equality. The ancestral legacy is directly African, and the amputation of those roots have caused much pain and destruction in the black American culture. The wholesale adoption of their slave-owners' Christian fundamentalism has undoubtedly contributed to this horrible state of affairs. Jordan's father is one of those disaffected African sons. He has lost his origins in the homogenising of white America. Even though they have recreated their own "tribal" grouping, it is still based on white slave-owners' bedrock.

Jackie: I am deeply aware of this, and ran into a brick wall when I was visiting him and his family. Saturn, hmm, brick wall. My idea was that he and I could travel back and forth, sharing our lives and giving our son a sense of global relationship. But I find the culture there too defensive, too stifling, and too rigid. And Jordan's father is one of them; he is a product of black American hostility.

Erin: Everything "over there" centres around a small, defensive,very protected, highly insular black community, based around the Southern Baptist Church. Now we have Jordan, with all his Aquarian planets and Mars retrograde – just like Martin Luther King, who had Mars retrograde. Is there any Caucasian blood in his father's family?

Jackie: Ultimately there would be, from slavery – it was so common to father children upon the female slaves.

Erin: It has not been that long since the emancipation of the black slaves in America. One of my favourite T-shirts commemorates the bicentennial of the USA, the two hundred years of American identity beginning in 1776. On this T-shirt was a fantastic, psychedelic stars-and-stripes – the cover of the Jimi Hendrix album – and the logo on the T-shirt said, "200 years of Jive". I thought it was brilliant. It is such a different ethos, the Black American situation, from what it is here in England, where it is much more worldly, cosmopolitan, and integrated. And South Africa completes the triangle, geographically and philosophically and politically.

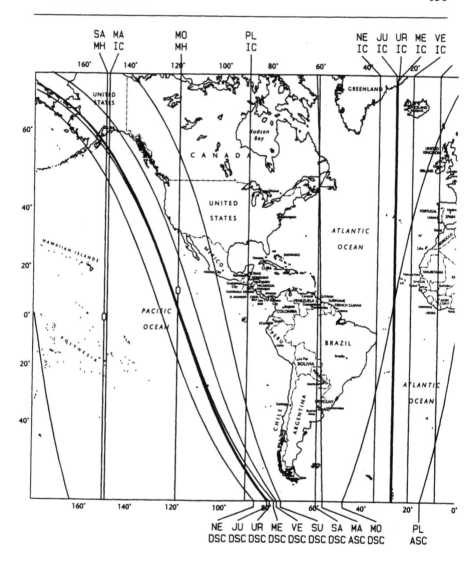

Figure 10a: Jordan

Astro*Carto*Graphy Map reprinted with permission of Astro Numeric Service

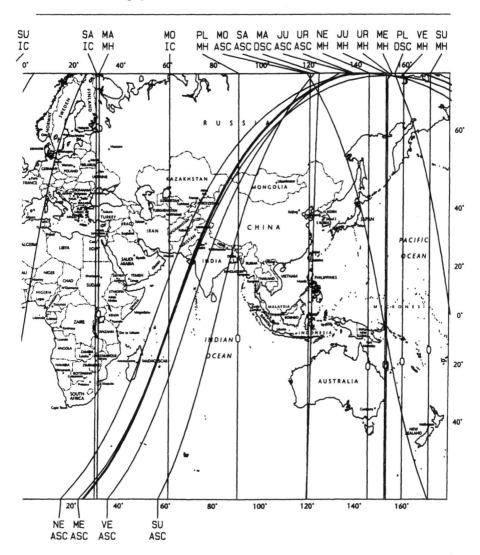

*Note: the SA/IC and MA/MC (MC=MH) lines appear as a "double" line running from the top left of the map on this page, from Finland down through South Africa.

Jordan was born during that wonderful weekend where we had that big conjunction of planets in Aquarius – the last time that many planets gathered in Aquarius was 5th and 6th February, 1962. He has Neptune, Jupiter, Mercury, Uranus, Venus, and the Sun in Aquarius in the 3rd house.

He has a tight configuration of Mars opposite Saturn. Mars is retrograde at 5° Libra, opposite to Saturn at 4° Aries, and it is that aspect that is so strongly marked, running right down through the dot of Johannesburg. We have Jordan's SA/IC (family responsibility, origins) in Johannesburg, with Mars retrograde at the MC. To me that epitomises, metaphorically, symbolically, and actually, the living, breathing, human manifestation of the breaking down of apartheid – the battle of the people (Mars retrograde) against the oppression of the past, the senex, the status quo of South Africa.

Mars retrograde opposite Saturn, the black-white situation which exists in Jordan's family, becomes polarised and open in Jordan's chart, and thus through Jordan. The merger is central in Jordan, with Saturn natally in the 4th house of the legacy from the family-of-origin to Mars in the 11th house of the collective political ethos. There he is, an amazing Aquarius individual with Pluto rising natally, and his PL/IC running right through Atlanta. His black American father will prove to be a profound and conflicting, but potentially healing catalyst. It is a different situation to have that kind of background than it is to be in Asia or to be in mid-London and be black, believe me. When Jordan grows up, and realises his amazing history, he will find something of power in Atlanta, but he may not want to go there. PL/IC lines have a bad reputation for violence. Jordan's father was born and lives on Jordan's PL/IC line, and his mother's complicated dual roots of black and white come from Johannesburg – his SA/IC and MA/MC lines. So you are thinking of going down there in February, perhaps for Jordan's birthday?

Audience: Will your husband go with you?

Jackie: He's not my husband. He's not my partner, either.

Audience: But will he go with you?

Jackie: Undoubtedly he won't!

Erin: This is where Jackie is the sole person responsible for the baby and his awakening. His awareness and his father may remain Pluto/IC, the unseen one, the haunting of the long past of the roots of slavery – the root that will have to be sought at some other time. This isn't a bad thing; it's just the situation. There is a remarkable configuration and confluence of lines that describe the living, actual situation.

Opening the doors for the future

Audience: The MO/ASC line in Jackie's map, crossed by PL/IC in South Africa, seems to me to mean she is being very generous to open the hidden doors of Jordan's exciting and unorthodox family. She is consciously going there to open the doors. It seems to me there is a bit of a difference from Christopher's case, where it was the PL/ASC line where all those threatening things happened to him.

Erin: You are absolutely right. Consciousness and generosity turn devils into angels. These are known ghosts. This is an important issue, to connect with the "racial problem", as it is still called down there in Johannesburg. As long you are in a safe place, you'll be fine. I've been down there numerous times. I have also been to Atlanta, and I live in London, so the trinity of the three cultures is known to me. I will show you my relocation chart next week, where I was intimately involved in a hijacking in a suburb of Johannesburg, so there's always that violent element about when emancipation occurs. It seems ironic, but when forces have been sequestered or ghettoed for a long period, their emancipation causes a chaos of violence. And South Africa enacts the irruption of the collective unconscious into the world. Apartheid is now not possible, but will take generations to settle – this is extrapolated out into all dimensions of being.

However, and most significantly, you are going down there to put something personal to rest, to open the doors of a family secret, to bring to the light of day the unseen quality of the PL/IC theme in the family – which Jordan is holding right in Johannesburg. You are going down there to unify. It's not your revolution, and Jordan is of the future. He is an Aquarius and he will live far longer than you, God willing. Therefore, what he has to live with is a unified globe, but where everything is still psychologically in apartheid. There is something here about the unification of the dark and Pluto and the unknown. If the world is an organic entity, then South Africa has been its unconscious. It has been the "dark continent" for centuries. Now that secrecy is blown open, the demons are flying out. But they are becoming increasingly more conscious, and the world is now aware of the dark continent of its unconscious.

I shouldn't think a two-week trip is going to be a physically dangerous thing. I think it will open something very, very important for your family situation. He has Saturn in the 4th house too, by the way. Houses move this way, so it really is in the 4th house. You don't read them into the next house.

Jackie: I have always wondered about that.

Audience: In February, Jordan has Chiron crossing over his Ascendant, which would be squaring all those planets in Aquarius. That symbolises him as the healer – this young baby is drawing them together over there.

Erin: Yes, this is the point, really, of taking him there, with Saturn in the 4th house, and your Uranus/Pluto in the 4th house, and his SA/IC. By moving him two hours east of Greenwich, it puts Saturn in the 4th house, making Saturn angular. By going to Johannesburg, his Saturn now sits on the IC, which is the reclamation and the cleaning up of, and the taking on responsibility for, the genealogical blending of the mixed race family. Now, the father remains unseen for a while in this picture, because Pluto is on the IC at his birthplace. But he is affected because there are very generous roots there, too, and he will go there to uncover them. So he really is a global baby. All right. Thank you so much. That's fabulous.

Post script

I have talked to Jackie since this seminar was given, and in September 1998, as I was editing the transcript, I asked her to write me about the trip to Johannesburg. This is what she wrote:

We arrived at Johannesburg airport in February 1998, to be greeted by a host of people from my family who last saw me thirty years ago. Aunties I'd never known, cousins younger than me, born in South Africa, too! Most poignantly, my childhood "best friend" in England, who emigrated with her family when we were both only eight years old, was also there to meet me!

Everything was there to greet us – and everyone. The departure of my best friend to South Africa was one of my most devastating losses as a child. I truly loved her, and that depth of feeling was reciprocal. I was lost for a large chunk of my childhood without her. The grief ran so deep that it set the tone for losses that I would later experience as an adult. Those that I love live far away, distant and elusive. Hard to get hold of. It can surely be no accident that I fell in love with an American citizen who lived thousands of miles away and had a child, who may never have a relationship with him either.

Meeting my best friend again was like old times. We had corresponded from eight through eighteen years of age. On her last trip to the UK we'd fallen out over the "colour bar" in S.A. Now, we were reunited on her turf, with some of the barriers stripped away.

I felt solid, complete, part of a larger family for the first time in my entire life. Jordan and I were warmly welcomed, and we will return, I suspect, on an annual basis. Our next trip is already booked.

Susie: all over the map

It's just after 5.00 pm, and we do normally quit at 5.00. However, bear with us, as I would like to share a couple of stories from Susie, whose horoscope (**Figure 11**) and A*C*G map (**Figure 11a**) follow.

In this natal horoscope there is an outstanding natal conjunction of Jupiter and Uranus, and an outstanding configuration between the Sun and the Moon – a perfect opposition. Those are the configurations that I am going to concentrate on. I have tried to get Susie to move all over the world, haven't I? Been working on it for a few years, we have – this is where astrologers have to be very careful. Because Susie and I have been doing work astrologically for a long time, I am fairly safe with taking some fantasy privileges with what life is about and what things can be done, because very often they are shared. I would never impose my belief about where one should go if I didn't know the person, but I was very strongly struck by the fact that the natal Moon in Sagittarius and the natal Sun in Gemini have a kind of city/country complex. It is not the most decisive of configurations, and has a multiplex of desires, needs and potentials. The "city" and the "country" are metaphors for myriad things.

On one hand, you want to be in the stimulation of the city, and on the other, the great boundless ranges of Artemis and freedom. It's the perfect chart for living abroad, in that the Moon in Sagittarius could enjoy living in a foreign country, easily making a home in a place where you spoke another language or lived in another culture or worked and studied with another culture. It's the same with the Sun in Gemini – a love of travel – and again with Sun in the 9th house and Mercury in the 9th at the MC, a great place for study opportunities.

Being born in England under her ME/MC line, there has been a lot of thinking, planning, ideas, and learning in her homeland. Susie has been an actress and an organizer, just to mention a couple of things. She has accomplished many goals, and still longs to try out new parts of her life. But now, she feels blocked, stuck, immobilised. Many ventures have not succeeded in finding her "place". One of the things you want to look for is SU/MO lines, because there's a Sun/Moon opposition in the natal chart. But also, look for this unusual Jupiter/Uranus conjunction. It is one of those double-barrelled planet configurations that we need to explore angularly in various parts of the world. I thought that San Francisco would be nice, because it brings her Sun/Moon opposition to the Ascendant. In San Francisco, she has Moon on the Descendant and the Sun on the Ascendant. That brings the split into a horizontal axis on the Ascendant and Descendant.

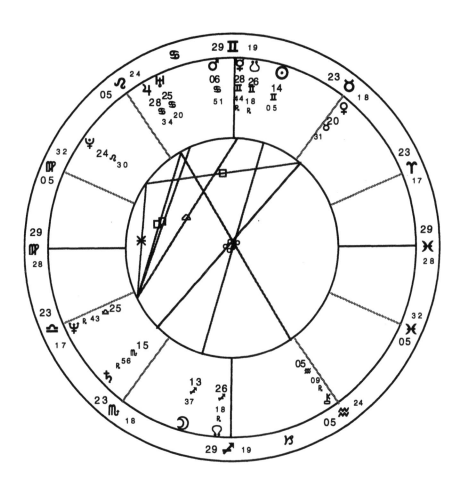

Figure 11: Susie

(Data withheld for purposes of confidentiality)

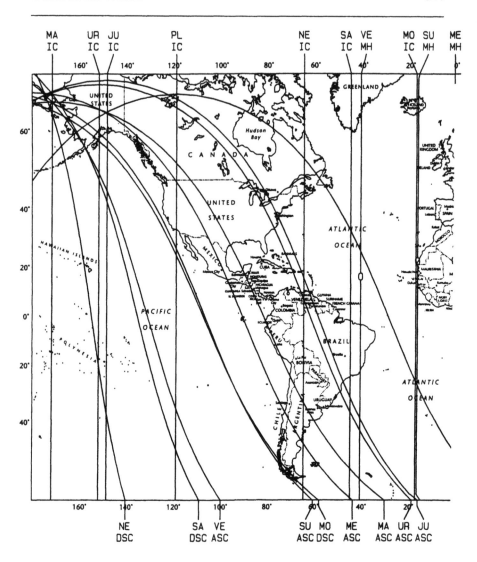

Figure 11a: Susie

Astro*Carto*Graphy Map reprinted with permission of Astro Numeric Service

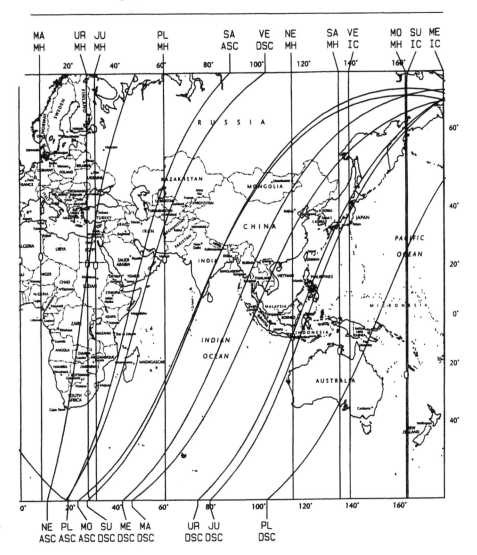

*Note: the SU/DSC and MO/ASC lines can be seen at the bottom left side of the map on this page, curving up through India and meeting over Nepal. As SU/ASC and MO/DSC they can be seen running up through the southernmost tip of Chile, meeting in the south Pacific and passing close to the coast of California.

Now, Susie, why don't you tell us some of the places that you have been, and why you were there, and what you discovered in those locations.

Right lines, wrong place

Susie: I went to Zimbabwe, and I was there working for a women's magazine. I was a travel writer. You were the one that said, "It would be wonderful if you could do journalism in Zimbabwe." And I said, "Well, I have. I was there a few years ago."

Erin: JU/UR/MC: something different, exciting, revolutionary, socially active, and travel-orientated. Zimbabwe is not only that culturally, but it is defined as such by you personally. This is where the individual is reflected in the culture and vice versa.

Susie: I loved it there. And I loved the work. I did try to go back to live there, but it was just not possible because of the masses of paperwork, the politics, and the level of income, which was not such that I could live there. Also, I went to Nepal, which is right where the Moon and the Sun cross.

Erin: The Sun and Moon are split by only a tiny bit, because their opposition is so exact. However, even that 20' of arc between a perfect opposition has its separation. Notice where the SU/DSC and MO/ASC start off at the bottom of her map and run up the Indian Ocean, hitting India at the southwestern tip, running up the eastern coast, and meeting and crossing perfectly over Nepal. Wonderful.

Now, this is interesting: this spot in Nepal is the opposite point from San Francisco, where she has her Moon setting and the Sun rising. If we take a moment now, and close our eyes and visualise the world, we would see sunrise in San Francisco while sunset was occurring simultaneously in Nepal. And on the opposite horizons of each place is the Moon – setting in San Francisco and rising in Nepal.

Audience: Oh, a good exercise. I see that perfectly, now.

Erin: Straight across her exact polarity is Nepal. Right there on the dot is the exact crossing or perfect angular relationship of the Moon rising and the Sun setting. I have to say that Nepal embodies everything we have ever imagined about enlightenment, from living in caves in mountains to high, high altitudes. To have the SU/MO/ASC/DSC lines go through there and intercept does strike me as a place of personal enlightenment. And what happened?

Susie: I just had a wonderful time. I went up to the Tibetan border, which is very remote and had only just opened up to other cultures. I had a wonderful time.

Erin: It had only just opened up?

Susie: Yes, when I went, which was five years ago, in 1992.

Erin: Your MO/ASC line must have been very emotionally responsive to the history and to the people, as well as feeling the heroism of the people via your SU/DSC.

Susie: I just remember feeling like a sponge. I couldn't absorb enough. I just felt happy.

The mutable dilemma - full Moon lines

Erin: And in San Francisco?

Susie: I liked it a lot. I have got friends there, and feel very easy and at home there.

Erin: So it's the flip situation. You have been to two polarities. Do you think you could live in either place?

Susie: I have a horrid feeling I could live in a lot of places. It is just getting out of the fantasy and into the reality.

Erin: Well, you have a lot of highly habitable lines running through very habitable parts of the world. This is the opposite dilemma of somebody who doesn't have any. And also, you have the Gemini/Sagittarius polarity, and thus could live almost anywhere – indeed, your map expresses that possibility. You have so much potential; you actually have to make a decision. God forgive that a

Gemini with Moon in Sagittarius should actually decide their fate instead of letting it happen.

Susie: That would be impossible.

Erin: Well, it so far has proved to be somewhat so. Now, here's another thing. Running through British Columbia, you have a ME/ASC line. It also runs through down through Salt Lake City, El Paso, and Santa Fe, down into central Mexico. And Central America is flanked by the MA/ASC and ME/ASC. This seems highly energetic and a lovely line to follow. Just off the cost of Vancouver there's a PL/IC-ME/ASC crossing. You went there; how was that?

Susie: I had a great time. I met some people who said, "Why don't you come out and spend some time and live here?"

Erin: A serious offer?

Susie: Yes. But again, a kind of a fantasy thing – "Just come and hang out and you could do massage on the beach."

Erin: Vancouver is so bloody cold. There is a nude beach in Vancouver, but most of the year it is cold and raining. It is 49°N14'. Now, any other places? I thought you might enjoy Adelaide. Let's look at Adelaide. It's a VE/IC line, but it is a SA/MC line as well. There's a Venus/Saturn opposition in the natal chart, which will show up as a split in the meridian lines of the A*C*G map. I think this exemplifies the splits you feel within yourself. You simply feel torn in all directions, or two at least, when you are in a place of power.

It is not really about you not being able to decide, or the world not being receptive. It is more that there are interior splits in the natal horoscope, dramatised on the globe. That would mean coming to terms with certain parts of the self that may be conflicting. Venus might like to live in Adelaide, but Saturn would probably say, "No, it's too beautiful, the sky is too blue, it's too warm and it's too comfortable." Yet Venus would say, "This is lovely. I feel so good. The sun is against my skin, the people are easy and friendly, and it is not a hard life." I do believe, if you don't mind me saying this, that it is possible that there may actually be natal issues unresolved that surface in places like VE/SA lines. You could swing more to Venus, and recognise that Saturn is a boring old man and is always going to be crabby and saying, "Don't be comfortable, don't be beautiful, don't be full of yourself and sensual." And yet Venus in Taurus wants to be – no, is – all those things. I think you need to be a bit more Venus.

Susie: I definitely think I want to be a bit more Venus.

Erin: And your Sun/Moon is saying, "Do you want to be more at home, or caught up in the solar drama of 'Where do I want to be? Where's my life force?'" When there are a lot of oppositions in the chart, one meets them in Ascendant/Descendant areas, especially at the crossings; and in conjunctions of IC/MC lines, which are always in polarised conflict by their very nature. When there is an opposition in the natal chart, which would be Sun/Moon and Venus/Saturn in Susie's horoscope, there are at least two archetypal and paradoxical messages. There exist both the desire to belong to the great collective, and the equal but opposite desire to be an exceptional individual and uniquely noticed. In some ways it is in the meeting of opposites that the beginning of healing splits, complexes, and issues that are out of balance lies. Using the world, or using travel, as a way of externalising these inherent personal issues is a pretty effective way – with conscious effort, mind you.

As Jimmy Buffet says in his song, "Changes in latitude, changes in attitude". I should think that might be exactly what the meeting of opposites in Astro*Carto*Graphy parallels in latitude: what we have in attitude. I have always felt that an opposition is a "split conjunction", and where an opposition becomes a conjunction via map-making, we might find unity. The opposition in this horoscope has become a form of conjunction on this map line, because we have SA/MC and VE/IC so close and parallel over a location. They are conjoined in the sense that they are linked together all the way down through the central part of Australia and Asia. This is a kind of conjunction, if you like. Yet in longitude, it actually is an opposition. There is a potential here of marrying oppositions and finding the ability to focus more on one planet than the other, and bringing them into a collusion with each other. Saturn and Venus can be happy if each respects the other. In your life, you would need to stop listening to the old parental saw: "Who do you think you are? You will never really amount to anything. No one will ever marry/love/care for you."

Susie: That is exactly where that comes from.

Erin: And that is exactly what you will hear wherever you go, until the issue is resolved internally – I mean, resolved to some degree. Remember, no matter where you go, there you are, and all the A*C*G map does is amplify by angularity that which is an issue. Maybe you should run off to Rio, where Venus is on the MC and Saturn on the IC, the opposite of Adelaide. Sorry, I am being silly now.

Audience: Would Susie's PL/MC line be more effective in Los Angeles than in San Francisco?

Erin: Oh, yes. Absolutely. It runs through Los Angeles exactly, but San Francisco is flanked by the MO/DSC-SU/ASC. PL/IC is running through the point just between San Francisco and Los Angeles. You would have to stay there longer for it to become an effective tool. San Francisco would be the kind of place where you could go and study and become an analyst or a therapist, or do some very deep soulful work and healing work. I wouldn't go to Los Angeles because it's a single Pluto line, and we have had some evidence of what takes place there if we are not comfortable with our dark side.

Susie, thank you for sharing your map and experiences with us – your full Moon illuminated a lot of landscape for us.

Audience: Would you go to your SU/PL line?

Erin: If the life I lived exemplified a Pluto mythos, yes. I wouldn't avoid a place because Pluto was there. A Sun/Anything line is about one's purpose in life, and must not be avoided.

Audience: I have a Pluto line running through Maryland, and I have always wanted to go there.

Erin: Well, then, if you go, take good care, and send me postcards from the edge!

We have to close for the day, and although next Sunday we will concentrate on relocation charts, we will continue on with some of the A*C*G principles. Bring your A*C*G maps with you, and any charts you want us to use. Thank you all for sharing your maps with us and making the day so interesting.

Bibliography

Campbell, Joseph, *The Hero With a Thousand Faces,* Princeton University Press, Bollingen Series, 1968.

Cornelius, Geoffrey, *The Moment of Astrology,* Arkana, Contemporary Astrology Series, London, 1995.

Filbey, John and Peter, *Astronomy for Astrologers*, Aquarian Press, Thorsons, London, 1984.

Lewis, Jim and Guttman, Ariel, *The Astro*Carto*Graphy Book of Maps*, Llewellyn, 1989.

Lewis, Jim, with Kenneth Irving, *The Psychology of Astro*Carto*Graphy*, Arkana, Contemporary Astrology Series, London/New York, 1997.

Reinhart, Melanie, *Incarnation: The Nodes and the Four Angles*, CPA Press, London, 1997.

Sasportas, Howard, *The Twelve Houses*, Aquarian Press, Thorsons, London, 1989.

Sullivan, Erin, *Saturn In Transit: Boundaries of Mind, Body and Soul*, Arkana, Contemporary Astrology Series, 1990.

Sullivan, Erin, *Venus and Jupiter: Bridging the Ideal and the Real*, CPA Press, London, 1986.

Part Two:

The Astrology and Psychology of Relocation – Finding your Place in the World

This seminar was given on 5 October, 1997 at Regents College, London as part of the Autumn Term of the seminar programme of the Centre for Psychological Astrology.

Introduction

Finding our place in the world can be complex these days, with all the options, possibilities, and freedom available to the majority of the world. The seamless globe allows transition from place to place, country to country, in a dizzying way. Accessing places remotely, through business, relationship, and now the internet, is everyday stuff to us. This is not always a good thing – it creates too much choice, too much potential, and engages far too much intellectual energy for many to cope with. The fact that we have all the options in the world is both a blessing and a curse. Much of civilization's neurosis stems from apparent choices.

Using astrology to better understand these choices, and using it sensibly, can reduce the anxiety about changing locations. Moving and relocating to specific cities and areas involves setting a relocation chart, that is, a horoscope for the new place based on your own natal chart time. There are going to be overlaps between seeing the relocation chart and the A*C*G map, and using them together effectively. Some of the technical material for A*C*G is going to be better digested now, after a week of thinking it over and examining A*C*G maps, so we can spend an hour or so delving into some of your queries regarding the material in the A*C*G seminar, if you like.

I will start by reviewing some of the material from the last seminar, and then take any queries that have arisen in the last week, specifically about Astro*Carto*Graphy as it pertains to relocation charts and your own experiences.

Relocating within Astro*Carto*Graphy lines

Last week we were talking about Astro*Carto*Graphy, emphasising angular planets and their power – on the Ascendant, MC, Descendant, and IC. This concept was graphically portrayed by lines that were overlaid on the map of the world. This is the "big picture", the global view of your birth time as it shows what is rising, setting, culminating, and at the nadir all over the world at the time of your birth. As you recall, aspects, signs and houses are not emphasized in A*C*G – only parans (crossings), zeniths, and the lines depicting angularity of planets around the world.

Relocation is more precise, and thus brings in the "local picture". It takes into account the houses, the signs, and the aspects between the planets, thus involving the intensely personal, central view one has of the heavens, and therefore of one's life. Though Astro*Carto*Graphy *is* personal, in that it is a chart of the angularity of each of your own planets seen on the world at the moment of your birth, it does give a specialised placement of planets – only planets on angles. So we look to Astro*Carto*Graphy maps not to see what is in the 11th house or the 5th house in a certain town or city, but to see what's on an angle somewhere in the world. A*C*G maps show where your own natal planets have a driving sense of power.

Not everybody is comfortable living in angular places, and I don't necessarily think that you should move to a place because you have lines there. I think that you should consider whether you really wish to deal with a place that demands a tremendous amount of awareness, consciousness, and effort relative to the planetary agency symbolised by the planet line. The places that I mentioned last week, lacking in planetary lines on your maps, are places which are intermediary places, places without urgency or specific tasks to complete. Jokingly, but possibly seriously, I call them "karma-free zones", because wherever you have a planet in your natal chart, you have to pay attention. It is an alert place. It is a place of intense focus and growth. This is particularly true of A*C*G maps, as they focus on the angles, which are the axes of intense purpose and direction. Having no lines through areas is rather like an untenanted house in the horoscope.

Obviously, if your horoscope has no planets in the 10th, 11th, and 12th houses, that doesn't mean that you have no career, no friends, and no interior life. It simply means that you are not absolutely determined to develop those areas. They will develop. You can go there, you have got to get things going, but the empty houses are not as strongly destined or fated, and do not present an obvious challenge. Wherever you see a planet, you see an agency where you will, whether you like it or not, be required to work on an aspect of your psyche, depending on which planet it is, and depending on the aspects involving that planet.

Thinking globally while living locally

Relocation can be subtle. You could move a very short distance and find a qualitative difference in your life. Moving exactly due north or south from your birthplace, the MC will remain the same, but the Ascendant will change. This is because the sidereal time remains the same down any given meridian of longitude. However, you will see a "yawning" of the Ascendant as you move from the equator, at 0°, toward 60°N or 60°S.[1]

---

[1] Refer back to the previous A*C*G seminar in this volume: "Astrology works differently 'up there'", p. 19.

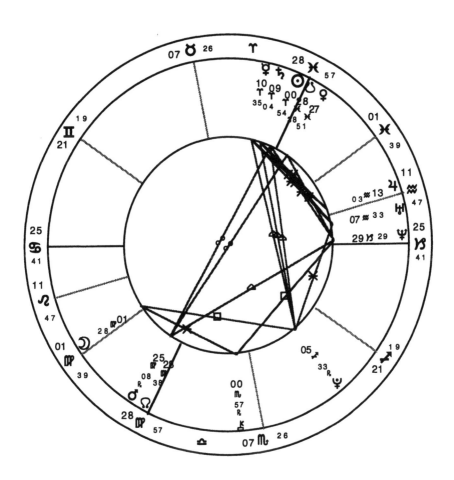

Figure 1

21 March 1997, 12.00.00 GMT, Greenwich, GB

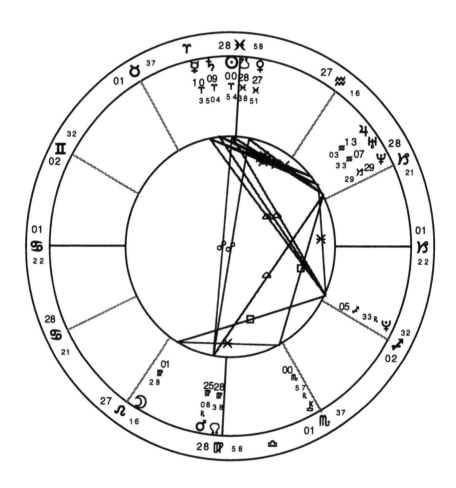

Figure 1a

21 March 1997, 12.00.00 GMT, Tema, Ghana

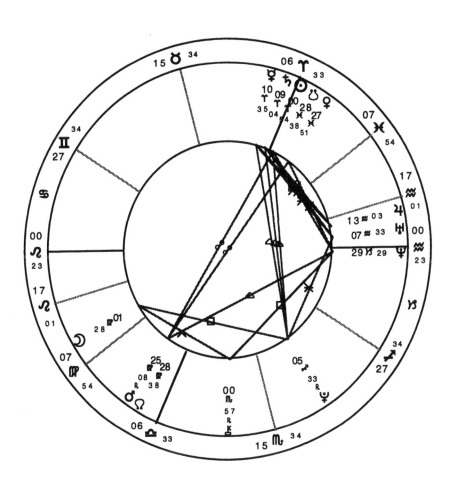

Figure 2

21 March 1997, 12.00.00 GMT, Cologne, Germany

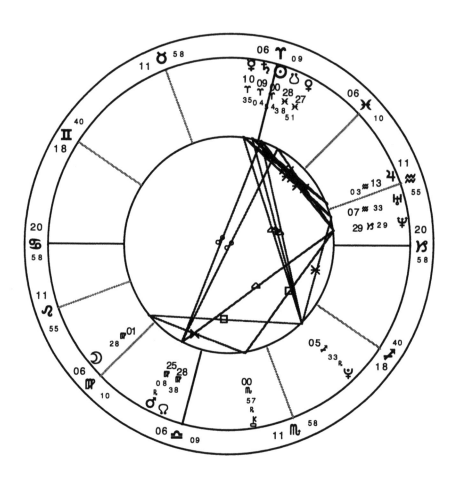

Figure 2a

21 March 1997, 12.00.00 GMT, Constantine, Algeria

At the spring equinox on 21 March, at a few minutes past noon at the Prime Meridian (0° longitude) in Greenwich, it is 00:00:00 hours sidereal time, and at that time the MC is 0° Aries. At the equator, the Ascendant is 0° Cancer, but as you move from the equator to 20°N, the Ascendant is 8° Cancer. At 35°N, the Ascendant is 15° Cancer; at 50°N, the Ascendant is 25° Cancer; and at 60°N, the Ascendant is 4° Leo.[2] I have set three examples here for 12.00.00 GMT on 21 March 1997, near the spring equinox, but at different locations.

In **Figure 1** and **Figure 1a**, we have a chart set for noon in Greenwich, and a chart for the same time but in Tema, Ghana, some 46° due south on the exact same meridian. The MC is the same, while the Ascendant has closed in by 24°, due to its proximity to the equator, where the Ascendant and MC are 90° apart.

In **Figure 2** and **Figure 2a**, we have two charts set for the same time and date, but this time relocated east of Greenwich by one time zone. However, Cologne, Germany is in northern Europe, and Constantine is in Algeria, Africa, which is due south of Cologne. Cologne is about 15° north of Constantine, but on the same meridian, as you see. Again, you can see the difference in the Ascendants of the two cities, while the MC remains the same. In extreme southern and northern latitudes, say between 45° and 60° south or north, there can be a great variance between the angular relationship of the MC and Ascendant in the course of a day. Closer to the equator, within 5° of it, the angle remains fairly constant at a square.

When moving, depending on the season and time of day, and in accord with the changes at the MC and Ascendant, the intermediate houses will shift as well – those being the 2nd, 3rd, 5th, 6th, 8th, 9th, 11th, and 12th house cusps. There are three main house systems most commonly used by astrologers – Placidus, Koch and Campanus – but there are many who use the Equal House system, which I do not favour because it is not based in celestial measurements. Those

---

[2]The reverse signs are the case in the Southern Hemisphere. See *The Practical Astrologer,* Nicholas Campion, Cinnabar Books, 1993, PO Box 1071, Bristol, BX99 1HE, England. The Tables of Houses on page 234 illustrate this phenomenon perfectly, graphically and visually.

three are the most common house systems used today that employ the same angles on the horizon and meridian, but use three very different systems of domification. Myself, I would stick with the one you use in practise. Be consistent with your house system, which does not mean do not try out others, as that is necessary in the first years of study. But do stick with one to work with consistently.

Houses are one of the theoretical measurements that people can argue until they are blue in the face about what's right or wrong. For the purpose of teaching this seminar today, I advise you to stick with your house system in both the natal and all relocation charts. Then you are working within the same system. My feeling is this: astrology as a system works if you stick to the system you are using. As soon as you start deviating and saying, "Oh, well, I'm going to relocate my chart and instead of using Placidus I'm going to Campanus houses," you are just going to confuse yourself. Stick with the house system that you use.

Changing places: why move?

Dramatic horoscope changes can occur when we relocate, but there are also subtle ones. For instance, if you move only a short distance and yet that move has altered your house system so that it shifts your Sun or your Moon into another house, that is important. Normally, you won't notice it the minute you arrive, because it takes some time and much energy to make a major move. You are unlikely to suddenly feel, "Oh, right, my Sun has now just moved from the 8th house to the 7th house, and therefore relationships are going to be really much better for me. And I'm not going to be dwelling always on the mysteries of life, but on friendship, relationship, and lighter-hearted things." That would be mad.

However, you might find that if you moved there and lived there for a couple of years – a Mars return is about the time it takes to take root in a place – that kind of subtlety will manifest. You will still be the same person and the Sun will have the same aspects – let's say it squares Saturn – so you still are that same individual with a strong challenge to the ego. You still will be required to develop under stress and hard work. But you may find that, in partnerships and relationships, you are much less interior and more involved – that you are not as isolated (8th house Sun) and are more capable of working with others.

The further away from your natal place you move, the more dramatic will be the way you play yourself out. I think that if we are going to consider relocation as a choice, rather than as happenstance, then it is good to be practical about the move, taking into consideration all the ramifications, and also doing the relocation charts. In other words, there are many reasons for moving. The basic two reasons are: you *must* move, or you *want* to move. Most people move because they are aesthetically and/or pragmatically attracted to a place. Work is better, education, cultural attraction, or aesthetics are more appealing, it is better for the family, and so on.

That is why I think Astro*Carto*Graphy comes in as an important tool, because if one is emigrating from one part of the world to another, then it is important to see the overall "tone" of the area. People who feel an urgent desire to move to other countries, for reasons other than just the kind of buildings and art that are there, are usually being called by their soul. There is some soulful attachment to the place, some deep work that needs to be done in that place. A*C*G might give you the big picture, but the relocation chart will give you the local picture. The global picture is Astro*Carto*Graphy, the local picture is the actual setting of the horoscope for the little village/town or major city where you want to live, say within a 600 mile proximity of the big line that has attracted you. You can use both. Because Astro*Carto*Graphy doesn't show you the houses, but the power energy, you will want to look at the houses.

For instance, if we are considering a choice of a couple of places because we love both, and a major A*C*G line runs midway between them, or is in the vicinity of both, then setting the relocation chart will fine-tune the places. Assuming that both are equally placed in our hearts as places to go, and the choice can be made rationally through mapping, then you will find using these methods helpful to you and your clients.

Subtle changes: same person, different perspective

Let's say you want to move to Sydney or Melbourne, Australia.
They are far enough apart that it would make a subtle difference in
your relocation chart. But initially, A*C*G might have drawn you to
that part of the world, and it would be better for you for various
reasons. Maybe a VE/DSC line crossing a MO/IC line is happening
just off the coastline, midway between the two very different cities.
The area is lovely to contemplate, but what are the details? If you
set a relocation chart for Sydney and then one for Melbourne or
Adelaide, you would find subtle differences between the way your
natal self, your "hardwired" self, resonates with the area, and how
the area receives your energy.

One of the cities you chose might dramatise the idea of a challenge
in career with the Sun in the 10th house, for example, whereas if you
shifted it further over to the west, so that the solar emphasis was
then placed in the 9th, it may well put you into a space of being
more open for learning and study – of being an enthusiastic student
rather than a driven, career-oriented person. The change can be quite
subtle. If I were considering relocating, I would consider the nature of
myself, my circumstances, the ethos of the place itself, and my
planets, and then try to find the best place for my planets' best
behaviour.

Where are the planets going to be much happier? Where are they
going to be more productive? Where would the individuation process
be better facilitated, especially if we are wanting to foster an
underdeveloped or shadowed side of ourselves? If we are thinking of
moving, then we would want to base it on aesthetic, practical, and
astrological pictures. For example, I think some planets are more
comfortable in quiet places, rather than angular. I would very
carefully consider locating to a place that has hard statements on
angles, unless you plan to exemplify that configuration in a socially
or politically useful way. By that I mean weighty, generational
configurations like a Saturn/Uranus conjunction, a Uranus/Pluto
conjunction, a Saturn/Pluto conjunction, a Saturn/Neptune
conjunction, or the T-cross that occurred with Jupiter, Uranus, and
Saturn that presented in the 1950's. These are important
configurations denoting a personal connection to a collective intent

or theme, and if they are too much for an individual to bear in an angular – conscious – fashion, then outstanding events will occur.

Choices: heaven on earth

Recall Christopher, in the previous seminar, with a Saturn/Uranus conjunction in his 10th house becoming angular in Africa.[3] Rather than being a voice of the collective, he became a victim of the external collective politics. Adventures of this level of intensity do not suit all of us.

When you are considering relocation, the best place to start is at home, thinking of your own self. How would you rather live out your celestial array? Where would you rather see the most challenging aspects enacted within the context of your life? Would you rather have them engaged in the 9th house, where it can become an argument with the gods or a philosophical pursuit, or would you rather have it enacted in your 5th house, where it might be interacting with your children or a lover, or taking speculative risks that could be very dangerous?

These are some of the most important considerations to keep in mind. There are individuals who have shifted a hard and ineradicable, inexorable natal aspect, from, say, the 4th house, where they are dwelling constantly on matters of the family and transforming the family and working all these aspects out in the microcosm of the family collective, yet could use them in ways which would transform society. One of my clients, who appears as a case in *Dynasty*, had ME, the immunodeficiency illness, for almost seven years. She was born with the Uranus/Pluto conjunction on the Ascendant, opposite Saturn on the Descendant and forming a T-cross to her Mars/Venus conjunction in Sagittarius in the 4th house. She was continuously processing her family dilemma through her psyche and her body,

---

[3]See Figures 8 and 8a on pp. 118 and 120-121 in the previous seminar on Astro*Carto*Graphy.

until finally it became somatic – she fell ill, and she has worked through all that.[4]

The good news is that at the end, as I was writing the story up for the book, I had to write a last minute add-in: she got married and has relocated to another part of the world, and she has really changed that drama into another, more enjoyable drama. She is now in a place where she has Uranus/Pluto at the MC, Saturn at the IC, and Mars/Venus on the Ascendant. It's a much more healthy challenge, living and working in an exciting place where she is offered diplomatic jobs and mediation work in the "war zone". She shifted her T-cross around to different angular prominence. You *can* shift the focus of yourself, by moving yourself. For Fiona, my client, the family dynamic still exists, her work still exists, and her T-cross is still there. But it is to a better cause, because she is using herself in another way.

I can see we are definitely going to use some of our work on A*C*G last week in this session. Hence the two projectors again – one for the natal chart and another for the A*C*G map or the relocated chart.

Spheres of influence: zodiac, ecliptic, equator

Audience: May I ask you a question? In the beginning you said relocation takes into account our houses, whereas Astro*Carto*Graphy doesn't. I wondered why? Why is it that relocation takes into account houses and not Astro*Carto*Graphy?

Erin: Good. Your question offers an opportunity to clarify something before we move into the more personal and experiential part of the work today. Horoscopy and A*C*G mapping are different systems, showing different views, depicting different astronomical pictures. A*C*G focuses only on angularity of planets, and accounts for both the latitude of the planets and their zodiacal

---

[4]*Dynasty: The Astrology of Family Dynamics*, Erin Sullivan, Arkana, CAS, London, 1997, p. 317.

longitude. Therefore, we have a more accurate visualisation of the planets in the sky, not just in the ecliptic.

The houses of the horoscope are based on an Earth view of the sky and the ecliptic (zodiac), whereas the angular lines of the A*C*G map are based on the sky's view – a planetary view – of the Earth. The houses are there, in the locations specific, but they are not the significance, the point, of the A*C*G map. Philosophically, it is based on power in angularity. In other words, if a planet is on an angle, it has more power than it does when it is in an intermediary house.

Audience: And so it does in relocation charts. I was born in London. I noticed that, although I have the SU/MC line almost on the dot of London on the map, I actually have the Sun about 2° into the 10th house natally. So it *looks* like SU/MC, but it isn't quite an exact conjunction. If I were to set a chart for, say, Dover, on the coast, would the exact Sun conjunct MC then show on the horoscope?

Erin: Yes, in fact, that is right – a perfect illustration. Your Sun is so close to the MC that the A*C*G line looks close to London, but to get the fine tuning down, you must find the place whereupon that line is precise. And it would be around Dover, a bit north of it, right on the tip of the peninsula. Perhaps you should put some energy into Dover and see what you can develop over there!

You see, the A*C*G gives a big picture, which we then can refine to houses and precise degrees on the angles by setting a relocation horoscope. But as you will see shortly, with Freud's examples, what you see in the horoscope with respect to angles is not always what you get in the more astronomically correct A*C*G map – especially with Venus, the Moon, and Pluto.

Audience: I have been looking at my map and my relocation and natal charts, and I see that, even though I have a wide opposition to Pluto from the Sun natally, there is actually a place on the earth where I have SU/ASC and PL/DSC crossing. It is in San Francisco. Now, does that mean that I have an opposition by paran? Are they are a "mundane opposition"?

Erin: Yes, sort of. Even though that isn't a real term – mundane opposition – that is precisely what is going on for you. Your wide opposition does not become a tight opposition – degrees don't change, but the view of them does.

Audience: Strange – I have the opposite situation in San Francisco! I have a pretty close conjunction of Sun and Pluto in Leo. They are only 2° apart. Pluto is right on the Descendant in San Francisco (PL/DSC), but the SU/DSC is apparently quite a bit south of the city, almost over Los Angeles.

Erin: Ah, again a good example. Your Astro*Carto*Graphy map shows the PL/DSC line running through San Francisco and your SU/DSC line running up south of it. This illustrates the "problem of latitude" I spoke of in the A*C*G seminar. Remember, this is particularly applicable to Pluto, especially in Leo, Virgo, and Libra.

Audience: Oh, I see. I have a virtually perpendicular VE/ASC/DSC line – and I have Venus at 8° Libra. But Mars is in Cancer, which is very curved along the ASC/DSC line.

Erin: Actually, that is a bit different – considerably different – because Venus is in the equinoctial sign of Libra, not because of its place on the ecliptic, as this situation with Pluto illustrates. Now, let's go back to your example of the close conjunction of Sun and Pluto, Susan. Yes, they are conjunct in zodiacal longitude, but when you see them on the A*C*G, map, you actually see the planets as they are according to their latitude as well.

Audience: And how does that work?

Pluto: what you see is not always what you get

Erin: Let me show you an example of Pluto's appearance on the Descendant of the natal chart, and its actual position in latitude. By example, I will use Sigmund Freud's natal horoscope (**Figure 3**). **Figure 3a** is his A*C*G map. **Figure 3b** is his chart relocated to London, where he spent the final years of his life.

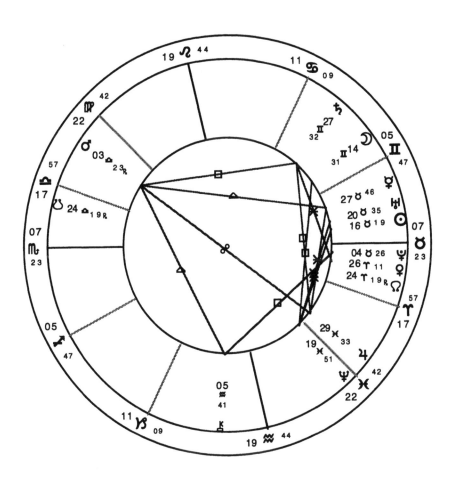

Figure 3: Sigmund Freud

6 May 1856, 6.30 pm LMT (17.17.00 GMT), Freiburg, Austria

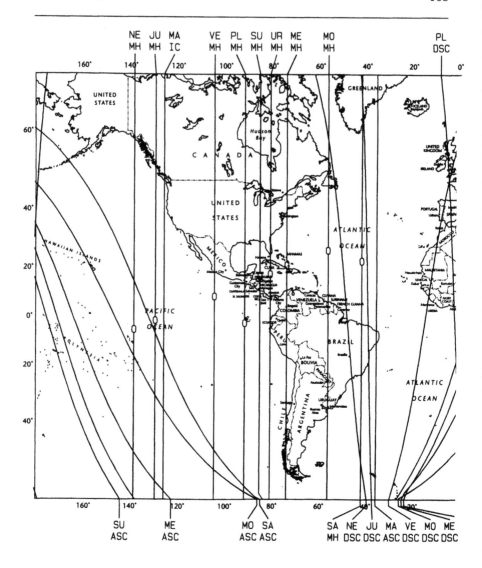

Figure 3a: Sigmund Freud

Astro*Carto*Graphy Map reprinted with permission of Astro Numeric Service

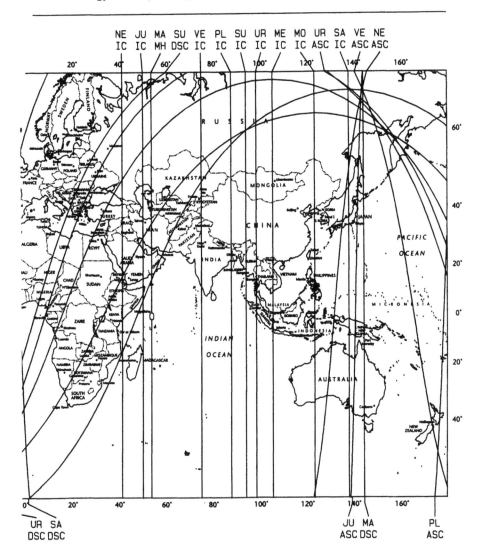

*The PL/DSC line discussed in the following pages may be seen running almost vertically from the top left-hand corner of the map on this page (also duplicated on the map on the facing page at the top right-hand corner), down through Great Britain, central Spain, and western Africa.

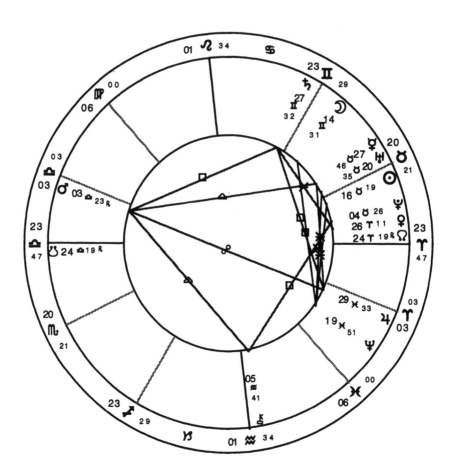

Figure 3b: Sigmund Freud in London

Freud has Pluto at 4° 26' Taurus, conjunct the Descendant, which is 7° 23' Taurus. When we look at his A*C*G map, we see that he does not have the PL/DSC line running through his birthplace at Freiburg, Austria. His PL/DSC line is running right through London, England. How can that be, you ask? Because although Pluto *appears* to be setting in the natal horoscope, which is according to the ecliptic (zodiac), it *actually* won't be setting for a couple of hours. Pluto's latitude is about 15°N, thus, a couple hours from actually setting. It is setting in London when he was born (west of the birthplace), but won't be setting in Freiburg for a couple of hours after birth.

Now, this is where the interpretation of this astronomical phenomenon becomes interesting. Freud had natal Pluto close to the Descendent in his horoscope, and he lived it out within himself and in his work. And certainly we know enough of his life and work to see what that meant – his depth of vision, his founding of psychoanalysis, his dedication to the "other" in himself and his patients, his pioneer work on the psyche.

Also, he was obsessive, observant, relentless, and a man of great power and influence over others. Though he lived in and loved Vienna, he was forced into exile in London (Pluto) during World War II, where he finished his life; most of his family were annihilated in Auschwitz, and his London home and office is now a museum to his family, life, and work. It is in Maresfield Gardens, and a must to experience.

To go to your PL/DSC line to finish your life seems appropriate. His cocaine addiction became profound in London. Eventually he died, after eighteen operations to his nasal passages, septum, jaw, and face.[5] And his daughter, Anna, founded the Anna Freud Institute in London, training psychoanalysts in the Freudian manner. He became immortal on his Pluto line. Pluto setting in London, though natally on his Descendant, says that he would be able to continue his Plutonian existence and work in London, whereas he would have died remaining in Austria. He was racked with guilt over this, and always

---

[5]*Cocaine Papers: Sigmund Freud*, ed. Robert Byck, M.D., with notes on the Freud Papers by Anna Freud. A Meridian Book, New American Library, New York/Scarborough, Ontario, 1975.

felt he had abandoned his home and family. But his legacy in London remains, and his contribution to the origins of psychoanalysis is vast.

Aspects recreated

We are talking about angles, and as we saw in all of the A*C*G examples last week, it is possible to have two planets in your natal horoscope which are completely without any kind of Ptolemaic or minor aspect. In other words, you don't have Venus trine or sextile Mars. But, due to what we looked at last time on the Astro*Carto*Graphy map, you could move to a place where those two planets will cross, forming a paran. There will be a place where the VE/MC line and the MA/ASC line will cross. Granted, it may be in the place where "astrology works differently". At that very place you would have Venus at the MC and Mars on the Ascendant, were you to set a chart for that location. [6]

Audience: Would it be all around the world at the same latitude?

Erin: The crossings' influence would be effective, but secondary to the actual paran location. The crossing itself, the paran between two planets, is found in four places – in all four crossing places. There is an MC/ASC, IC/DSC, MC/DSC, and IC/ASC for each planet, and if you pinpoint them on your map you will see that they are in precisely opposite points on the globe (map). The JU/IC will cross PL/ASC in a diametrically opposite place on the globe as the JU/MC will cross the PL/DSC. The theoretical example that I am using for you to grasp this is someone who has Venus at 10° Gemini and Mars at 29° Virgo. Now, in a natal chart, that doesn't have any particular aspect. However, if this person who has Venus at 10° Gemini and Mars at 29° Virgo moved to a place where Mars is rising and Venus is culminating, that would mean that, on that A*C*G map, they cross and would therefore form what is called a mundane square – a very powerful place, indeed.

---

[6]Refer back to Part One of this book, "Crossings", p. 39.

Moving house: relocation

Taking up more interpretive material, I want to emphasise that the houses are very important in relocation. We have very good class examples of moving ourselves around the world to incorporate more of our whole self in life. When you move house, literally you move astrological houses. I would say that with relocation, shifting your houses is probably the first, most important consideration.

Solar return relocation charts

Another consideration with relocation is solar returns. A solar return is a horoscope set for the exact return of the Sun's degree, minute and second as it was when you were born. And solar returns are another story which have their own interesting cycle. If you set consecutive solar returns for the place of birth for, say, twelve years, you will notice that the position of the Sun moves about three houses back each year, thus in the same place in each quadrant as it was natally. By that I mean, if you were born with the Sun in the 2nd house, the Sun will be found either in or very close to succeedent houses in every solar return. It is a pattern. Again, the more squared the Ascendant and MC are in the natal chart, the more regular is this pattern.

The day we are born, we are zero age. Then, on our first birthday we are one, and so on. For instance if you were born at zero age with the Sun at the MC, your first solar return will present the Sun at the Ascendant or in that area. Your second solar return will present the Sun in the area of the IC, and your third Solar return will present the Sun somewhere in the area of the Descendant. Your fourth solar return will bring it back up to the approximate place it was when you were born.

There is an annual rhythm. It has to do with the passage of three signs over the MC in the course of a solar year, and that is part of the solar return phenomenon Because of this astrological event I always set the solar return for my natal place – "Thou shalt be judged in the land of thy nativity." But I also set a solar return for my relocated place – but only if I live there and have a real life there. I look at my natal birthplace solar return as "the way it is", and my relocated Solar return as "the way it is here". The aspects between the planets are not different, but the view of the world they occupy is. And both work. However, I would recommend doing this only if you actually live in another place than your land of nativity.

The solar return is a renegotiation of the solar contract you have at birth. You have the same soul purpose in life, but a different way of executing it each year because the angles and the relationship between the planets will always change. Your purpose in life is unchanging – the Sun is the body that is brought to precise return – but all the other planets generally are in different locations by sign and house. Also, the dharmic path – the angles – will present a new focus every three solar returns, and on the fourth, the Sun is very close to where it was at birth, so there is a four-year cycle of return to solar position. This rhythm is worth paying attention to, and you won't get it in the relocated return, unless you live there for at least five years.

A friend of mine always goes away for his solar return. He likes to have his solar return in a location where Sun will be in a place that he likes – a way of moving himself to the environment that he wants to imprint for the rest of the year. If it were possible, I would imagine people doing this a lot. However, if you were to go for a week only, and then think that your whole year is going to be different because of this, then I think you will be mistaken. However, if you live in a city other than your birth place, then you are indeed advised to experiment and set solar returns for birthplace and relocated place. For instance, even though I lived fully in London for eight years, I still set my solar return for Vancouver, but because I lived here in London, and for eight years had a fully engaged life, I set my solar return for London as well, and I watched them both.

I watched what happened, and saw the feelings and the moods. They were interesting because they both worked. Now I have begun setting them for Tucson, Arizona, because I live there now, have bought a house, and am investing life into the area. But because I am still attached in London and life goes on here for me, I still set solar

returns for London because it is still a very influential place for me –
and I watch it for the connected events. Still, natal is the strongest
interior chart to use.

I had a rare experience where my solar return occurred in an
aeroplane above North Africa. I was flying back from Johannesburg
to London and my solar return actually occurred about an hour and a
half from Heathrow – while we were flying over North Africa. I
thought to myself, "This is getting really weird. This is really out of
it, because not only do I have no earth in my chart, I don't even
have a solar return place. I just ceased to exist on some important
level." I set the solar return for London and I set it for Vancouver, as
usual, and I just thought about it and wondered what it meant, because
I wasn't sure of the coordinates above North Africa. But anyway,
that happens.

At around twenty-seven to twenty-nine years of age, you will get the
Sun and the Moon in their birth signs in your solar return – a repeat
of your birth lunation. Periodically you will get Venus in the same
degree, and Mercury, and sometimes both. Every two years you will
get Mars in the same place. This isn't as predictable as I am making
it sound, because Mars returns every two years and two months. If
you have Mars in an early degree of the sign, then for several two-
year cycles you will have Mars returns in your solar returns every
two years. It will stretch out after several returns. And in the time-
period of your Saturn return, age twenty-eight to twenty-nine, you
will have the re-statement of your Sun/Saturn relationship. You could
even have two consecutive solar returns with a Saturn return in
them! Then, every twelve years you will have Jupiter in the same
place as when you were born. There are some years that are more
loaded with restatement of natal place. This is just within the
planetary arrangement, and some solar returns will be very similar to
the natal chart, depending on the number of returns.

I always relocate my solar return to where I am living, and
sometimes think, "Gad, if I were at my birthplace, this or that would
be going on there, and aren't I lucky that I am living here!" Or *vice
versa*. That's just another thing to explore with relocation. I do
know that relocated solar returns are expressive in that way. In the
deepest essence of relocation, I am subjectively experiencing my

own inner life, my planets in signs, in aspect, but my outer world can be dramatised or externalised in another way by shifting myself. The primary consideration in relocation is to keep your natal chart in your mind as the inexorable, absolute conditions of the incarnate self and its view of the world. Your arrival, your reception, your psychology, your family of origin – all of the absolutes that exist in your life are your natal chart. Then move it around to see how you experience the world according to different horizons, meridians, and house emphases.

Planets in the relocated chart

Planets, being agencies of the self and the ego, work to unfold the nature of your being, whether it is your Mars – your self-assertiveness and your ability to cut through life and to individuate – or your Venus – your inherent values, the way you perceive the world as a relative experience. These things don't change. This is who you are. They are the aspects of your self-organisation and the challenges which have been placed before you and within you to fulfil a life. The sign the planet is in is the way you cloak the archetype of the planet. You will "wear" the same Mars wherever you go. However, by relocating it to another house, you put it in another arena for it to explore another dimension of itself. Rather, you then explore another dimension of yourself.

The voice of an angle

The other factor of great importance in relocation is the angles. Naturally, the angles set the pattern for the rest of the houses. Your natal angles represent the expression of challenges that are based on your origins, your genetic code and family-originated destiny. If you move and your angles change, then it doesn't change your DNA structure and your family and your origins. But it will give a new advantage, a new way of looking at your horizon, a new way of achieving your MC, and a new way of nesting, rooting, "creating" a new IC.

Moving and changing your angles will not change your natal self, but how you organise your capacity to exercise options will have a distinctly different angle. From the earliest days of your astrology study, you all know that the houses are realms of individual experience, which was Dane Rudhyar's way of putting it.[7] Houses are the areas of life wherein our planets' presence activates more attention and requires more consideration than houses that don't have planets. By relocating you will place your same old planets in new areas of challenge, in new venues, and sometimes in places where they are more suited – say, where they are much less deeply enmeshed in mysterious origins and process.

Planets moving house

For instance, somebody with a couple of planets that remain troublesome and haunting in the 8th house, may, by relocating, put that set of planets or planet from the 8th house into the 7th house, where he or she might find that the complex that lies in the 8th house is more easily addressed. One might find that one might be able work with that troublesome 8th house mystery better in the 7th house, having it in enacted through relationships, demonstrating it in a way which is more open or externalised, because it is an air house rather than the watery realms of the 8th. Shifting a planet from the 8th to the 7th just might bring you to a mirror. You are going to meet the issues face to face, often in another person or in the public in some way. It is not then just some inner pool of process, but it is more externalised in a relationship house.

Audience: I have seen that very thing.

Erin: Oh, have you done that – moved to find a planet translate from the 8th to the 7th house? What aspects do you have?

---

[7] *The Houses: The Spectrum of Individual Experience*, Dane Rudhyar, Doubleday and Company, 1972. Also see *The Twelve Houses*, Howard Sasportas, Aquarian Press, 1988.

Audience: No, but a client of mine has. Natally she has a Saturn/Venus conjunction in the 8th house, and one of the key words for Saturn is lessons. In the 8th it is a very lonely place for her, a lonely way to approach life emotionally. I thought that in the 7th it would be more about relationship – it is an airy house – so she might have a greater understanding of herself and her isolation after moving here to London.

Erin: Yes, ideally, that is so. One would meet it more directly, if only by projection. It would be less of an internal process, less of a theory, less of a possible mystery and round-and-round-you-go complex. It would be thrown out into the 7th house, where she would be likely to meet it face to face. The combinations of Saturn and Venus together speak of a sense of impoverishment when it comes to love, beauty, and aesthetics.

But if it is in the 8th house natally, it means she would be more inclined to be caught up internally about it. This is a thing she will always process, a symbolic state rather than an active, externalised state. Her theories about relationships, about the value of them, about her own worth, her own investment into relationship with others, could just remain theoretical, or even blocked. One might be less inclined to throw one's lot in with others than if the conjunction were in the 7th. Then again, it could become very difficult to sustain an intimate relationship with Saturn/Venus in the 7th, if she projected her needs for love entirely onto one person. If she moved it into the 7th house, then she would have to come face to face with, "Why do I have this feeling? Why am I existentially isolated? Why do I feel impoverished?" Her relationships then would become much more dynamic, and she would likely meet people who make her aware, or find herself becoming more conscious, of why she has feelings of abuse, lack of love, and intimacy.

Audience: Her first experiences in relating here were pretty horrible – she really had a hard time. But now, it seems, she is very happy on her own, and has begun a new business.

Erin: Good. Do you think some of her lessons – as you said, her work – are not so much about intimate love-affairs, but about her relations with her own value and her work in the public? Finding her own authenticity and authority?

Audience: Yes. Theoretically, I think it might also be work involving relationships. It could be a lot of things, couldn't it? It could manifest in problems in relationship, or with a co-worker. It seems to me that in the 8th house one prefers talking about the structures of relationship, theorising rather than acting them out.

Erin: There is a lot of theory in astrology. It all depends, doesn't it? We talked earlier about Astro*Carto*Graphy and the idea of a self-realised planet. You could have a comfortable relationship with two planets which are challenging, like a Uranus/Pluto conjunction or a Saturn/Neptune conjunction or a Saturn/Uranus square, all of which create dynamics centring around rebellion against authority. If external figures always seem to impose their sense of order on your own unique individual needs, then that can be a cause for anxiety or, conversely, it might be a path of individuation. It may be what you were born to do. Not everybody who has a Saturn/Uranus square is miserable because they always have to fight authority in order to become themselves.

Some people do that kind of thing for a living, or as volunteer work – law, medicine, mediation work, prison work, hospitals, criminal justice, international politics. Now, with the world undergoing such profound change, we need those people with the hard social aspects to get to work on a new order of global equilibrium. If everything we do is related to a negative complex, then we aren't fulfilling a larger destiny. Ideally, relocating should have to do with fulfilling a larger destiny, and by the by, creating a more self-realised existence.

Audience: Yes, it is said that we have to walk toward our fears, challenges and anxieties, to face them and meet them and befriend them – then they become our allies.

Erin: Absolutely. Some people do. The degree to which a relocation is going to alter it at all would really depend on one's comfort with one's own self. Some houses are much less personal and emotional when you have difficult collective aspects like Uranus/Pluto opposite Saturn, or Saturn/Uranus square the Sun.

A Uranus/Pluto conjunction in the 12th house would probably be harder to reach consciously than if it were in the 1st house. I might rather have it in the 1st house because at least it is in the open, and isn't lurking in the shadowy realm of the unconscious, waiting to be born. It would not be jumping out at me from corners when I least expected it.

All of those big configurations I would rather have in the 9th, to tell you the truth, because then the war is on a bigger level. In that case, the fight is with the gods, with the divine. It is not always with your lover or your daughter, or something like that. If we could all move to where our most awful unrealised self was relocated into the 9th house, then we could at least turn it into philosophy or write a book, or become a tyrant or dictator in another country. If anybody has any of those secret aspirations, by the way, we could find a place for you to rule!

Audience: If you notice, people who don't physically move to a place still seem to be attracted to certain parts of the world, reading books from there, constantly meeting people from there. In that case I would also draw a chart for the place.

Erin: Yes, you could. That's where Astro*Carto*Graphy plays a role – it is the global picture. It shows you, within a six hundred mile radius on either side of the line, a place which is attractive to you, and why. But if you want to get to a specific place – let's say you are attracted to India – you might want to set a chart for Bombay or Madras or Pondicherry to get specific. Then you would be able to see more detail. Astro*Carto*Graphy gives you angles, and relocation gives you a specific locus and view of the planets.

I was brought up in the colonial-ish atmosphere of a British grandmother who, though she loved her life in Canada, longed to return. But she was never was able to come back to London. All my early reading, by both availability and attraction, was centred round Trollope, Dickens, and the Brontës. I was brought up on English literature and I loved it, and the attraction has always been very powerful. London is my MO/NE/DSC line. You can see that certain houses are more personal and others less so, and if there are areas of your life that you find more difficult, you need to know more about yourself. Relocation alone won't do it for you.

Relocating an event: the "long-distance phone call" charts

Another thing I want to mention for relocation is really interesting. You can extrapolate this idea into several concepts. The main idea is this: *An event is happening objectively, but is being experienced subjectively in a different way by individuals in different places. The time is the same, but the place is different, and the relationship between the two is unique.*

Let's say something of great importance has occurred, and you receive an urgent phone call from abroad. Perhaps your grandmother has died, or a new baby is born to your sister, or a friend's house has burnt to the ground. Set a chart for the time you received the call at your home, and also a chart for the location that the call was initiated from. You end up with two horoscopes – the same planets in the same signs to the degree, minute and second – so the objective event is the same. But the subjective experience of the time is very different. The caller is calling for their reason and you are receiving the call for yours. The caller knows the event, but you don't – or *vice versa,* if you have to make an important call from London to Hong Kong, to see what is going on there about a volatile business venture. The instigation for the call is the time, and you set charts for that time in both places.

Regarding remote events, let's say, for example, you own a house in Los Angeles. You are in New York and there is an earthquake in Los Angeles, and the house collapses. You set the chart for the time of the earthquake, both for New York, because that's when it affected you subjectively, and for Los Angeles ,because that is where the objective event occurred. You then have the event and your experience of it.

I am thinking of a phone call that I received at 1.30 am, from San Francisco to my house in Oxford. It was from a friend, about a mutual friend of ours who had died two hours earlier. I had been expecting this call for over a day or so, so I set a chart for my receiving the call and for my friend initiating the call. The charts spoke to me about what was happening for him as he was telling me, and my experience as I was hearing it. When I received the call in Oxford, the Sun was in the 3rd house for me, and when he was making the call the Sun was in the 8th house for him. He was calling me about my friend's death, and I was getting the news through the 3rd house – he was like a brother to me. There was a lot to those charts.

That's definitely a form of relocation astrology. It affects you, it's your life, and it will describe the conditions of the person who is sending the call, or the event and its deeper meaning. Let's say you are the recipient. You get a call saying you are accepted into a university or are receiving a new opportunity. You are going to have something on an angle, or an aspect that really points out the information. The other person will also have something remarkable in their chart that will say, "This is why I am calling you." If a friend called up saying, "The baby was born at such and such a time," I would definitely set charts for that moment in both places. It's not all doom and gloom. But if you ever get a shocking phone call or a revelatory phone call, make a note of the time and set the chart. You increase your understanding that the content is the same – that is, planets don't change, the information is identical – but the purpose, the intent, and the impact are different.

Audience: It becomes a bit like horary doesn't it?

Erin: Indeed, it is a form of horary. The quality of time is different in all parts of the world, but the quantitative aspect of time is the same from a global viewpoint. Are there comments or questions at this stage?

Global sympathy: feeling the world inside

Audience: It's a bit general, but what if one has strong reactions to news from a foreign country?

Erin: What do you mean? World news?

Audience: Yes. I'm quite interested in the fact that Chicago and Indonesia and Singapore are each covered by fog right now, and I've been to those places and can feel it, literally. I am getting the news here, and I am actually affected by this personally.

Erin: That makes sense to me. Some people are highly susceptible to *Weltschmertz* or "world pain". If there is an event of great significance, like the mid-1980's oil spill off Anchorage, Alaska, or the Chernobyl nuclear accident, and your heart is thudding and you are deeply affected at the thought of it, you are in tune with the global mind, the global body. This is where Astro*Carto*Graphy proves that we exist in all places at the same time.

Now, this isn't far off quantum theory, where energy and mass are one. It has recently been discovered that photons of light, hundreds of miles apart, respond to the same stimulus as if they were twins, and will come to the same conclusion or terminus or end result without any previous information. They do exist in all places at all times. Why astrology works is not about planets, signs, and houses. It is about something much deeper. Fractal maths and chaos theory are the closest explanations for how or why astrology works in myriad ways.

Other places, other lifetimes

Audience: I was always attracted by Greece, from a very early age, and I studied ancient philosophy at university. I was very much involved with Greece and Greek thought. When I began with astrology, I discovered that Jupiter, which I have in the 10th house, was exactly on my MC in Greece. And I have never been there – not yet. I don't remember which part of Greece the JU/MC line passes through.

Erin: How interesting! Jupiter/Zeus is the god of the ancient Greeks who was paramount in the origin of western religion and western philosophy. Zeus is the greatest dogmatist in the entire pantheon.[8] That you have a JU/MC line through Greece should suggest that, whether you ever went there or not, the origins of western civilisation, western thought, as seeded in 5th century Athens, are going to be very important in your own world-view. Your myths,

---

[8] *Venus and Jupiter: Bridging the Ideal and the Real*, Erin Sullivan, CPA Press, London, 1997.

beliefs, philosophy, and education are tied in with that era, and include pre-Socratic philosophy. That's a Jupiter experience, yes?

Jim Lewis himself was very practical. But at the same time, we once had a conversation about Astro*Carto*Graphy being used as a reincarnation tool to invoke places where we have resided in previous soul experiences. You are perfectly at liberty to play with this stuff. It's not sacrosanct. It could be that reincarnation plays a role in the attraction to location, and A*C*G could be the demonstration of that.

Audience: I've been attracted to places that I associate with my Mars/Saturn conjunction. It is just off my IC natally. I am now thinking of moving. It is one of the things that attracted me to New Orleans. It is right on that Mars/Saturn line. It scares me, but still...

Erin: Actually, no, because New Orleans is a Pluto/Saturn/Mars type of place. You realise that it is seven feet below the water table and that the Mississippi river has got a bank holding it up. As you walk through the streets of New Orleans, especially the French Quarter, the old part, the underground is steaming up through manholes. It is unbelievably, fabulously Plutonian and Saturnian, full of voodoo and obeah. It's a very, very interesting place, rich with amazing history, especially the Black and Cajun lifestyle. The free blacks and the aristocracy that originates from there are terribly romantic.

It is an amazing city. If you have got MA/SA/IC running through there, it strikes me that you might be able to form something quite solid as far as work, ambition, or life direction go. It sounds quite stable, but you would be very, very in touch with that aspect of it – with the fact that it was a steamy, underground, very Plutonian place. Do you know New Orleans at all?

Audience: I know what you are talking about.

Erin: It is an amazing place.

Audience: With seedy joints and dirty music.

Erin: There are a lot of exquisite accommodations in the French quarter, converted into guest houses and suites that used to be slave quarters. What we are looking at here is a place that was probably once the most liberated place in America for the socially prominent blacks. It was a very complex hierarchy, though, that seized up and became oppressive again. Only through law, which is not a very stable force, has it become integrated again. I wouldn't necessarily be afraid of going there because of your Mars/Saturn – it depends on Mars and Saturn in your natal chart. Where do you have the conjunction?

Audience: In my 3rd house.

Erin: Has it got aspects to other planets?

Audience: It is almost unaspected.

Moving with intent

Erin: I would go to a place with intent, and if the planets describe the intent and you work hard at it, then it will work. If you do go, then realise that MA/SA/IC is not a place where you go to lay around and have a good time. You go with a purpose (Mars) and with a structure (Saturn), and the potential for establishing something really hard and rock-solid is there. If you went there saying, "Well, I really like the weather and it's really pretty, all that lovely New Orleans-style architecture and baroque housing and French Quarter area," you would probably be in for a shock. I think it would be really hard. But if you were going to establish a business, or you were going to create a real structure where your ambitions were about the area itself, then it would work. You need intent, a purpose, if you go to a place with planets on angles.

Audience: Would you use the waxing and waning Moon when you make a decision like that – for instance, going on the waxing Moon?

Erin: Well, decisions to relocate are not usually made that abruptly. This kind of thing is usually an evolutionary thing, arising slowly and being evaluated over time. I don't think the waxing of the Moon would have much effect.

Audience: Would you work at all with lunation?

Erin: Yes, if you are dealing with the question as a horary query. To really apply astrology, you would want to take the lunation cycles into account – the new Moon as the meaning for the instigation of an idea, the seed, and the full Moon for decision making, or the outcome.

Audience: I have an example. I have been very involved with Far Eastern culture, and with Japan in particular. I've been studying Japanese. My Sun is on the IC in Japan. It is also interesting because my ex-husband is a psychologist, and it is through him that I became aware of this aspect of myself. He is an expert on China. In his birthchart he has a very close Sun/Mercury/Uranus conjunction. He is Canadian by birth, and this conjunction is in the 4th house at birth, but he moved to London, where that Sun/Mercury/Uranus is on the Ascendant. But if you relocate his chart to Beijing, it is at the MC exactly.

Erin: Wonderful. See how we are called to these things. That's a really excellent example.

Audience: But if you relocate my chart to Beijing, Pluto is on the MC and Jupiter is in the 7th. I was more interested in Japan, where my Sun is on the IC.

Erin: That's exactly the kind of thing that demonstrates most actively how the astrological principles of the planets work. Your Sun on the IC in Japan instinctively attracted you to that culture, and then you pick a partner who is born with his Sun at the IC, but who then relocated to London where the Sun is at the Ascendant. Your Jupiter falls into the 7th in your relocation in Beijing, where he is an expert – and you have Pluto on your MC in Beijing. You can learn so much astrology through exploring these things than you can from reading books. Learning in this way is the way of the soul and the way of the psyche, and the way of the relationship that we have with the world. It reveals so much.

Audience: Just how precise can you be in a large metropolitan area? Can you fine-tune the location?

Erin: Your question is about being finite. Finding location within a large metropolitan area, or within a 30-mile radius, is quite acceptable. But I am not sure about the degree to which it is going to make a difference. In Canada we have telephone poles of wood, and on each telephone pole is a little brass label upon which are the exact coordinates, so you can step outside your house and see exactly what the coordinates for your house are. I could set my horary fixed coordinates in my computer for right outside my house – degree, minute and second. You can find that on local ordinance maps, or by checking.

Progressions and transits to relocated charts

Audience: Do you use progressions and transits to the relocated chart?

Erin: Yes, and they work, especially to the new relocated angles. If you are working with a relocation chart, your secondary progressions will be identical to your natal progressions. You would then see, for instance, where your progressed Moon is progressing over the MC in your relocated place but is progressing through the 8th house in your natal horoscope. I should think it does make a difference. We could look at Tina's chart now, because it is a good time to talk about transits to the relocated place. So let's look at a relocated example.

Nita: Saturn on the move

Here are Nita's natal chart (**Figure 4**) and her relocated chart in Tenerife (**Figure 4a**). This chart example illustrates the progression question rather nicely. Nita moved from London to Tenerife, which is south and a little bit to the west. In her natal chart she has Gemini rising, and by moving further south and west, we end up with Taurus rising.

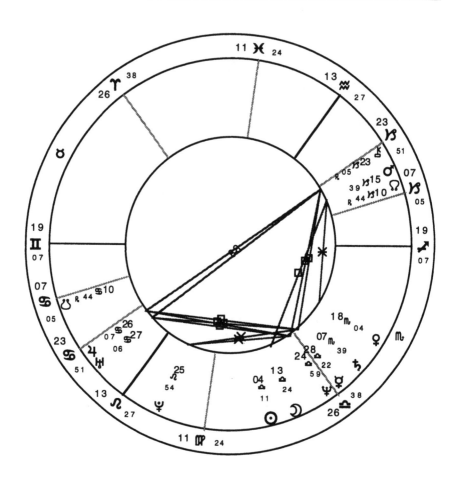

Figure 4: Nita

(Data withheld for reasons of confidentiality)

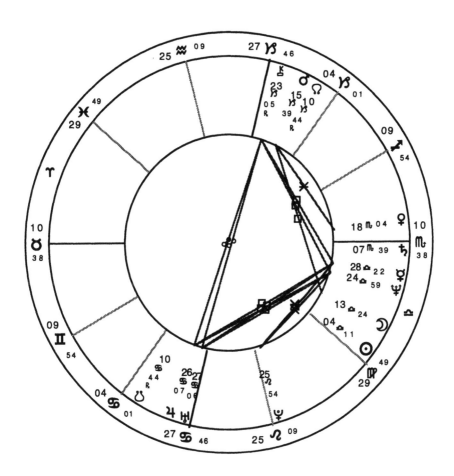

Figure 4a: Nita in Tenerife

Nita: Actually, my progressed Moon is now at 10° Taurus. That's right on my relocated Ascendant, and I am having strong feelings about going back there.

Erin: The natal chart has a fairly insignificant Saturn. It is sitting there in the 6th house, not doing a whole lot.

Audience: It is not aspected, except by a quintile to Pluto.

Erin: It is a virtually unaspected Saturn. By moving to Tenerife, it changes the MC from 13° Aquarius to 27° Capricorn. It changes the Ascendant from 19° Gemini to 11° Taurus. The relocation places Saturn at the Descendant, and the Jupiter/Uranus conjunction at the IC. Now, Jupiter and Saturn do make an extremely wide square, not one that people would normally consider an exact aspect, but they are pretty much angular on this relocated chart. So you have Jupiter/Uranus/IC on the relocated chart and Saturn at the Descendant, which means that it is likely that in your A*C*G map, Tenerife is close to the crossing of a JU/UR/IC line and a SA/DSC line. Right?

Nita: Yes.

Erin: This is a powerful place for you, filled with complex urges which say a lot about an exciting domestic life and a root connection to the land and the people. But it brings a note of seriousness and possible difficulty in personal relationships. Now, tell us what happened.

Nita: I went there for a holiday.

Erin: Where and when?

Nita: I went to Tenerife for a holiday in February 1982, and fell in love with the island. I decided I was going to live there. I came home, put my house on the market, sold it, and went. I moved there on 16 November 1982. I had two suitcases, my son, my husband, and a push-bike.

Erin: At least you got to take your husband, your son, and your push-bike.

Nita: Well, he wasn't my husband at the time, but he became my husband later. We came back to England the following winter, and I got married on the day of the Jupiter/Uranus conjunction on 18 February 1983, in London.

Erin: How interesting.

Nita: My marriage went one full Jupiter/Uranus cycle and finished earlier this year.

Erin: Fourteen years – I wonder if this has something to do with your longing to return, and the progressed Moon at the Tenerife Ascendant.

Nita: Yes.

Erin: I see. IC. Or I don't see, as the case may be.

Nita: I was escaping my roots. It was freedom from my very oppressive family in England.

Pluto in transition

Erin: Well, you do have natal Pluto in the 4th house, and it is just barely on the cusp of the 5th in your Tenerife chart. Excuse me for interrupting, but this is what I mean by shifting something in a move. You didn't escape your family, you escaped the interior *process* which you undergo. Pluto in the 4th house means that as long as you stay wherever Pluto is in your 4th house, the process of the family returns and returns, cyclically. But by shifting it so that Jupiter and Uranus are on the IC, your process of family becomes different. It is more about individuating out of the family, and finding a philosophy about the family. Pluto hovers, always requiring a deep, psychological process. Now, as I said, it is a hair into the 5th according to the relocation chart with Placidus houses, and so we will assume that it has moved out of the 4th, because of your experience. You see, you didn't escape the family as such, but your process of the family became different by relocating.

Nita: I put a lot of miles between them and me.

Erin: Yes, now you can keep that aspect of yourself, even though you have come back to the natal Pluto in the 4th.

Nita: Yes I have.

Erin: It is possible to change by going to another place, because you can develop new habits. Your habitual reactions to your process can change. What was once Pluto – gripping, fated, addicted to the family mystery of, "Why am I like this and what is going on? And I have to carry it!" – has now shifted to something with a little more freedom, even though you are still involved to some degree on a deep psychological and DNA level. In fact you may have worked out a family complex by going away and living in a zone where the main focus around family dynamics is Jupiter/Uranus/IC. You are now looking at it with a clearer, more concise perspective, initiating radical change, individuating out of the family mystery or secret – making a new family. Cancer is on the IC.

Nita: I came back a different person from the one who went there.

Erin: So you moved back here eight years later. That is a Venus cycle, by the way. Why?

Nita: I got thyrotoxicosis when Jupiter was going over the relocation Descendant and opposing Saturn, which natally is in the 6th. My thyroid blew up like a balloon in my throat, and I could have died from it.

The manifesation of illness

Erin: Taurus rules the thyroid and neck area, and there it is on the relocated Ascendant. What are the symptoms?

Nita: It is an overactive thyroid. I gave out too much thyroid hormone, and it speeds your metabolism up.

Erin: Interesting. And with Saturn on the relocation Descendant in Scorpio, which is the polarity to Taurus (throat)...

Nita: It went undiagnosed for a year in Tenerife. When I came back to England over the Christmas holiday and decided to see a doctor here, she instantly knew what was wrong. She could see it. I had a tennis ball in my throat and I hadn't even noticed it growing myself. I came back here and had radiotherapy in Westminster Hospital, and it seemed like a good time to buy a property here. I was wrong, but it seemed like it.

Erin: In your natal chart Venus is in Scorpio in the 6th house. Scorpio is the polarity to Taurus. Venus is the ruler of Taurus on the Ascendant in Tenerife, and rules Libra on your 6th house cusp in London. Venus has to do with thyroid, hormone, and glandular secretions. By relocating to a place where Venus becomes powerful in that it rules the Ascendant in Taurus and it is found in Scorpio in the 7th house, with Saturn descending, you get the manifestation of what is inherent in the natal potential.

Your Neptune moves from the 5th to the 6th house in Tenerife – it is very difficult to get proper diagnosis or a clear understanding of body issues with Neptune in the 6th. Oftentimes the illness is misdiagnosed, untreated, or simply an evasive symptom.

Also, with Venus in Scorpio, I would see the thyroid problem as a reflexive disorder which I suspect had to do with deep creative frustration and some marital problems. There is a correlation between the throat and the genitals in both development and in our reactions to things. It manifested in the Taurus rising place. You then came back to the place in which Venus is in the 6th house to be cured, to be healed.

I don't believe in the now stereotyped, blatant concept of cause and effect. I think the emotional side – relationship problems, sexual frustration and a weakness in your relationship – was confluent or synchronous with, but not necessarily causing, the physical problem. The whole thing is really about relationship, even though obviously thyroid problems are something that may run in the family – Pluto in the 4th. You are probably safe to go back and not re-experience the same thing, but we now come to the possibility that you may want to return.

Nita: I went there in 1982 and came back in 1990.

Erin: So your marriage broke down since the return.

Nita: This year.

Erin: And now you are going to go to Tenerife to check it out?

Nita: In a fortnight. I have been back there, but I haven't been back for a couple of years now. And with Jupiter/Uranus on the IC, I worked for an estate agent and for a property developer while I was over there. I made thousands of pounds. I was their top sales person.

Audience: Uranus and Jupiter – luck and fortune, literally.

Nita: I never even worked it out. Somebody asked me once what I was earning and I sat down and got the commissions book out and ended up with about £62,000 per year. I came back to England and carried on spending money as if I was still earning it at the rate of £1,000 or £2,000 a week. Here Jupiter-Uranus is sitting on the cusp of the 2nd and 3rd, and I was spending money like I was earning it over there, but not earning it here. Within a couple of years in England I was in pretty deep financial trouble. Back to Pluto in the 4th house.

Erin: That Jupiter/Uranus conjunction is square Mercury/Neptune. And that is another manifestation of the 4th house – property and homes, real estate and development, are a much more objective reading of a 4th house condition.

Nita: And Mercury is my chart ruler as a Gemini Ascendant, conjunct Neptune. I really fell into the illusion of a bottomless resource.

Erin: In your natal chart Mercury is in a weakened place, one that is hard to realise because of its house. It is in strong aspect, mind you, but it is not a very strong house placement. Mercury and Neptune flank the 6th house cusp. It doesn't seem very dynamic or alive. Do you see what I mean? I am getting a feeling – I'm not telling you a rule, but I get a feeling – that the natal chart is not activating the hard angle between Jupiter/Uranus and Mercury/Neptune in the same way that you demonstrated in Tenerife. Natally you have Mercury/Neptune in the 6th house of work and job, square Jupiter/Uranus on the cusp of the 3rd. In Tenerife Jupiter/Uranus is at the IC. It seems so obvious as to be embarrassing – but the fantasy of houses, property, and land is real there.

Work and play

There are two more significant house shifts by relocation. The first one is from the 5th house in the natal chart, into the 6th house. Natally, in London, you have Mercury, Saturn, and Venus in the 6th house. Well, Mercury is so cusp-y, one wonders. Technically, it is also in the 5th house, leaving just Saturn and Venus in the 6th. But in Tenerife, you have the Moon, Neptune, Mercury, and Saturn in the 6th house, while Venus has moved into the 7th house. Only the Sun remains in the 5th house in the Tenerife chart. It seems to me that work and play are issues that are dramatically played out in both charts. In Tenerife, your nature found work to be equivalent to play, whereas in the natal placement, work is hard – it is all Saturn/Venus. The relocated chart suggests that work *is* play, and that the intuitive Mercury/Neptune comes into a strong place, right in the centre of the 6th house rather than straddling the 6th house cusp, uncertainly wondering if one should play or work.

The second planetary shift I mentioned is that the relocated chart puts Mars in the 9th house of foreign interests, while in the natal chart it is in the 8th. Now, remember that the Moon will always square Mars, no matter where you are, so there can be volatility and a sense of restlessness. In the natal chart the Moon squares Mars from the 5th to the 8th house – which can mean a carelessness about invested interests, whether that is time, love, or money. In this case, it seems to have been about money. It can also mean a deep rage over how you were nurtured as an infant, and a longing for passion to replace the lack of nurturing. By shifting the Mars into the 9th, and the Moon into the 6th house, we have real foreign work, and – even if it was fun – a striving for success, comfort, nourishment, and a passion for work, travel, and life. You may have given away your power (Mars) before this stay in Tenerife, and now have learned to contain it more for yourself.

Audience: But Nita has Mars in the 8th in Capricorn, which is a very focused energy in terms of other people's property. Probably the realm of making money, managing property, is there inherently, but didn't wake up until the move.

Nita: And Jupiter/Uranus is in Cancer, which is connected with property.

Audience: Are you going back to that job?

Nita: No, I am going back for a visit to see some friends. I really feel like I want to stay even before I get there.

Erin: I understand that, because of the transits under which you are returning. Remember, Mars in Capricorn is in the 9th in Tenerife – work and business in a foreign country went very well, as you so found it, and likely will find that to still be the case – if you wanted it, that is.

Clearing the past

Nita: I wonder more about that progressed Moon on the relocated Ascendant now. And I have got Chiron exactly conjunct my Saturn on the day I arrive.

Erin: This could mean reawakening some of the old feelings you had there, and a process of clearing the past. Fourteen years ago it was moving over the Descendant. Unfinished business can be cleared up.

Nita: When I moved there, there was a Pluto/Saturn conjunction on my natal Mercury, which is my chart ruler, so it really was like a new life for me. And, of course, it was in the Saturn return period in my life.

Erin: The transit of Chiron over your natal Saturn now, coinciding with the return to that place, just might open up some old issues that need to be explored. Also, it is likely you will get a clear insight into your old holding patterns, or even your current holding patterns, and certainly, if there is a draw to living and working there again, you will want to examine that.

Nita: I have to admit, when I saw those transits, which was only this week, I had second thoughts about even going.

Erin: Oh, dear, don't do that. Your instincts are taking you there for a reason, and the astrology can help you understand why. People are so often brilliant instinctively – they seem to be doing the right thing at the right time. It's funny – I was saying to somebody the other day that even if it's horrible, if the transits are describing it, then it is working.

Nita: That's encouraging!

Erin: I hope so. I think it means that you are living your life, rather than someone else's, or a life of denial. That is the most important thing about being alive – that life is being lived as it should be. It's about being in tune with your own needs and your own destiny and life-force.

Nita: I am leaving on the seventeenth of October.

Erin: Not bad. It's a 23° Libra Sun. Does that do anything?

Nita: It's 2° from my natal Neptune.

Erin: And guess where the transiting Moon is?

Nita: In Taurus, on my progressed Moon and relocated Ascendant when I arrive.

Erin: Looking at the action in the relocated chart, we have the superior conjunction of Mercury and the Sun right on your natal Neptune in the 6th house, so the fantasy returns to be explored. The transiting Moon will be on the relocated Ascendant, conjunct the progressed Moon. I think that is a great deal of the draw back to that place. There are also the transits to consider in both the natal and the relocated chart. Uranus is trine your Sun, Pluto is sextile it, and Neptune is wavering back and forth at the relocated MC, squaring natal Mercury. I think you will find your return somewhat confusing, and therefore, I wouldn't make any sudden decisions at this time. But do look at what might still be there for you – if anything.

Audience: Nita, you are not considering moving again to Tenerife?

Nita: No.

Audience: Saturn is at 17° Aries.

Erin: Right. And it is retrograde, so it will pass back over the opposition to the Moon before it corrects its path forward, simply adding more serious consideration and maturation to the feelings of past and current stuckness and future possibilities. Saturn's retrograde cycle from first contact to final passage over a degree is around nine months, always – a gestation period. Allow the seed to mature.

What we are looking to see is if the dream is real. You will probably find that it is based in reality. Neptune's transit opposite to your Jupiter/Uranus is done. The long growth process of retrogression has completed its journey – an eighteen-month cycle. Fabulous. Eighteen months ago Neptune stationed retrograde on your relocated MC. Whenever an outer planet stations retrograde on a degree, it will make three (or more) passes, and then station direct on that same degree exactly eighteen months later, which marks the end of the process engendered by the transit.[9]

Nita: Eighteen months ago is the last time I was there, and I sold the last property I had, which was a shop. It really wasn't a good sale, but I just wanted rid of it. I gave it away for far less than it was worth, just to get shot of it. Neptune is at the MC down there, too, not really working for business decisions in a positive, energetic way.

Erin: I probably would have suggested you wait until now, only because Neptune has just finished the final pass – the one where you know that the coast is clear, that you are more likely to make sensible decisions. However, you are going as Jupiter stations direct, Neptune stations direct, the progressed Moon is in the same degree as the transiting Moon, and Mercury is on Neptune. I think it indicates that this is an auspicious time. It looks to me like it is going to become crystal-clear whether you wish to remain there or return here. Depending on what your practical concerns now are, you will find that this is going to be the time that any illusions and fantasies will be pretty much exposed. Either you love it and that's where you

---

[9]*Retrograde Planets: Traversing the Inner Landscape*, Erin Sullivan, Arkana, CAS, 1992, London.

want to be, and you create a "double life" – in which case you would then come back and organise your life to be there – or you will realise that that was a part of your life in the past. However, you look very comfortable there, and more powerful somehow.

Nita: Actually, that's what I thought. I have got this gut feeling. Anna and I did my Tarot cards last week. I have a feeling that I am going back there to meet a man from my past.

Erin: From your past? Well, with transiting Chiron on your natal Saturn, it just may be that you do, and that meeting could be part of the healing process. You know, the progression of the Sun coming to natal Venus will really put your priorities, values, and needs straight, which may indeed coincide with the meeting of someone with whom you can have a partnership with mind, body and soul. Very often the progression of the Sun to Venus or Venus to the Sun does bring in the love of one's life – or, at least, love of life!

The progressed full Moon in the relocation chart

Also significant to me in this case is the progressed Sun at 18° Scorpio – you will have a progressed Full Moon in eight months. This precipitates a new lease on your life. In looking at the whole big picture, let's look at the transits in eight months.

The progressed full Moon is an illumination point, a major turning point in one's life path. That cycle will change the focus of your life. A progressed full Moon is always amazing because it illuminates the results of the last fourteen years, since the last progressed new Moon. The full Moon and new Moon phases of the cycle are most always eventful, whereas the other, more subtle lunation cycle changes – for instance, the transition from crescent Moon to quarter Moon – aren't as dramatic as the two progressed lunations. The progressed new Moon phase and the progressed full Moon phase are dramatic. And it takes place in the relocation chart from the 1st to the 7th house, on your Venus. This will definitely bring illuminations about relationships, commitment, values, needs, work issues, and health.

What is relevant is that you will be feeling more aware and conscious of relationships and their value in your life. Now, no matter where you go, you are going to have a full Moon cycle right across your natal Venus this year, in eight months. In London, in the natal chart, it happens from your 12th to your 6th house, and I wonder what we would say if it were going on here? It would have to do with your work and your values and the amount of time that you spend alone.

Nita: And the amount of time I spend working on natal charts, and what I charge for it.

Erin: It is the evolution from your present progressed lunar phase, which is called gibbous. That phase is about learning, absorbing knowledge, experiencing and feeling one's life and environment. It leads to the awareness of what has been absorbed, digested, and learned in the full Moon phase. The progressed lunation cycle is very informative, and when you see progressed Moon to progressed Sun's change of phases, you will notice marked evolutionary changes in your interests, attitudes, moods, personal growth, and areas of expertise. The progressed full Moon blows open full understanding of what your life has been about for the last fourteen or fifteen years. Wherever you are, the awakening will happen.[10]

Nita: But progressed Venus went retrograde, and is still retrograde in my chart. It's retrograde for the rest of my life now. It is on natal Venus, but 1° away, at 17° Scorpio. It was exactly on natal Venus last year.

Erin: And your progressed Sun is at 17° Scorpio. In May and June you will have the progressed full Moon and a "return" of progressed retrograde Venus to itself, and Uranus stationary direct, trining your Sun. That is a unique combination – one that can only occur with this chart, specifically. Hence there is a specific message to you about relationship, purpose, and life-direction. This is a marriage of opposites, in the inferior conjunction of the progressed Sun and Venus right on your natal Venus.

---

[10] *The Progressed Lunation Cycle*, Leyla Rael and Dane Rudhyar, CRCS Publications, 1978.

This is where, in the Mayan myth, the goddess of the underworld meets and conjoins with the Sun, giving birth later to a new form of the self through marriage and fertilisation by the opposite.[11] It looks to me like a very serious relocation question coming up or, at the very least, a "What do I want to do, and where?" issue. I would allow the entire process to evolve over the next five to eight months, and see what happens. Don't do anything hastily, because Neptune is still at the relocated MC. You still could be enchanted, with Neptune opposite Jupiter, but I would take a good solid look at what your practical and aesthetic needs are. By May or June, it may be time for you to make a decision, but that will come step by step.

Nita: I started this course a year ago, when the progressed Moon was opposite my natal Sun.

Erin: The progressed Moon making a contact to *any* planet is profoundly active, and symbolic of a process involving instinctual and habitual responses changing or being disrupted according to the planet it is aspecting. Progressed Moon to the natal Sun involves a new way of looking at one's purpose in life, but the illumination of the progressed full Moon is the strongest of all the lunations. That is why I am saying you have to consider practical matters and aesthetics. You don't have to jump to do anything in a hurry. There is time. I have a feeling that you will be drawn, perhaps to work or to do something there, but you don't have to instigate this immediately.

Nita: Well, actually, when I go out there, I am doing a few chart readings for people, which my friend has set up for me.

Erin: Why can't you go back and forth?

Nita: That was the idea. If I could establish a small clientele over there, then it would pay for me to keep popping out for holidays.

Erin: It isn't that long a plane ride.

Nita: No, it's four hours.

---

[11]*Retrograde Planets, op. cit.* Note 8, see the chapter on Venus retrograde.

Living in two places

Erin: There's no jet lag. It's perfectly feasible to contemplate living your life in two places.

Audience: And she has a Gemini Ascendant, so it's wonderful for her.

Erin: Exactly. The dream is of creating something that gives you an alternative lifestyle, where everything isn't so intense and subterranean as Pluto in the 4th implies. You could use this relocation as an alternative place to rejuvenate and enliven yourself. In the next year you could look very carefully at how you might create a life in two places.

Nita: I would love to have a life in both places.

Erin: Well, it would be ideal, and you are reaching a point in your life where it would be good to start thinking in terms of a summer-winter lifestyle. Uranus will pass over your natal MC in the next couple of years, and this one is also an eighteen-month process.

Audience: Librans also like two things.

Nita: Last week, you said something about not actually having to go to the place to experience the energy. Somebody who was born there could bring it to you. Does that mean that my son, who was born there, will always activate my relocated chart?

Erin: Yes.

Nita: And he would activate Jupiter/Uranus on the IC, instead of Pluto in the 4th.

Erin: Yes, because he was born on your JU/UR/IC line. He is a living, breathing embodiment of that aspect.

Nita: Natally he has Moon conjunct Uranus, both at 0° Capricorn, conjunct Saturn at 2°. He has Moon/Uranus/Saturn, so he would experience me with a mundane square that I don't have natally, but that I do have in my relocated chart. That is interesting isn't it?

Erin: Yes, it is. He also experiences your ambivalence about where you live. It's terribly interesting. That would be one way of settling his psyche down – by his having both places to live as well.

Nita: Oh, would it? Get rid of a bit of that rebelliousness.

Mars out of hiding

Audience: Mars in the relocation chart in the 9th is that kind of a son.

Erin: This is a good example. I take your point about Mars in the 8th house in Capricorn being very practical and working with others' resources.

Nita: If you own it. But I never did.

Erin: Maybe you do have a shadowed Mars. I think it is unrealised to a great degree, by your own description. By shifting it to the 9th house, it stops being a complex and starts being a process.

Audience: It is exalted. It is a good Mars.

Erin: Mars in the 8th is pretty hidden, watery, to some degree subterranean. It can be more of a psychological experience than an externalised force. Mars in the 12th and the 8th and the 4th is a family matter. You may need to be the one to bring ambition, direct action, force, passion, and drive out into the open. Certainly, you need to be very clear about ambition and drive and aggression and assertion – which may not have been part of your earliest teaching.

Audience: So is it stronger by house than by sign? It is very positive and focussed when it is in an earth sign like Capricorn. Do you think the house placement is more important?

Erin: I wouldn't say it is more important, but I think that having Mars in the 9th would result in the 9th house being clearer in expression of one's deepest desires, rather than those desires "just happening".

Post script: Diana

Erin: There's something I forgot to tell you before lunch. I was going to do this as soon as I came in this morning. The controversy remains controversial about Princess Diana's birth chart. Yet another time has arisen. It is a real exercise, this one. It is a bit awkward to phone up someone in the family and say, "I hope you're not busy, but why don't you just tell us what the real birth time is?" The 2.15 pm time came from an astrologer. So did the second time, the 7.25 pm time which gives Sagittarius rising. Now there is somebody else who claims to be close with Diana and the family, a reasonably reliable source, who has said that there is a time in there which would give Scorpio rising. That could be very interesting. God knows when it will be finally settled, and perhaps one of the family will actually put it to rest, but it does leave the whole thing open to speculation. And speculation is interesting, especially considering that all of the times are alive on some level, surely. In Geoffrey Cornelius' book, *The Moment of Astrology,* he deals with the business of relevancy, radicality, and wrong times.[12]

The 2.15 pm time comes from Penny Thornton, as well as Roger Elliot, who rang up the Palace. The 7.25 pm time was given by Debbie Frank, and the third time I am not at liberty to disclose, because it hasn't come out yet. So there is another time which produces a Scorpio Ascendant. Who knows? I still feel the exercise is valid, because we are looking at something that now is public domain. It just remains interesting – watch that space. If anybody else has claims to being close to Princess Diana, don't be shy, because a whole lot of other people are too, apparently.

Audience: I read something about her position in the family, and how her mother wanted a son– she didn't want another girl.

Erin: Family secrets, family mysteries – it's phenomenal. I think her position in the family – whichever family we are putting her in, whether the collective, the family of origin or the royal family –

---

[12]*The Moment of Astrology,* Geoffrey Cornelius, Arkana, Contemporary Astrology Series, London, 1996.

means we are looking at a pretty hefty 4th house. There are lots of secrets.

Pars Fortuna: you can take it with you

Audience: I have got a general question about relocation charts. The only thing that actually moves, or changes houses in the relocation I am looking at in my book of personal horoscopes, is the Part of Fortune.

Erin: Yes, because it is related to the Ascendant and the Sun and the Moon. The *pars fortuna* is a nodal point, and it is the most important of the various parts handed down from the Greeks through the Arabs – hence called "Arabic Parts". The most common derivation for the Part of Fortune is the one devised by Manilius. The Part of Fortune is the same distance of zodiacal arc from the Ascendant as the Moon is from the Sun. It is calculated by figuring the degrees of the Ascendant plus Moon minus Sun. That is why the Part of Fortune will change position along with any change in the Ascendant.

Audience: Do you use it?

Erin: Not normally. But it is the bit that changes signs and houses most radically in relocation. It is a valid point, having the connotation of the life force meeting the personality and incarnate path. If you change locations and thus your relationship to the horizon, zenith, and MC, then clearly your Sun/Moon – your purpose in life – is going to produce a different fortune. It would make sense, if you use the Part of Fortune in that way, that it would shift its house.

Audience: Can it shift signs?

Erin: Yes, because the relocational shift can put the relationship between Sun, Moon, and Ascendant in a different zodiacal degree.

Relocation stories

Ari: coming home

Let's look at Ari's natal chart (**Figure 5**) and her relocation chart for London (**Figure 5a**). You people have brought fabulous relocations, which I want to put up because they exemplify some of the things that I was trying to express about changes in the MC and changes in the Ascendant. Now, these two charts perfectly illustrate how a move further south and further west moves the Ascendant and the MC respectively and simultaneously. Ari was born at a low-to-moderate latitude, around 38°N. These low-to-moderate latitudes periodically produce a radical aspect such as a sextile or a trine from the MC to the Ascendant. But generally speaking, the nearer the equator you are, the more likely there is to be a square between the Ascendant and the MC. In fact, right on the equator, the MC and the Ascendant are *always* square, because the angle of the sun is direct. It rises at 6.00 am, culminates overhead at noon, and sets at 6.00 pm.

At the same time as her birth in Athens – where the MC and ASC are in a square, separated by 92° – in London, the MC and ASC are separated by a slightly greater angle of 100°. The MC in London moved back 22°, to 20° Taurus, and the Ascendant moved back 14°, to 0° Virgo. You end up with the Ascendant and the MC yawning, opening a bit, in this relocated chart. It is later on the clock in Athens than London, so the Sun is already in the 9th house there, while it is earlier in London and therefore the Sun is in the 10th. All the planets have changed houses, except Venus and the Nodes.

What this move has done is relevant to the power of angles. It has shifted the 9th house Sun at 24° Taurus into the 10th house, very close to the MC – certainly closer to the MC than it was when you were born. Thus you have relocated to your SU/MC line, and you haven't moved off your MO/DSC line, but simply moved to the "other side" of it. On your A*C*G map, it would show that you have in some way shifted the focus from 6th house/9th house Sun/Moon placements to putting the lights in angular houses, reinforcing the MO/DSC and amplifying the SU/MC.

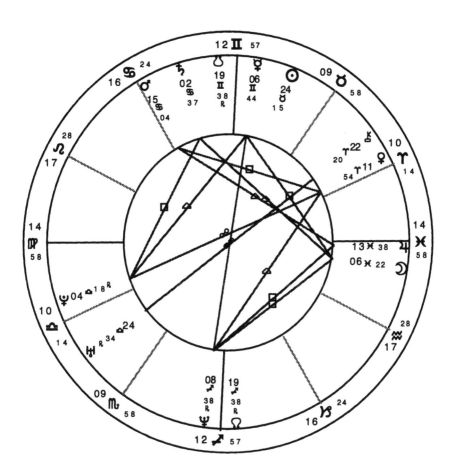

Figure 5: Ari

(Data withheld for purposes of confidentiality)

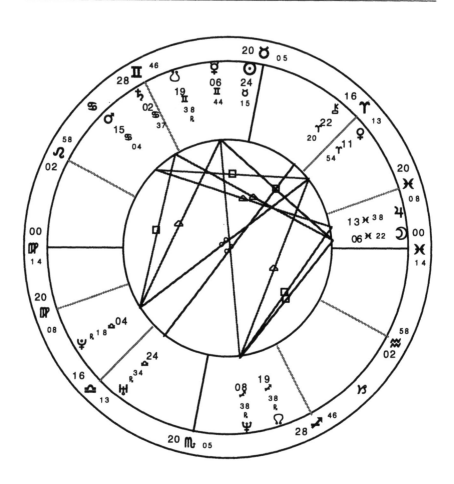

Figure 5a: Ari in London

Your inner needs of the 9th house, as they are in the natal chart –
the desire to meet new cultures, languages, and studies, and exploring
and professionalising your metaphysical ideas – have been brought
into strong professional focus, rather than remaining a study or a
pastime, a hobby or simply an interest. Moon/Jupiter having moved
from the 6th (thought still influencing the angle of the Descendant)
to the 7th house, I am wondering if that, too, is something that you
have noticed.

Ari: I have definitely noticed that I have shifted more from a
JU/DSC to a MO/DSC line!

Erin: Oh? Does this mean that you resonate more personally and
emotionally to the world and your environment here? More so than
in Athens?

Ari: I *am* more emotional here, and responsive to the collective,
and most definitely things always came more easily to me in Greece
than here. But with the Sun in the 10th house, I am more easily
accepted by authority, here in London.

Erin: That may well be due to your own sense of confidence, your
inner authenticity, having done an heroic thing – leaving your own
country and "conquering" London! The 10th house Sun is a more
environmentally and socially adventurous placement than the
introspective 9th house placement.

It also strikes me that the Moon in Pisces makes you more aware of,
or susceptible to, health matters. That it is in the 6th house natally,
in Athens, suggests that you are acutely responsive physically to
whatever is occurring around you. However, you might experience
more physical weakness or tiredness or vulnerability here. With the
Moon angular on the Descendant, I should think that you would be
more likely to register your Piscean unconscious responses to the
environment and your inner state more openly here in London.

Ari: That's definitely true. It probably has to do with transits as
well, but since I have come here I have had a big depression and am
going through a dark, dark phase. I am expressing it much more to
the people around me. I am not so shy any more, in the sense of
expressing it.

Erin: That's interesting. The feelings and responses are no different, but your ability to externalise them, to tell friends, is. And yes, transits to planets are occurring no matter where you are – thus, you will undergo that process regardless. However, the *housing* of the process is very, very different in your relocated chart.

Ari: I am not shy here. The first time I came, I was ten years old. For some reason, the very first day I stepped foot in the airport, I thought, "Oh, I like this place," though I had never seen it. Since then, I always wanted to come back and study – I did, and that was it! Even in Greece I always had Irish people that I immediately liked. So I have always had an affinity with the UK.

Erin: That speaks of instinctively responding to the SU/MC line that lies in the 9th house natally. The natal horoscope does talk about wanting to live abroad – Sun/Mercury in the 9th – and an enjoyment of other cultures. By the way, this is also in character with your Moon/Jupiter, which is about making a home in any foreign land. That you have brought your Moon/Jupiter to London, where it is happily in the 7th, says a lot about the comfort you find in the habits, the people, the ordinary things here. Again, about the Sun – because of the 9th house Sun, there is an inherent draw to foreign places. That is the inherent condition of the Sun. Therefore, on your A*C*G map, the places to which you would be attracted would likely fall under Sun/angle lines, and, also Mercury/angle lines.

Ari: It is a very weird thing, because the SU/MC line passes exactly through Paris, Marseilles, and Brussels. I found Paris really, really distant and cold – it never attracted me. I found it much more at ease here. Maybe it has something to do with the latitude.

Audience: Crossings?

Erin: Or maybe something even more subtle, because Paris is your exact SU/MC line. That would mean that your Moon would be exactly on the Descendant there too, forming a mundane square.

Ari: Paris was too much for me. I had good times, but I couldn't live there, or stay longer than I did. Here I am actually thinking of staying, and not going back to Greece. I feel much better away from my family. Saturn in the 10th house gets transferred to the 11th, and

Pluto goes to the 2nd and Uranus to the 3rd. And as you said, only Venus stays in the 8th house, while Chiron moves to the 9th.

Erin: It shows us that the angles and angular houses are more demonstrative than the succeedent or cadent houses. Let's look at the shift of planets into the earlier houses.

10th house change of tenants

Natally you have Saturn/Mars in the 10th house. That means that your sense of individuality and presentation needs to grow into a place of authority. It is individuating toward assuming your own authenticity and running your own life – being the author of your own destiny. This is something that is usually much better demonstrated as one gets older and matures, which is Saturnian. When that configuration shifts into the 11th house by relocation, though your inherent, natal promise is toward finding a strong authoritative purpose, that's not the dominate focus of behaviour here in London. Your inherent seed will evolve this whether you are conscious of it or not. Consciousness can bring more free will to bear on your ambivalence about your and other's authority. However, the move has put the Sun in the 10th, with Mercury, so your sense of acceptance in society and as an authority is much more graceful.

This is where I was saying you have played down Mars and Saturn as a strident, battling force, by placing them in the 11th house. This is very different in its manifest action than in the 10th house. It means that you are mirroring your power and authority against a collective or a structured group who will feed that back to you, and you will have to actually deal with it on a pure level as opposed to a police-principle Mummy-Daddy level. And your Sun/Mercury in the 10th is a much nicer goal to achieve in a 10th house sense, especially in the first half of life. It may be that you haven't abandoned your birth place, but you may need to be more matured to go back and fully appreciate it.

Ari: That's what I was thinking – that I would like to go back over there when I feel I have become much more of who I know I am inside.

Erin: Yes. When your Mars and Saturn are really secure and you have got a bit of Saturn internally, and your *gravitas* is more developed, then nothing will shake you.

Audience: There is another shift through the relocation that reinforces the sense of comfort. Mercury, the chart ruler, is now also in the 10th.

Erin: That's more comfortable.

Audience: Where would she have to move to place Leo on the Ascendant, and the Sun the chart ruler?

Ari: Just into the Atlantic! I don't think there is a place for that nearby.

House cusps

Audience: Don't you read the natal Mars into the 11th when it is just on the cusp?

Audience: We had an argument last week about this.

Audience: It is 1° away from the cusp of the 11th in the natal chart.

Erin: There are a few ways of perceiving this dilemma. Firstly, the very next day after her birth, Mars was beginning to transit and exert its influence into the 11th house. But if she were born a few minutes earlier, then Mars would be in the 11th house. However, should she have been born somewhat later, then it is in the 10th more firmly. There are a lot of different ways to look at this, all of them speculative. Generally, people seem to say, "If it's on the cusp, read it into the next house." But they have several reasons for this, none of them in agreement. Myself, I tend to keep it in its house, and think of it as moving toward the next house by transit and progression.

Audience: Why not both?

Erin: Indeed, why not? Why not just say, "It's on the cusp."

Audience: Jupiter is also on the cusp in Ari's natal chart – within 1°.

Erin: Ah! Now, with angles it's absolute – it is in the 6th house, but it is angular.

Nita: I've got a lot of planets on the cusp, and they feel like they are in both houses.

Audience: I have Neptune 5' from the IC in the natal chart.

Erin: And do you feel Neptune on the IC? Or in the 3rd or in the 4th?

Audience: Definitely as an angular influence. That's what I identify with – Neptune on the IC, rather than in the 3rd or 4th.

Erin: It is about being very attached in a romantic and fluid way to your roots – and the roots are, I think, found wherever you flow. Home has a shape-shifting nature. Now, Ari, natally you have Sagittarius in your 4th house, but by coming to London you have Scorpio there. Natally, this says that you can live abroad, or anywhere, but living in London, you get to the real nitty-gritty of your roots. Your existence is more intense, more psychoanalytical, and more extreme here. You would feel your Pluto more intensely and personally, even though natally it is in the 1st house, and in London in the 2nd house. You still would be more aware of your existential issues: "Why am I here? What is my purpose in life? Who are my ancestors? Where are my resources to be found?"

Ari: I feel that anyone can scold me into anything, but I feel much more stable after this morning, when I came round here to the class.

Erin: You have got more angular planets here. You are more cardinal, more substantial. All this cadent material, where so much is mutable and falling away, is not only shifting more strongly to angularity by relocation. It also puts Pluto in the 2nd house, rather than rising. When you were born in Athens, Pluto was the first planet to hit the horizon after your birth. It still was in London. But in Athens it lives in the 1st house and it really colours the more secretive, hidden side of your self. But Pluto in the 2nd isn't as strong in a personality sense – it is more interior. Pluto in the 1st house is a loner, an observer, a person who watches the world – this is pretty much what it is about when in the first quadrant, but in the 1st house it can feel very isolated.

Ari: I am also thinking of the Sun/Uranus quincunx – which is the only aspect the Sun makes – from the 9th to the 2nd in my natal chart. It moves to the 10th and 3rd here in London. That is really what the astrology actually did – all the nitty-gritty things I have done in London, and the studies I really went for in the open, as opposed to the 9th/2nd house, which was private, interior, and largely unshared.

Erin: Open communications, thinking, writing, speaking, being involved in a collective sense. The unaspected Sun is a real hook for whatever the masculine/authoritative collective dictates. I do know that Greece isn't very accepting of astrology as a practice, and it is still very influenced by the Orthodox Church and the Reformation. A client of mine was telling me that it's very difficult for her as an astrologer, and she wouldn't dream of setting up a practice there.

Ari: Never, never.

Erin: She does practise for her own friends, but that's it. As far as a professional arena for you, Sun in the 10th at the MC, with an angular Moon on the Descendant, strikes me as a more viable place for you to work toward your purpose in life. This clearly calls you to help and not be a victim of your own illnesses. The Moon natally in your chart is squaring Neptune on the IC, acting as the agent for carrying the family's uncertainty and insecurity. This way you have shifted it into a whole other space. Is there anything else anyone has to say about this? Thank you so much for sharing your chart, Ari. Gad, you will all go away and only remember that I can't tell east from west or Ascendant from Descendant.

Audience: Isn't your MO/NE/DSC line also here? You pick up all the indecision.

Erin: Yes, but I won't blame that. I suppose I could just say it's all London's fault – it certainly can't be me!

Aven: looking at a new place

I'm going to put your charts up now, Aven. This is another marvellous set of charts, involving birth in New York, life in England, now in London, and possibly considering a move to San Francisco.

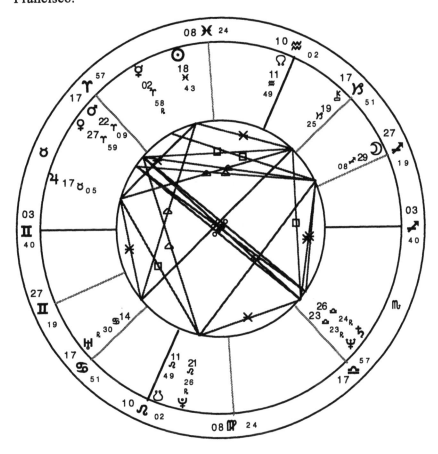

Figure 6: Aven

(Data withheld for purposes of confidentiality)

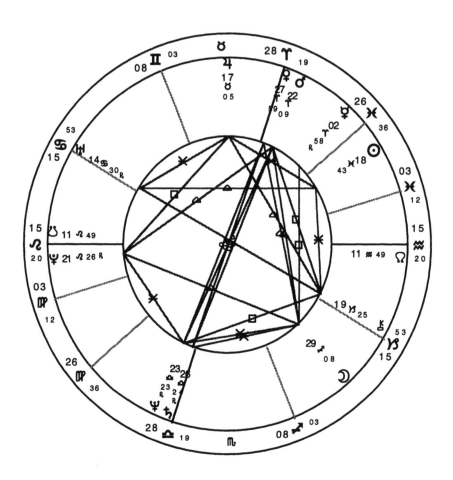

Figure 6a: Aven in London

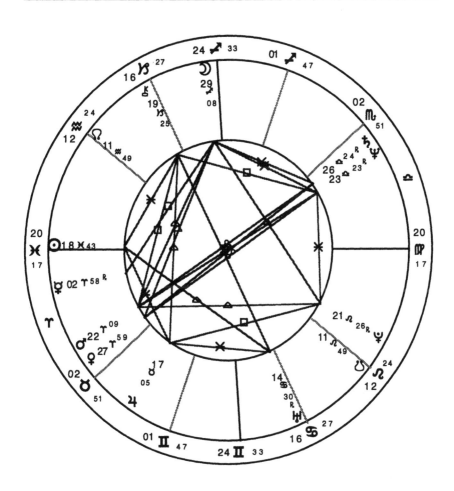

Figure 6b: Aven in San Francisco

Tell us a bit about the situation with the charts, Aven.

Aven: I lived in the North of England for almost twenty years, and have only just moved down to London, but I am quite attracted to the idea of moving to California. I have never been there.

Erin: That's what we are going to do with the charts. **Figure 6** is Aven's natal chart; **Figure 6a** is her relocation in London; **Figure 6b** is her relocation in San Francisco, California. First, let's look at the natal chart, which has got lots of strong planetary aspects. If Aven moves them around, they will likely manifest in very different areas in her life. There is a Mars/Venus conjunction, and the Sun is in Pisces trine Uranus.

The Moon is interesting because it is in the very last degree of Sagittarius, and thus is the receptacle of all life's experiences. Now, the Moon is quite important in this chart, because it receives the last transit from any planet as it applies to the horoscope. Wherever her Moon is will be a significant place of final realisations and results from her life experiences. This shows her to be a very responsive person after all is said and done – she really does process her life through the feeling function and the instincts.

Transits to the planetary story-line: first and latest degrees

The other factor with a late degree planet – anywhere from 27° to 29° 59′ – is that there is little "void" time, almost no space between the last aspect made in the chart to the change into a new sign. Because she has Mercury at 2° of a sign, this means she is a very busy woman, in her head and in her life.

Audience: Can you explain that again, please?

Erin: An example, using Aven's chart, is this. When Saturn transited Pisces, it made the following primary aspects to each planet, from its entry point at 0° Pisces to its departure at the last minute of Pisces:

1. closing semi-sextile to Mercury (earliest degree planet)
2. trine Uranus
3. sextile Jupiter
4. conjunct the Sun
5. sextile Chiron
6. quincunx Pluto
7. closing semi-sextile Mars
8. quincunx Neptune
9. quincunx Saturn
10. closing semi-sextile Venus
11. square Moon (latest degree planet)

When we look at our natal planetary degrees in that way, we have a story-line. It is always in that planetary order – from the earliest planet to the latest planet. Just think of this pattern as one that becomes ingrained after years and years of transits. The Moon will create this order of contact thirteen times in a year; the Sun reinforces it annually, along with the inner planets; and Mars, every two years or so, and on and on.. Hence, my theory that the last degree planet is the recipient of the sum and total of our transits, progressions, and life experiences.

Also, she has several cuspal planets – Moon on the 8th house cusp in the 7th house side; Mars on the 12th house cusp, in the 11th house side; Saturn on the 6th house cusp on the 5th house side; and the Sun just into the 11th house side of the 10th house cusp. This strikes me as showing some ambivalence, because when we have a few cuspal planets – within a degree and a half of the cusp – the chart is one which is poised for change, for experiencing a sense of uncertainty.

Now, by living in England, what have you done with your planetary pattern? You have moved your Venus/Mars opposite Saturn/Neptune from the 11th/5th house to the MC/IC axis. You have made them angular – very specifically, Venus/MC and Saturn/IC. Mars and Neptune are now in a more mental house axis, where thinking and beliefs dominate.

Also, the Sun in Pisces in the 8th house is very different from its natal place in the 11th. The Sun in the 8th is more accommodating, especially as it is a Piscean Sun. When it is in the 8th, you might find yourself feeling that sacrifice is part of intimacy – that close bonding, or merging with another, is mysterious, ego-threatening, and difficult to understand. Natally, you do understand people, because the 11th house Sun is very much involved with the group mind, the collective psyche. And your natal 11th house is very busy, whereas here, in England, it is not. In London you have Uranus in the 11th, which sets you apart from "the group", or from making friends and a life that feels substantial. How have you done here, these last twenty years?

Aven: Well, a lot of things have happened emotionally. I have had a lot of very difficult experiences. Of course the Sun is in quincunx to Pluto.

Erin: But it is quincunx Pluto wherever you are. It is a matter of *where* it is quincunx. And this is what we must always recall: you are yourself no matter where you are. The substance of the planets is the "real" thing. It is the planets and their conversation that are the archetypal core. The array of those planets is what changes. Thus, our perspective and the planetary agency shift according to location. And Pluto is close to angular here in London – indeed, it is the existential Pluto placement. Wherever we have Pluto we have the existential question, but when it is angular it becomes our *modus vivendi*. In the Ascendant, it is the way we feel our way though the path of life.

Aven: It has been quite an 8th house experience.

Erin: Please, what kind of an 8th house experience?

Aven: I am a very 8th house person, with Moon on the cusp anyway. I think the Venus/Saturn, with Saturn on the IC, has made it a difficult place for me, even though I have been here twenty years. I have stayed here because my son was born here when Saturn transited my IC in my birth chart. That really rooted me to the ground. He has just grown up, you see. There are massive amounts of change, because he and I are very deeply bonded. His Sun is on my Jupiter in Taurus, and we are unbelievably close. I have transiting Pluto on my Descendant, and Uranus coming to my MC, so I could really do anything. Because he was born when Saturn was in Leo, and when it was transiting my IC, it means that his Saturn is on my IC. And I got stuck here.

Erin: Ah, yes, we must be very careful where we find ourselves when Saturn is at the IC, and for about the first year of its transit through the 4th house, as that is when a major tap-root is sunk. It is a time when we can relocate and/or work toward a major settling down. But if you are in a place where you feel trapped or uncomfortable, or you have outgrown it, and you do not make conscious, assertive efforts to move, then it is not surprising if you stay for many, many years, like it or not.

Looking at the natal chart, you have Pluto transiting your Descendant and Saturn about to conjoin your Mars/Venus and oppose your Neptune/Saturn. Now, looking at the English chart, the London chart, Saturn will be transiting over your relocated MC by the end of this year. That Saturn is about to pass over your relocated MC three times in the next year, and station-direct in December of 1998.

This gives me a feeling that your concept of adventure and life-direction is about to undergo a long, retrograde process of reevaluation. You may well change your direction while it passes back and forth over your relocated MC. This may seem like mixing metaphors, and it is, but you can do that if the various symbolic signatures are strong and stating the same point in the same way. Pluto is currently transiting your natal Descendant, which it finally clears this month. That is a transit that has been in effect since March 1996. Where are you living now?

Aven: I had a home in the north of England. I gave that up to come down here to London. Now I have done that, I feel I can do anything.

Erin: Well, it is very powerful, this stuff. Have you thought of San Francisco in an astrological context only, or did you like the idea anyway?

Aven: I feel very hemmed in here. I like open places and I find England very repressive, even though I have been here a long time.

Erin: Are you and your partner or husband in agreement about this?

Aven: I haven't got a husband. But I have an American passport.

Erin: That could prove to be better than a husband. Priorities, please!

Aven: I was wondering what you made of the fact that I have never been there, but my mother went there. I'm not very close to my mother, I have to say, but she tells me it is very nice out there.

Living lunar links

Erin: It *is* very nice out there. It's wonderful. However, you must be practical. Charts are one thing, but actualising them is another. That your Moon is on the MC in San Francisco has something to say about your mother's dream. There are many ways of coming to terms with our mothers, without any conversations, confrontation, or direct action. When we live our lunar links, we are in some very primal way living out the mother.

That you say you aren't that close to her is revealing, and in the light of the Moon's placement, you might find that the link between you and her is present if not very direct. There are no rules for parental links, and San Francisco has both lights, the celestial parents, so to speak, at the most extraverted angles. Maybe your parental images can be reconciled in this place – where you can be adult, both mother and father to yourself.

Aven: What do you think of the Sun/Moon square on the angles in San Francisco?

Erin: I think it is a good thing. As I said, it is about being your own "Lights", your own parents. To have the SU/ASC line and the MO/MC line in the same place is a good omen for externalising your deepest self. Seriously, having the Sun in the Ascendant and the Moon at the MC, and moving there with a sense of purpose, you would find that your anxiety, depression, isolation, and existential *angst* would be alleviated. It shifts your big axis of Aries/Libra planets into the 1st/7th house. Mars and Venus rule the 1st and 7th houses, and the polarities of relationship will be in their natural syzygy.

You may find yourself able to work out more of the attraction/repulsion, freedom/closeness relationship issues that arise with a Mars/Venus conjunction opposite Saturn/Neptune. You are already less isolated in feeling by just having come to London from the North. Again, having the aspects in angular houses is slightly more in favour of working on the issues consciously. It may be my imagination, but the San Francisco chart looks like a much more dynamic and actualised potential, if we consider the Sun/Ascendant and the Moon/Midheaven. More of your life purpose can be enacted in a way which feels easy and comfortable – after allowing time, a year at least, for all this to settle in.

Audience: The focus of the London chart strikes me as being the Mars/Venus conjunction opposite Neptune/-Saturn on the MC/IC axis. It has been highlighted by virtue of living here twenty years, which I think must deepen its impact. What do you make of the combination?

Audience: Whatever Pluto represents must be very prominent in England also.

Erin: Yes, I agree. That is what I want to get back to. It brings up the feeling of struggling hard and getting nowhere. Now, what I really wanted to know in the beginning was this. What is your perception of living in a place for twenty years with Mars/Venus opposite Saturn/Neptune on the MC/IC, and Pluto rising?

Aven: It has been quite frustrating. I have got involved with the wrong people. I have been living in a small town in the north of England by circumstance rather than choice.

Audience: I get the impression that, by moving to San Francisco, you could somehow incorporate that experience into your own sense of value. Two lights being angular – that could be a real boost in terms of what you do and what you achieve.

Aven: I just have this idea in my head. As I said, I have never been there. People tell me that it is a good place to live, but I don't know.

Erin: Really, if you are seriously considering it, I would definitely make a trip out, because you should never go anywhere unless you have been there, even for a couple of weeks. You could get a car and drive around and start imagining, dreaming, what life would be like and what the practical realities of it are. Having done that, and finding it a workable place, only then could I say honestly, "Do it." If you have the ability, then do it, because this is an excellent relocation horoscope and a very good time to uproot and change your perspective and your horizons.

Aven: That's what I seem to be doing.

Erin: And you are going to change anyway, because that is what is going on in your planetary gestalt. So give yourself a year in the place to self-reorganise. I would think that within a year to two years, your comfort level in yourself will be much greater, and also the ability to work out the issues that are too complex to go into here, with relationships. I think you are going to be able to see a lot.

A grand fire trine looking for earth

Aven: I have a grand trine in fire signs, with Venus/Mars trine Moon trine Pluto. In the San Francisco chart they go into the earth houses, with Venus on the cusp of the 2nd. That's what I need – a place where I feel more at home, and can get to grips with what I am doing.

Erin: Right – a fire trine with an air outlet. Grand trines are closed circuits. The planets therein are only speaking among themselves, and can be somewhat autistic with respect to the rest of the planetary gestalt. In fire, a grand trine manifests in a lack of enthusiasm without stimulation from others, a stuckness in the creative sphere, unless their are external forces to encourage the excitement, the inspiration and creativity, to emerge. The air outlet – that is, the Saturn/Neptune kite-tail – says you need a solid grip on your imagination in order to create. Now, most grand fire trine people need others to fan their flames, and isolation is very dangerous to fire. It smothers, smoulders, smokes, and chars, but it does not work well on its own.

And you have earth as your inferior element. Jupiter in Taurus is found in the 2nd house in the San Francisco chart, which really supports the Sun on the Ascendant. That natal Sun is beautifully aspected – it is trine to Uranus, and Jupiter is at the midpoint. Inherently you have a great sense of yourself, your value and your worth, but it is not well grounded.

This may well be simply a matter of maturing into yourself. You are geared to individuation in both radical and practical ways, but finding the radical part may be difficult because of the inversion of the fire trine. You must invoke Jupiter in earth to bring you your sense of worth and value, and Uranus to bring you to your own sense of identity and find the external sources of stimulation to help you bring out your creative side.

The feeling I get, from your saying you have sacrificed something for twenty years, is that it is coming from the underbelly of Pisces the victim, and the closed circuit of the fire grand trine. You need others to turn you on, to light your fire. This is a good thing, not a neurotic thing. Staying in a place in which you are unrealised and unfulfilled, and not making a major change toward finding stimulation and outlets for your interiorised extraversion, *are* neurotic – even if you are doing it for a so-called good reason.

Audience: What strikes me is that she has got all the personal planets above the horizon in her natal chart. In London, it is mostly that, but with the exception of the Moon – maybe children, as it is in the 5th. But in the second chart, for San Francisco, the Sun is right on the horizon, and the personal planets are underneath, with the exception of the Moon in the 10th, which seems to say she might be whatever she wants to be. It is a kind of coming out, where she might find more fulfilment in response to both to the area and her inner needs.

Audience: Is the Moon important? What I mean is, you were saying it is a strong receptacle of life's experience. But as it is in the grand trine, does this make it more difficult to externalise?

Erin: Yes.

Audience: Well, if you think in terms of placing a really important planet in a strong place, then the San Francisco chart puts the Moon at the top. And her Moon is trine the Mars/Venus and sextile the Saturn/Neptune. That strikes me as a possibility of bringing out her Sagittarian excitement – what you say is locked into the grand trine – in a very open way. Both the natal and the London chart have the Moon in a quiet place, not in strong angular or dramatic places.

Erin: That is brilliant. The Moon in the MC, and the Sun on the Ascendant, seem to be the most productive placements of the rather scattered array of planets. This would remain to be seen, however, by actually taking the challenge and moving. If one were advising about this matter, tossing it back and forth in a consultation, I would confirm, Aven, that your feelings – your attraction to this place, to San Francisco – are instinctively based on your desire to be more self-realised (Sun/Ascendant), and to be much more in tune with the people and the collective in the way which you need to have in your life (Moon/MC).

In the spotlight: is that comfortable?

One of the more interesting relocation cases in *The Astro*Carto*Graphy Book of Maps*, repeated in *The Psychology of Astro*Carto*Graphy*, is Yogananda's story. He moved from India, where he was born and lived on his MO/ASC line, to his SU/ASC line, which runs through the dot of Los Angeles. He went to Los Angeles, bringing his cultural and religious values with him – Moon in Leo on the Ascendant – and he never returned. He founded the Self-Realisation Centre. His foundation is one of the most benign, long-lived, pleasant spiritual retreat centres that exist.

Yogananda was an extremely kind and social person. His SU/ASC line drew him, in the 1920's, to a place where he spent the rest of his life being famous, but not ostentatious – and all this on gut instinct. No Astro*Carto*Grapher told him to do that. Sun rising is about long life, much exuberance, and recognition from others of who you really are. Thus your sensitivity turns from being a victim to being a helper.

It could be an incredibly gentle and lovely place, Aven, especially surrounded by water, which your Pisces Sun cries out for. I think this could be an excellent shift from a deep, introverted, self-exploratory country – England, with the Sun and Mercury in the 8th and Pluto rising, where you are really looking inward. You were raising your child – Moon in the 5th – and doing some kind of root work for Saturn at the IC. But suddenly this other chart is there, this other opportunity at this time in your life – a perfect opportunity at midlife to shift you into a much lighter, more illuminated part of your own life.

Aven: Do you think San Francisco is a good place to do astrology?

Erin: Yes, it would be. It is very complex. It is rich with astrologers, but in terms of using ideas and work you would find an unlimited horizon. That is why you have got to take a year to look around and see what is going on, and meet some people. There is a lot going on there, and it is a very open place. There are many very interesting astrology people there, and good groups. The teaching is excellent.

As for the Pisces Sun, I'm all for bringing it out into the open, as opposed to suppressing it and leaving it languishing in the 8th house in London. Natally the 11th house is more compatible with the Ascendant and 1st house, as the need for friends and support systems is better realised when you move from the 11th house Sun to placing it on the Ascendant. Bringing it into the Ascendant is like saying, "Look, this is what I do. I work with people. I work with the psyche. I am interested in philosophy and metaphysics. I want to be responsive to the collective." Thank you for giving us this example, Aven. Let us know where you go!

Fitting in with a country's horoscope

Audience: Erin, if when you relocate to a country, do you ever consider your own synastry with the chart of the country?

Erin: Oh, yes, definitely. The research Nick Campion has done for *The Book of World Horoscopes* provides you with as many possible horoscopes as we have been able to get for the astrology of countries, cities, and places.[13] I would definitely superimpose my chart on a country just to see what it is like.

Audience: I came here when transiting Pluto opposed my Sun for a few years, and then conjoined my progressed Moon. In two of the horoscopes of London, the city's natal Pluto is conjunct my natal Moon. I just came here to go for it, I think – and to do it under the resonating transit.

Erin: That's really true. And it is often that literal. You will find, if you do have work to do in a particular country, that there will be precise planets in that country's horoscope that are related to your natal chart.

Ulla: nature versus culture

Now we have got a natal chart and a relocated chart to London that Ulla has provided. **Figure 7** is her natal, and **Figure 7a** is the relocation horoscope.

Ulla, when did you move here to London from Cyprus?

Ulla: I was two.

Erin: So you really have lived here all your life. Have you visited and gone back to Cyprus?

Ulla: Yes, I know Cyprus well.

Erin: Interestingly, this brings up a point that we talked about in the tea-break. This might illustrate a situation where a country is too weak for the personality. You are not going to move somewhere just because of the Astro*Carto*Graphy. If you have great lines in the middle of the Sahara Desert, or off the Galapagos Islands, you cannot always do it. It is entirely possible that the personality of the individual doesn't suit the place in all practical ways.

---

[13]*The Book of World Horoscopes*, Nicholas Campion, Cinnabar Books, 1995.

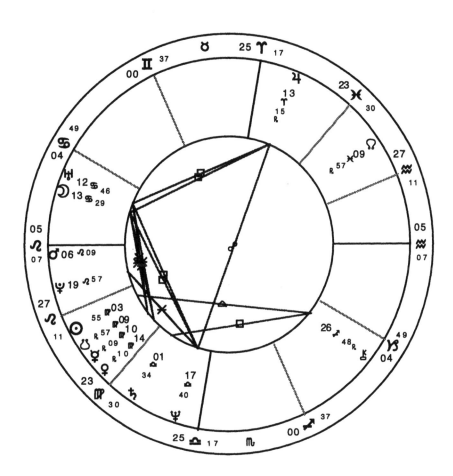

Figure 7: Ulla

(Data withheld for purposes of confidentiality)

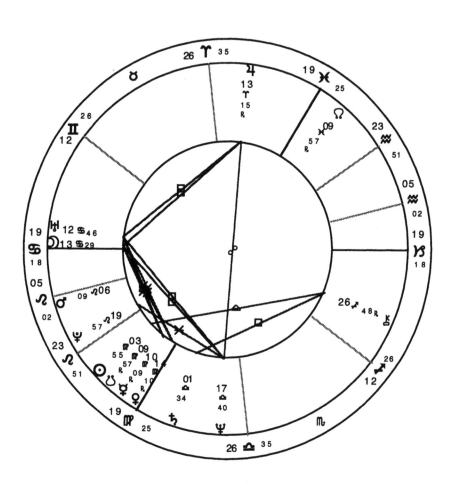

Figure 7a: Ulla in London

Being born in a place with Mars angular, Mars on the Ascendant at 6° Leo in Cyprus, could have produced a personality more in need of drama, excitement and edge, a kind of fight, than the birth place can provide. Let's imagine that Ulla was born in London, and then relocated to Cyprus. Look at the charts in that way, and imagine what would happen. We find that Cyprus is her MA/ASC line. Maybe the striving, difficult, harsh, exciting, dramatic, masculine sort of things that arise under MA/ASC lines are expressed in different ways in different cultures. Cyprus-type Mars is different from London-type Mars. You would need to use your Mars rising wherever you are, but in Cyprus it is very close to the surface, and affects you in a personal/personality way. In London, Mars is located in the 2nd house, which, though personal, is more to do with your capacity to carve out your own identity in private. The fights of Mars in Cyprus may be very different from the kind of excitement you need. So you may find that this Mars line turns into one of frustration, as opposed to one of dynamic action and exercising the will.

Ulla: The way men treat women there can make me very angry. I feel frustrated with the women who seem to be happy taking on the "woman's role". If I lived there I would be very cross most of the time.

Erin: It brings up the masculine archetype as animus, but in a way which angers the magisterial Mars in Leo on the Ascendant. You need to feel free and equal, and know that your masculine and feminine sides are both recognised. Yet the country's culture does not suit those needs.

Ulla: Yes. I suppose that Moon/Uranus in the 12th house states that I have to live in exile from my country because I can't be the kind of woman that my culture says I can be.

Family of choice

Erin: Moon/Uranus needs to change the dynamics of the family – not only the family-of-origin, but the cultural family. The generation of Uranus in Cancer is all about that anyway. It is the foreshadowing of the global family, the still chaotic, seamless world community. Yet to have your Moon there as well states that a new way of building families must be created from your own self and generated family. Also, you have Jupiter singleton retrograde, which in itself means that one is not at home in one's own country. It is like being a stranger in a strange land wherever one goes. More often than not, one is much more comfortable outside one's culture-of-origin. It is as if you are a foreigner within your own territory. And that Jupiter is in the 9th house only amplifies the possibility of finding yourself or your cultural norm in another country. The natal chart expresses the frustration of the culture in which you were born. You yourself might have taken years in coming to terms with it. You have emphasised it by coming to London. The watery, feeling side of your life is more hidden in Limassol – Moon deep into the 12th – but it is brought closer to the Ascendant and in the same sign in the relocated horoscope. The Moon is in the Ascendant, with Cancer rising, here in London.

Ulla: I have lots of family here in London. The Moon is more angular in England, and the system of values here is more at home for me. In Cyprus the masculine was activated. Women have no place to express themselves, and men are oppressive in their aggression. It would have been a frustrating place. Here the feminine is focused in a more unorthodox way.

Erin: Even in the relocated chart, the Moon and Uranus remain in the 12th house. But it has moved the need to wander (Jupiter) into the 10th. It has moved that strong singleton Jupiter retrograde into an angular house, giving you a greater latitude for your beliefs, studies, and practice in metaphysics. It has also shifted Saturn and Neptune into an angular house, so that the family becomes more of a solid place. Saturn is the midpoint of Venus/Neptune, and natally Saturn is in the 3rd house, symbolising problems with early learning, siblings and primary relationships. Relocated to the 4th house, it offers roots, and a solid foundation for creating a family of your own. Natally, there are no planets in the 4th house – it is a kind of "free space", with Libra on the IC. You have three children and other family here for you – and that has been the greater part of your life, really. If you had stayed in Cyprus, perhaps you might have found that very difficult because of the social situation there. Your natal 3rd house with Saturn and Neptune becomes your relocated 3rd house with Sun, Node/Part of Fortune, and Mercury/Venus. You can do it all – live, work, study, and raise a family.

This is where we see an interesting shift with Pars Fortuna. It stays in the 3rd house (the relationship between the Sun, Moon, and Ascendant has only changed a small amount), but it moves significantly by degree to conjoin the lunar south Node. This could be interpreted as the necessity to do the opposite to the "family thing", to evolve your south Node purpose. You would have been battling and fighting the system with your Mars in Leo energy in Cyprus – all that good energy going to waste!

Ulla: I wouldn't have been able to survive there.

Erin: In the old books they say, "Mars in the Ascendant rules blows to the head." When you think of it metaphorically, it *is* rather like having blows to your head, with Mars in the Ascendant. Whatever you think or do, or whatever your willfulness, you are going to get hit in the head (or mind) for it. It isn't always a great thing to have a planet on an angle in a place where the culture doesn't suit the planet and your nature. You may have had to fight your way through the cultural bias, and it could have ended up in quite an abusive relationship in ways associated with the culture itself. But by being raised here, you can process different ways of fighting what is inherent. You cannot change your cultural background, even if you left it at two. It is still there – it is bred in the bone.

In this way consciousness is much more available about families and how families run, because that does seem to be a great part of what your own evolution has been at this stage. This brings up an important issue about the family, your family-of-origin. In the natal chart, Libra rules the 4th house. There are no planets therein. Relocating to London gives a Virgo IC with Saturn and Neptune in the 4th. What has that done to your family-of-origin – your brothers, sisters, mother, father?

Ulla: I have one sister and one brother. I don't even know where my brother is right now. My sister and I are not really close. She was a part of my life. She prefers her children to me. That's it. My parents are both dead, and although I have got lots of family in Cyprus and here, I never see them.

Erin: That may be a part of Jupiter retrograde – all so far away. When I was doing the book[14], I did a lot of research into retrograde planets. With the singleton Jupiter retrograde, an individual often feels that they have literally been found under a cabbage, or dropped by accident through the neighbour's chimney rather than into their own family. The search for the family of culture and family of ideology, the family of the tribe, begins very early in life. I wonder – if you had stayed in Cyprus (this is all total speculation), would your family bonds have remained any stronger? But further to Jupiter's message, by living here in London, with Saturn and Neptune in the 4th house, has it brought right to the fore the feeling that your family of origin may not be your family of soul?

Ulla: Maybe. Even my situation when I was younger seems to say that. A cousin of mine, my Mum's sister's daughter, came to live with us from Cyprus, and the only time in my life I have ever got into a physical fight was with her. She was in bed after that, and I was in bed for a week because I put so much energy into it. I don't know. I think I must not have family of that kind, and must leave it as it is.

Erin: I agree. I think that is very wise.

Audience: This upsetting theme is in the chart anyway, with Moon in Cancer conjunct Uranus as part of a T-square with Jupiter opposite Neptune. It doesn't matter where in the world Ulla is. That T-square is always working, and it would suggest that there is an uncertain or even severed relationship with home and origins. There is something turbulent there, or even a sense of loss.

Siblings

Audience: The relocation chart has Sun, Mercury, and Venus in the 3rd. The Sun rules the 3rd. Mercury rules siblings, and all those planets in Virgo. I would never have looked at that and said, "This is

---

[14]*Retrograde Planets, op. cit.* Note 8.

somebody who doesn't have a lot to do with their brothers and sisters."

Erin: Okay, fair enough. But what about the natal chart? What do you think, focusing on the 3rd house?

Audience: I would look at Saturn and Neptune in the natal chart and say, "Well, maybe they don't get along too well, but I think those would be important relationships."

Erin: Well, maybe they are.

Audience: There are important issues around siblings.

Erin: An important distinction. Thank you. Relationships as an active thing are not always necessary for there to be large issues abounding. The very lack of relating is in itself an issue, and Saturn in the 3rd will always have a sense of responsibility and concern, whether or not the siblings are present to receive it. And psychological astrology tries to probe under the surface, and there is a lot of that here. Also, Saturn in the 3rd is sometimes the eldest or the only child, and that is an issue in itself.

Ulla: I am the eldest.

Erin: It is so often the case that it is weird. It is one of those things that you don't want to say is a law, but it is so commonly the situation. It runs in an order of priority: Saturn in the 3rd is the eldest or only child; Saturn on the Ascendant is another level indicating eldest/only child; and Capricorn rising or Capricorn on the 3rd house cusp is yet another level indicating it. It is very distinct. The Neptune presence is more confusing, more subtle. Saturn in the 3rd can literally isolate one from their brothers and sisters, in the sense of feeling so terribly responsible that you have to abdicate – if the sibling constellation is psychopathological, that is. If it is not, then there will be major disagreements over the maturation process, but the bond becomes stronger, deeper, and more mutually responsible as the siblings grow up and share life. However, Neptune is a loss, a disappearance, a feeling of sadness and uncertainty, and a cloud around the sibling set.[15]

Audience: But to relocate that isolation and loss to the 4th house in London – what is that?

Audience: That may be even more isolation from the family sense of brothers and sisters, going into the 4th. I couldn't honestly say that I would expect that to be the case. I would have expected the exact opposite to be the case. I am surprised.

Erin: Maybe it resulted in abdication of responsibility for the sibs because it was too great, or because of that sense of alienation. Ulla?

Ulla: When I was growing up I was burdened by my sister. I was forced to take her over, to become a parent.

Erin: You were a replacement parent. That does make sense, with the natal Saturn in the 3rd house of sibs moving to the 4th house of parents.

Ulla: It was like an albatross round my neck – a struggle to throw off.

Erin: I usually advise people who have a child who has Saturn in the 3rd house to not remind the child, eldest or not, how responsible they are for their siblings, because they already know it. It could have separated you, because there wasn't that kind of communication in the cultural and generation gap between your parents and you. As the elder daughter, you are the one that has to do everything.

Ulla: I won't let my children do anything at all.

Erin: Oh, dear! Compensation! That *is* interesting. Freedom for the children – Sagittarius in the 5th house. Restructuring family boundaries has been very much part of shifting your T-cross – shifting it into more angular places where it gets worked out more clearly. Moving Jupiter/Neptune from a cadent to a more angular

---

[15] *Sibling Constellation: The Astrology and Psychology of Sisters and Brothers*, Brian Clark, Arkana, CAS, London/New York, 1999.

place brings out into the open whatever complex and mysterious issues there are about family, freedom, children – creating a new style of family is more pertinent to the 10th and 4th houses.

Now, the Moon is *not* in the relocated 1st house, but it *is* closer by degree and in the same sign as the Ascendant. There is a subtle comfort in that shift, in your unique ideas about how you want to create your heterodoxical Moon/Uranus in Cancer family. You may well have been stuck in cultural law in your homeland, with Jupiter in the 9th retrograde. Though you are a heretic, by cultural law you would be in the same position as every woman in your culture. Jupiter in the 9th opposite Neptune in the 3rd doesn't have much to say, or if it had, there would be no one to listen. At least this way, in the privacy of your own home, you can say what you want.

You said earlier that you hadn't really done much on relocation charts, and now you are about to set off to do everybody in the world's relocation chart, which is very good. It is better than being bored with it. Tell me if you have any questions. It is a quandary trying to interpret Ulla's relationship with her siblings, which is an odd one.

Ulla: I only looked at this relocation chart when I printed it out the previous day. I was surprised to have Cancer rising.

Audience: Didn't you say you went to America and had a really good time there? If you go to America you shift the whole thing to something different, which may be more fun and give you more freedom.

Erin: Then we run into the practical things. One does not have to move, lock, stock, and barrel, to access a place. Remember remote access through the philosophy of A*C*G?

Ulla: There are still the children which keep me here.

Erin: Of course. A good reason.

Audience: What about the shift of the Sun, Mercury, and Venus from the 2nd house into the 3rd, and Mars and Pluto from the 1st to the 2nd?

Erin: Mars/Pluto in the 2nd house does suggest great losses and gains of resources. There are often great crashing losses of personal resources, and then a rebuilding. That is an aspect of Pluto in the 2nd house.

Ulla: Yes, that has happened here, too, through partnership.

Erin: It is a more self-examining chart in London than it is in Cyprus.

Ulla: The more I see it, the more I like it.

Erin: It looks more dynamic to me, just generally. And I much prefer the 9th house Node in Pisces to the 8th house Node in Pisces. We are looking a lot more at issues of self-worth and being reliant on other people in the Cyprus chart, whereas here you can grow into a strong sense of self-worth on your own. The move is a subtle example of relocation. It is not glaringly dramatic. It doesn't have to be. Drama is not always what we are looking for. Well, thank you very much for that, Ulla. The charts really make a strong point.

Françoise: relocation for a purpose

This next example is also a subtle shift in relocation. It is Françoise, born in Belgium, near Brussels. **Figure 8** is her natal horoscope, and **Figure 8a** is the London relocation chart.

In moving to London from Brussels, the MC has shifted back 6°, and the Ascendant only 3°. But it has done the reverse of Ulla's chart, and moved Mars from the 12th house in the natal horoscope to the exact Ascendant in London. You two are exactly one Mars cycle apart in age, by a few days, as the two Mars placements are only 3° apart. I like that in a seminar – synchronicity with a twist. It's a bit sibling-like. Your relocation chart has also shifted some planetary house positions, which has a lot of bearing on what goes on for you here as opposed to your homeland.

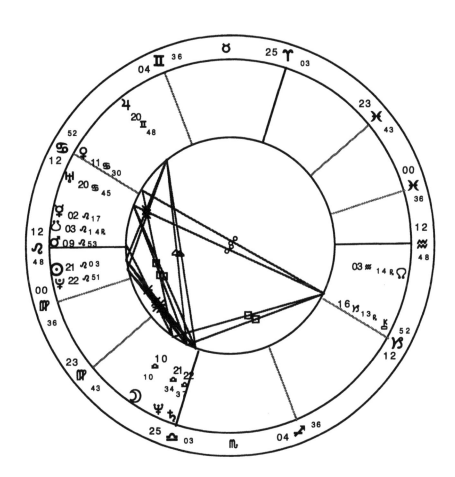

Figure 8: Françoise

(Data withheld for purposes of confidentiality)

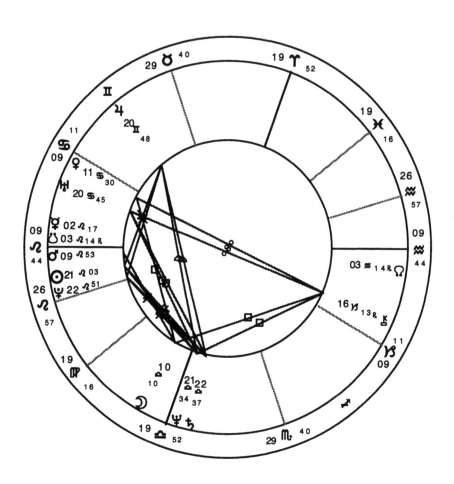

Figure 8a: Françoise in London

When you came to London, did you come with a purpose?

Françoise: I still live in Belgium, but I come to London for the CPA certification course.

Erin: Specifically? Oh, good. Now, in this situation, we are looking at a relocation chart based on choice. This is about choosing a place in which to activate a specific purpose. The purpose preceded the choice of city. Now, how does this work for you, Françoise? You live on the continent and travel here for studies only.

Françoise: I come for the course about seven or eight times every term. The question is, "Is this a good place for me? Does it bring me extra energy, or is it a battling place with Mars on the Ascendant?"

Erin: No, that's very good. You see, you came because of the course. You are specifically here to study astrology, taking the CPA course. It strikes me that flying over from Belgium six or eight times a term is pretty Mars-like – lots of energy and drive and passion put into travelling. But that doesn't have to mean it's bad, because you are working toward a purpose. London itself, with Mars right on the Ascendant, you might actually find very harsh, but at the same time, you are fulfilling a strong need for Mars in Leo to conquer a place or an idea, or develop a trait within yourself .

Pluto again: remote control

Françoise: In my A*C*G map, Brussels is right between my MA/ASC and PL/ASC lines. The PL/ASC line is even nearer than the MA/ASC.

Erin: In Brussels? But it bypasses London?

Françoise: I don't know. In London, I am very near MA/ASC. But when I am in Brussels, PL/ASC is just as near as MA/ASC.

Audience: That is because the horoscope doesn't show the declination of the planets. Pluto has the greatest angle to the ecliptic and creates the greatest distortion. If you are looking at the line in the A*C*G map, you are looking at a three-dimensional horoscope.

Erin: Quite. Now, Pluto may already have risen, but it will not be in the same degree of longitude. It is in fact on the Ascendant in real space – but its zodiacal longitude degree is vastly different from the Sun, which it is conjunct, because Pluto can be 17° degrees in its angle to the plane of the Sun's orbit.

Françoise: So Pluto in Belgium is not that strong, even though it is near the Ascendant? But where is the SU/ASC line?

Erin: Can I look at your A*C*G map? Oh, I do wish we had an acetate, because this is another brilliant example of Pluto's eccentricity. The Sun and Pluto are within minutes of each other in zodiacal longitude, and thus conjunct in your horoscope. But on the A*C*G map, Pluto is very wide from the Sun, and they only cross in both longitude and latitude over Cairo![16] Sun and Pluto are so distant that we have the SU/ASC line running through Copenhagen and the PL/ASC line right through München, Bonn, and just a bit above Belgium. They are separated by a considerable amount, half an inch, and they cross in exact conjunction by declination and longitude to the left of Cairo. I have given up on east and west! The conjunction by latitude and longitude takes place over Cairo. Belgium is where Françoise was born, but by the time you get this far north, it looks as if Pluto is much further south than the Sun.

That's why you get that kind of apparent distortion with the Astro*Carto*Graphy map. I would say, looking at the map, that the subterranean power of Pluto, as it runs through where you live, is much stronger than it is on an obvious level. You have your MA/ASC line running through London. Now, *that* works – same longitude, very little deviation of latitude. The MA/ASC line runs smack through London and a bit west of Brussels. Let's get back to how you feel about all this. The examples are brilliant here. You live in your home, Brussels, and have every intention of staying there. You come to London for a very specific and pointed reason – to gain an education, explore astrology, and undoubtedly complete the course. To me, that seems like a very good thing to do with Mars on the Ascendant. It really does.

---

[16]Refer back to Part One, p. 45-48, to review the "problem" with Pluto.

Focusing on the planetary house changes, we see that in the relocated London chart, your Moon is in the 3rd house, while your natal chart has Moon, Neptune, and Saturn all in the 3rd. Your natal mind, your learning skills for what you want to do, required your coming here to London to find it. Saturn and Neptune in the 3rd house inhibited your finding what you wanted in training at home, and London shifted Saturn/Neptune into the 4th, placing the Moon alone in the 3rd. To me, that has much to say about the way you are receiving your education, your training, in a nurturing group – a kind of family situation. You are coming here to be in a kind of family group that is in some way harmoniously working together – not always, but hopefully, at least some of the time.

Coming home

Françoise: It feels like that to me. Families have all sorts of positive and negative things. Sometimes, it feels like coming home.

Erin: Well, it would, because your Moon is on the Ascendant of England's horoscope, which is 7° Libra.[17] Lunar locations are familiar to us. Looking at the Moon relative to England is another interesting feature. The Moon in the 3rd house is there to learn, to study, to pick up – not just intellectually, but intuitively and instinctually – the emotional human concerns and issues. Your explicit course of action, that of training and education, is also an implicit learning experience.

Françoise: With Saturn and Neptune in the 4th in London, is that a reason to not actually live here?

Erin: Those two are shifted into the 4th from the 3rd by relocating the chart to London. There are other significators of explicit changes made too. Your natal chart has both Jupiter and Venus in the 11th house, indicating your dedication to serving and working through the collective, through tribal or specific-goal groups. But in London, Jupiter is the only planet in the 11th house, and Venus

---

[17] *The Book of World Horoscopes*, Nicholas Campion, *op. cit.* Note 12. I am using the most commonly used horoscope, the 1 January 1801 chart.

moves into the 12th. It retires, so to speak. By using London as a place to work through a study program, involving a group situation with a philosophical focus, you are really doing what you must do here. Gemini is the "early learning" sign, Jupiter the "higher learning" planet, and here you are doing that very thing.

Françoise: I would say that I have experienced the MA/PL/ASC line very heavily at home. I have experienced my masculine side in a certain way. I really want to experience my Sun more. Do you see what I mean?

Erin: The Astro*Carto*Graphy PL/ASC line is on the border of Belgium. The most powerful angular relationship between the two planets is much closer to Belgium than it is to London. You would experience the subterranean effects in Belgium more than you would here. You may be able to bring the uncomfortable unconscious material that lies in the natal region more to consciousness when you are away from the exact line. I do not subscribe to a policy that living on a line is good – it may render your objectivity useless.

If you live on the Pluto line, and come away from it to study matters of the unconscious – living a mythic and symbolic life – you may find that the function of Pluto is more conscious here than in Belgium. This is an interesting way of using the knowledge of A*C*G – once you know you are using it, that is. Even if you were *not* aware of it, it would be working, but it is better to work with it as consciously as possible than to sleep your way through a good opportunity. Also, by coming to London from Belgium, you are bringing Mars out of the 12th house of hidden enemies – which often are within one's own psyche – into the 1st house where you confront fears, primal rage, and passions, instigating a real one-to-one relationship with Mars. In this type of study, the study of archetypal astrology, unconscious material arises much more readily than it might do otherwise. It is like being in analysis all the time – or it should be. In this way, you can fight your way through things that are just whisking around the corners of your psyche in Belgium.

You are also coming here for reasons that are implicit, rather than just the obvious ones. The explicit reason is to study, to gain skill, to relate to people who think astrological and planetary thoughts like you do. Perhaps implicit in that, tacit and hidden, is the potential to actualise a rage for life by bringing it to the Ascendant. This is not as accessible in the 12th house. Rage isn't about throwing tantrums and getting mad and irritable. It is about being able to cut boundaries between yourself and other people – making your statement clear, feeling your power. The "masculine side" does not have to dominate you. You are much more in touch with it because it is right up front on the Ascendant. This is on a very subtle level, because we are only talking about 3° of movement by Mars to the Ascendant. Some people might not even differentiate. Here you seem to be shifting yourself that much further west, bringing Mars into the 1st house and saying, "This is me! This is who I am! I am going to study this, even if it means battering my way through some psychic pain and bringing it out into the open." You may resolve some dilemma by coming here consistently over time for specific reasons. You may never want to live here, though, with Saturn/Neptune in the 4th house. You may not want to end up here.

Ancestral inheritance in the light

Now, has this changed your family dynamic, considering that we are looking at a similar situation with Libra ruling the 4th house? Have you understood more about your origins and roots by coming here to study? This reflects back on Ulla's reverse situation, where she now lives in her new location with Saturn and Neptune in the relocated 4th house.

Françoise: Astrology has definitely opened up doors. I have a family background that is really reflected in the 12th house as you see it natally.

Erin: It made me wonder if you have been violated in certain ways by the family condition.

Françoise: Certainly, yes.

Erin: Then maybe that is what this threshold is about – cleaning out any of the buried rage and mistreated *eros* in the family by bringing it into your own life and power on your Ascendant angle, as opposed to locked in the 12th house. Perhaps you now see things more objectively. Although one does need to find a space to forgive, one should never forget what has happened. You might be able to detach yourself a bit more by coming away and looking at it from Saturn/Neptune in the 4th, as opposed to it being more mushed up in the sibling house. I am sure you weren't the only one to experience it. Is that right?

Françoise: No, I am not the only one. We are six children.

Erin: I see.

Françoise: I come from a family with very old values. I have Uranus in the 12th, so I have always been a revolutionary in my family.

Erin: A subversive! You and Ulla should talk.

Françoise: At the same time, Saturn/Neptune is also in the 4th when I am here in London, so now I am more conscious of it.

Erin: It is a very responsible family fate. What place are you in the family – are you the eldest?

Françoise: I am number four.

Erin: You are really in the middle, then.

Françoise: My family comes from aristocracy. That might be the 12th house – all these ancestral values, as you say in your book.

Erin: Hmm, old ideas in a new mind. The dynastic family line and the ancestral values can really violate one's sense of individuality. It can be abusive, really.

Françoise: Abusive because everybody in the past behaved the same way. And no one in the present can act to change that.

Erin: You need to cut your way out of it, or through it. By coming just a few miles west of your birthplace, you have brought Mars out, so you can develop it much better here. In the A*C*G seminar last week, I told you that I moved thirty miles west to put my Sun right on the Ascendant, and from there I really shone from within. My work, purpose, and inner awareness developed rapidly. I didn't know about A*C*G then, but I did relocate the chart, and that was the significant shift. Thirty miles – half a degree – can make a huge difference.

Audience: Oh, is that another mundane square, then, between Mars and Neptune? Is it a paran?

Erin: Yes. NE/MC is actually crossing MA/ASC just a bit south, in France, so the paran doesn't occur in her chart here. In actuality the *paranatellonta* lies just south of Paris. So yes, that would be a mundane square, a paran. Yes, Françoise?

Françoise: I am rooted with my family. It has been a struggle coming to England. Do you think that England is a bad place for me?

Erin: No, no, no. But as you say, the family dynamic might get more activated. You may be making it more conscious, which to my mind is a better thing. But you do not have to live here – just use the place for what it can offer you.

Audience: Erin, when you say abusive, are you looking at Saturn on the IC? What makes that abusive?

Erin: I am looking at her natal Pisces 8th and 9th houses, and the connected stellium of Moon/Neptune/Saturn in Libra. The Moon rules the 12th house, the hidden cultural and ancestral issues, in which we find Uranus, Mercury, and Mars. Neptune rules the 8th, another ancestral house, but closer – the family ancestral league. And Saturn rules the 6th, which contains Chiron in Capricorn, another indication of the patriarchal wound.

It appears that her instinctive feelings, beliefs, and values were sacrificed on behalf of the family. Now, it can be overt violence, like being hit, or it can be an unconscious violation of the soul – it is the same root word. Violence is the Mars and Sun/Pluto. The abuse is the victimisation of a Pisces 8th house and the Moon/Neptune conjunction just sort of falling into it by rulership of both 8th and 12th.

Audience: Even though she has Saturn/Pluto in sextile?

Erin: That is a survival aspect. Sun/Pluto is a hard legacy from the father, for a woman especially, because she is meant to overcome obstacles beyond belief. It is an heroic legacy. It is like having a father who is a sorcerer, a magician. Someone with such vast power is mythic in his dimensions.

It is hard to overcome that – in fact, it is something one must grow into. Perhaps, by bringing Mars to a more cardinal placement, and with your relocated Aquarius 8th house, Françoise, you could intellectually work through more of what it is that you have gained from the family, as opposed to what has suppressed you and will always be with you. Uranus and Aquarius can mean liberation through objectivity.

Growing into Pluto

Audience: What do you mean by "overcome"? You said Sun/Pluto is a strong father, which is hard to overcome.

Erin: Well, it is.

Audience: Then by putting everything in cardinal positions, you can overcome it. Does that mean a separation?

Erin: Sorry, it is not that cut and dried. I mean that more consciousness makes for more understanding. It doesn't mean "getting over it", whatever "it" is. Overcoming things is relative. I don't mean that it ceases to exist. It just becomes more part of one's own personality in a successful way, so that one doesn't feel so victimised by the solar figure in the family. You yourself become the solar figure. That takes time and age. Pluto is one of the last planets we grow into. It is the furthest planet out. Solar system individuation states that, for the deepest self to emerge, one must come to terms with Pluto and what lies beyond. That takes one right into midlife – sometimes later, sometimes never – before anyone can achieve the sense of deep calm that a Plutonian type of person can have when they finally realise two things: first, you can't control the universe, and second, it doesn't matter that you can't.

Once those two things are accepted within a Plutonian type of person, the sense of peace that falls upon him or her is phenomenal. That's the kind of power that Pluto is all about, not about running for political office or making oneself super-visible. Pluto is unseen power, and it is something which does sometimes take forever. Generally, probably until midlife, it is a struggle. The god Hades was invisible. His name translates roughly into "unseen" – he was "the Unseen One". Usually Sun/Pluto is a father issue because we are still involved with male and female archetypes, and fathers are still male. We usually respond to that solar figure in our lives as heroic. "Overcome" is not a good word. I don't like words like "transcend", "overcome", or "get over".

Audience: It will go away.

Erin: Yes, right. Ha, ha. Let's say "grow into". Accommodate. Incorporate. Work with.

Audience: Then putting Françoise's Mars angular will make it easier for her to grow into Mars through conflict.

Erin: It is hand-to-hand battle instead of sneaking around in the 12th. In the old books, the 12th house was "secret enemies". As soon as you bring it out into the 1st, you became yourself. I have always seen the 12th as the inner secret enemy – one's own shadow.

Audience: It's called the house of self-undoing.

Erin: At least now we know where the conflict lies. The more frequently you come here, Françoise, and the more comfortable you are as you continue to return to your relocated place, the more things will rise to the surface, allowing you to process increasing levels of your Mars. The hidden sense of violation or violence is now in the open, and you can talk about it, because you are safe.

Audience: So you have one more ally.

Erin: Yes. That's beautiful for Mars in Leo. The warrior has been awakened to come and join the king. It's fabulous on the Ascendant. Thank you so much, Françoise!

Mysterium coniunctionis: the meeting of opposites

Audience: I have a strange situation in my relocation chart. I was born and raised in New Zealand, and my Ascendant and MC are virtually the exact opposite up here to where they are in my natal chart. Can you say anything about that?

Erin: Really? That is the next story we have, the next example. What is your question about that?

Audience: I have Mars in the 9th house in my natal chart, in Auckland, and here it is in the 3rd house. Everything is opposite.

Erin: By nature, Mars in the 9th questions authority, arguing with God. You are going to look at dogma and fight it. You battle your way through whatever dogma centres around beliefs, ethics, cultural law, religious issues, and your ethnic background. Relocating to a place which puts Mars in the 3rd house is a way of using the inherent need to do all that in a way that will articulate and clarify the universal questions through study, reading, talking, communication and learning new methods of expressing yourself. By coming to a place that reverses the natal chart, you are destined to take your self, turn it inside out, and meet the opposite within you in order to heal a split. Now, you may be aware of that, having come here. Do you think you will go back to New Zealand?

Audience: I think I will remain fairly split.

Erin: Perhaps it is more productive for you.

Audience: I have had too many experiences. I feel I need to get back to life. I still have got some travelling to do. I have filled out every possible variation of Mars in Scorpio while travelling. It is true that when you look back on it, you really learn from it.

Erin: Mars in the 9th wants to explore every possible corner of the earth, whether that is philosophically, ideologically, or geographically. If you can do that, then that's great. You have to do it anyway. The fact that you have settled in a place where Mars is in the 3rd means you can make more use of it intellectually and mentally, through communication and the written word. Some day you may write articles, or you may be able to use this in teaching.

Even if you never told anybody you had been in any other place, someone who has experienced the world and other cultures is far more comfortable in almost any social situation than another person.

The 9th house is not only about one's local dogma, but also about a global world-view. You may well have got stuck in small battles, local dogma, all your life, as opposed to going out and challenging other world-views. By travelling, you managed to do that. There will probably be a point where you do need to settle down, though. For now, I would really "work" my relocated chart by looking at it as the *mysterium coniunctionis* of time, space, and relationship, and think about how this horoscopy might be a major part of your process of individuation.

Maya: relocation and the family

You know, sadly, we are looking at closure – it's almost 5.00 pm. And here I am with Maya in India (**Figure 9**), Auckland (**Figure 9a**), and London (**Figure 9b**).

Maya: Could you say something about it if you have the time? I was born in India, moved to Auckland at three months old, was raised there, and moved here ten years ago, around 1987.

Erin: I would love to. These three charts all produce vastly different views of the world. All your natal planetary oppositions fall along angular axes, and this should be very interesting for us.

Maya: I also have planets which make it difficult being here. The Auckland Descendant is only few degrees opposite the relocated Ascendant in London. And I have Jupiter singleton retrograde in the 8th house natally, and the Moon is alone, too. I find the similarity by opposition of the charts for London and Auckland really strange and disturbing. Having lived through it, I would be interested to know what you think. This is particularly the issue: what is the strange connection between London and Auckland?

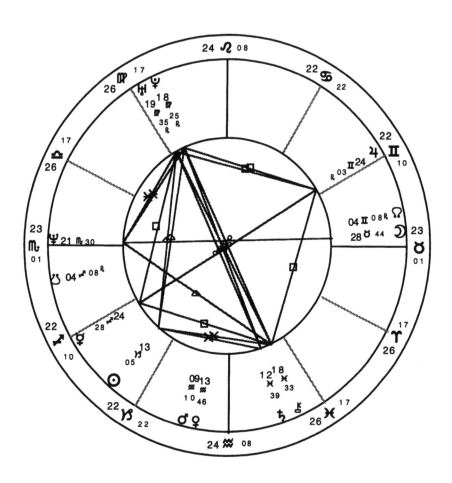

Figure 9: Maya

(Data withheld for purposes of confidentiality)

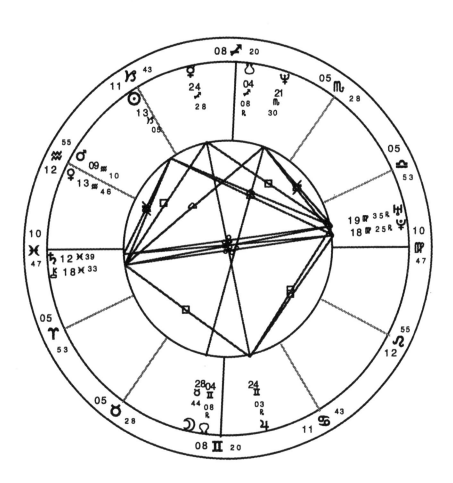

Figure 9a: Maya in Auckland

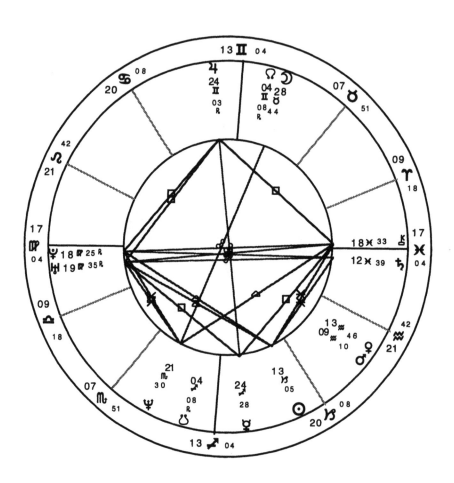

Figure 9b: Maya in London

Erin: You are right – this is very interesting. For the technicalities: Auckland is 175°E, and London is virtually 0°. Auckland is almost half the world away, almost at the International Date Line. And the angles are reversed because when Auckland is in midsummer, it is midwinter in London. The difference between the latitudes puts the median latitude at about 45°, midway between the equator and the poles. The seasonal angle of the Sun and its risings and settings produces this polarity of horizon/meridian – so you are going to get the same kind of distortion at the same time of the year.

Let's think. The angles are about your orientation and your navigational coordinates on earth, and your natal chart is what you were born to pursue. It's flipped by moving to the north latitude from the south latitude, and I would think that you had done this either on a whim, from necessity, or because of a profound inner urge from the deeper self to explore your opposite. I am not being facetious. This is done to explore the experiential side of you where you remain "yourself". The arena in which you enact all of your life destiny, dharma, and focus meets its opposite. Your interior self meets your exterior self, and *vice versa,* by moving to London from your home in Auckland. Now you will act out your 9th house in your 3rd, and so on. Give me an example of what concerns you.

Maya: Well, we can use the 3rd and 9th houses if you like. That is where my Moon/Neptune opposition falls, whereas my birth chart has the Moon/Neptune opposition along the Ascendant/Descendant.

Erin: Auckland and London, from India...Look, it is 5.00 pm now. If everybody voted for another ten minutes, we could look at this example. I'm going to leave it up to you. I don't mind. I've probably got about ten minutes left in me anyway.

Audience: Would you mind? It's very interesting.

Erin: Okay. It's very interesting because this is just what we were talking about with you – the meeting of opposites.

Maya: Auckland is really close to my SA/ASC and UR/PL/DSC crossing in the A*C*G map. And London is close to the UR/PL/ASC line.

Audience: So you were born in India and moved to Auckland at three months old?

Maya: The only time I went back to India, I was right on my Neptune line in New Delhi, and I got really, really ill. I got bad food poisoning, even though I had been very careful up until that point about what I ate. But there I drank from a tap.

Erin: You didn't take your lomatil. One never goes to India without their lomatil. Everyone has a Neptune line through India and gets the runs. It's too late in the day, Neptune must be on the Ascendant now. Neptune rising in India doesn't strike me as being a very certain source of origin. It would make the identity as an Indian in India not that thick. But the family roots are very strong with Saturn in Pisces in the 4th, so the origins and culture are powerful, especially with Cancer ruling the 9th house and Saturn in the 4th. The culture went with you. Were you raised in an Indian community in Auckland?

Maya: Not at all. We were just completely alone. My parents were quite eccentric, not traditionalists.

Erin: So there you were in Auckland with Saturn rising. But we carry our natal charts within us, and with Saturn natally in your 4th house, the origins and roots are powerful, though tradition is shattered by the opposition to Uranus and Pluto in the 10th house. That very configuration is the one that was heard around the world. All the old order began to crack – it was instigated by the Saturn/Uranus conjunction in late Taurus and early Gemini, at the beginning of World War II, and blew into the open, global mind by the mid-1960's.

Maya: I didn't realise that until recently, until I set these charts for the seminar. I can't believe that the two places I have lived most of my life, Britain and New Zealand, both have Saturn on the angles.

Erin: You are one of those Saturn opposite Uranus/Pluto people that I was mentioning earlier. Not only is it angular where you were taken as a three-month-old child, but then you consciously moved to a place where you would experience the opposite, with Saturn on the Descendant.